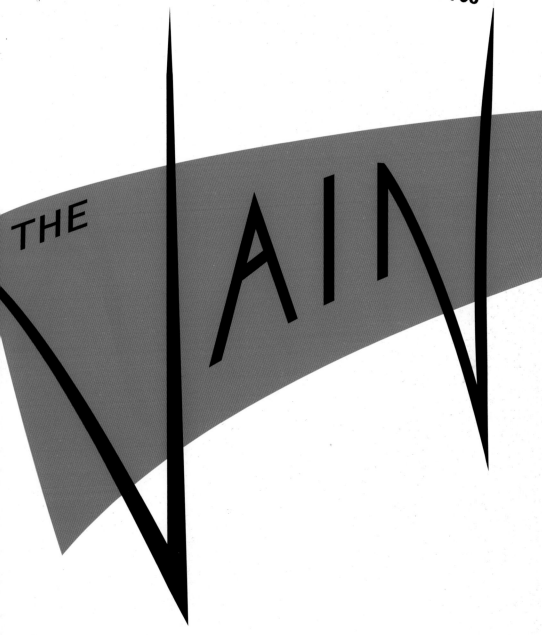

THE VAIN

THE

VA

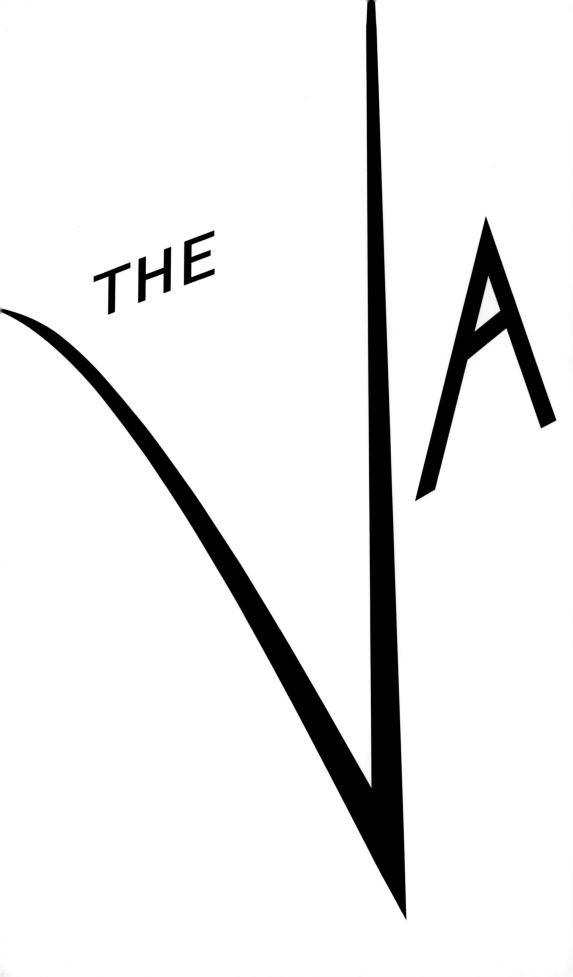

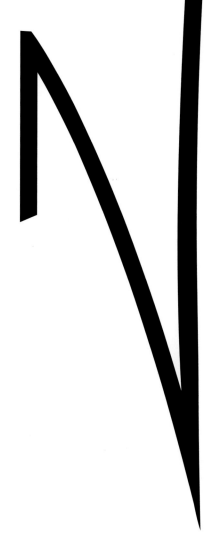

WRITTEN BY
ELIOT RAHAL

ILLUSTRATED BY
EMILY PEARSON

COLORED BY
FRED C. STRESING

COLOR ASSISTANT
MACY KAHN

LETTERED BY
CRANK!

COVER BY
EMILY PEARSON
WITH COLORS BY
FRED C. STRESING

ONI PRESS

AN ONI PRESS PUBLICATION

—
——
———
DESIGNED BY
KATE Z. STONE
——— EDITED BY ———
DESIREE WILSON, ROBIN
HERERRA, & JASMINE AMIRI

PUBLISHED BY ONI-LION FORGE PUBLISHING GROUP, LLC

James Lucas Jones, president & publisher
Sarah Gaydos, editor in chief · Charlie Chu, e.v.p. of
creative & business development · Brad Rooks, director
of operations · Amber O'Neill, special projects manager
Margot Wood, director of marketing & sales · Devin Funches,
sales & marketing manager · Katie Sainz, marketing manager · Tara
Lehmann, publicist · Troy Look, director of design & production · Kate
Z. Stone, senior graphic designer · Sonja Synak, graphic designer Hilary
Thompson, graphic designer · Sarah Rockwell, graphic designer · Angie
Knowles, digital prepress lead · Vincent Kukua, digital prepress technician
Jasmine Amiri, senior editor · Shawna Gore, senior editor · Amanda Meadows,
senior editor · Robert Meyers, senior editor, licensing · Desiree Rodriguez, editor
Grace Scheipeter, editor · Zack Soto, editor · Chris Cerasi, editorial coordinator
Steve Ellis, vice president of games · Ben Eisner, game developer · Michelle Nguyen,
executive assistant · Jung Lee, logistics coordinator · Joe Nozemack, publisher emeritus

1319 SE Martin Luther King, Jr. Blvd.
Suite 240, Portland, OR 97214

onipress.com
lionforge.com

@onipress
@lionforge

First Edition: April 2021 · ISBN 978-1-62010-887-1 · eISBN 978-1-62010-888-8

Library of Congress Control Number: 2020938366
1 3 5 7 9 10 8 6 4 2
Printed in China.

CHAPTER 1

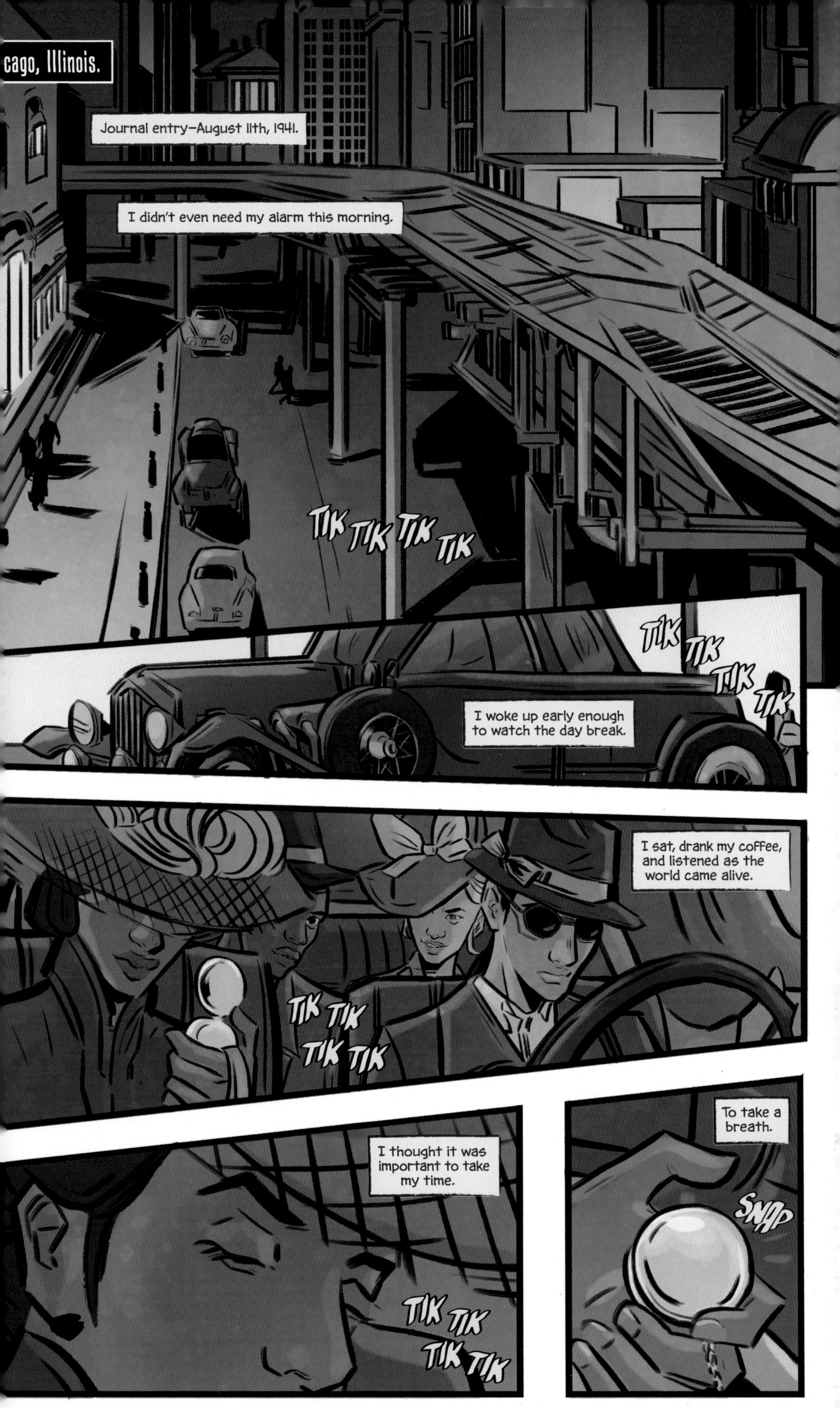

cago, Illinois.
Journal entry—August 11th, 1941.
I didn't even need my alarm this morning.
TIK TIK TIK TIK
TIK TIK TIK TIK
I woke up early enough to watch the day break.
I sat, drank my coffee, and listened as the world came alive.
TIK TIK TIK TIK
I thought it was important to take my time.
TIK TIK TIK TIK
To take a breath.
SNAP

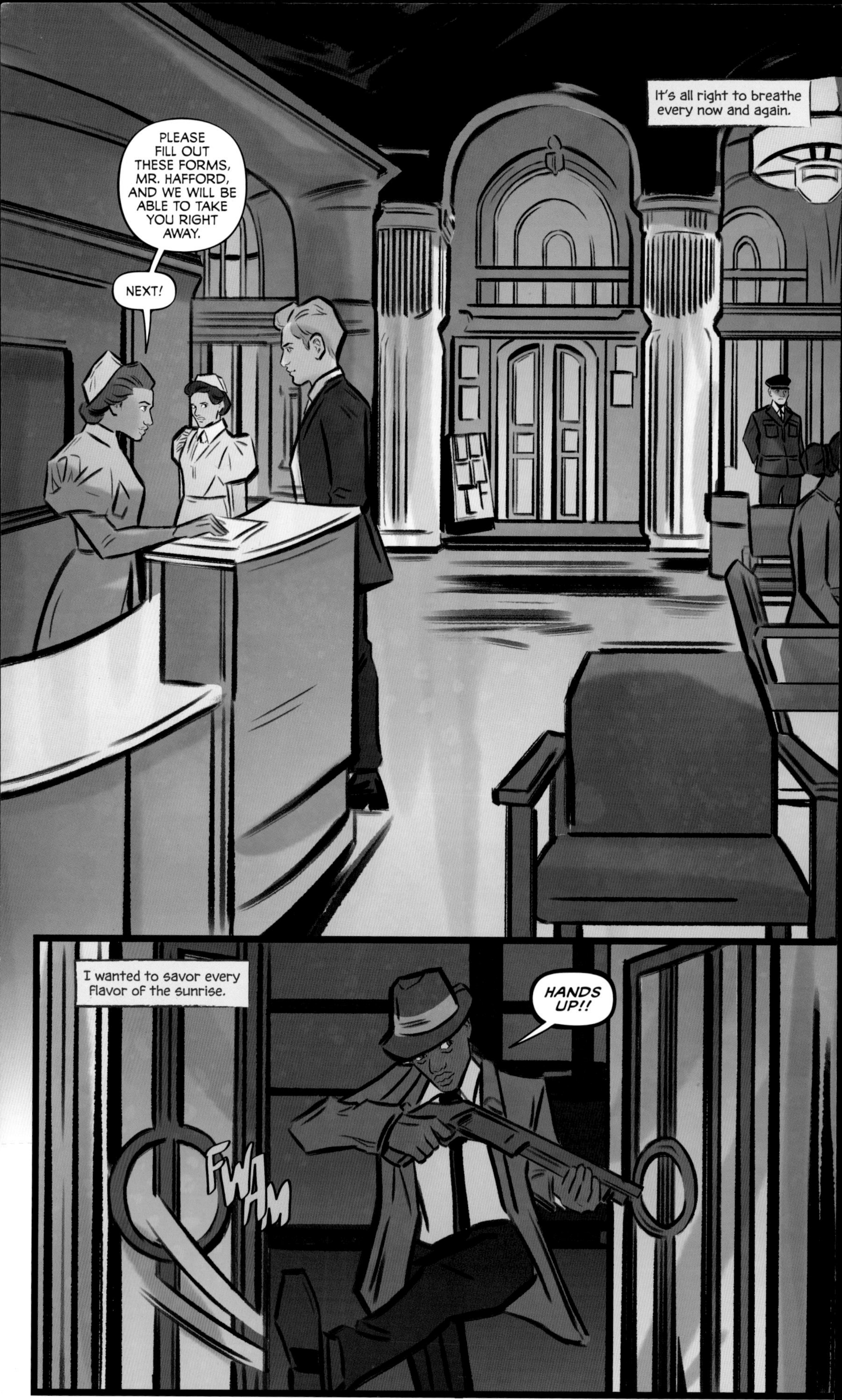
It's all right to breathe every now and again.
PLEASE FILL OUT THESE FORMS, MR. HAFFORD, AND WE WILL BE ABLE TO TAKE YOU RIGHT AWAY.
NEXT!
I wanted to savor every flavor of the sunrise.
HANDS UP!!
FWAM

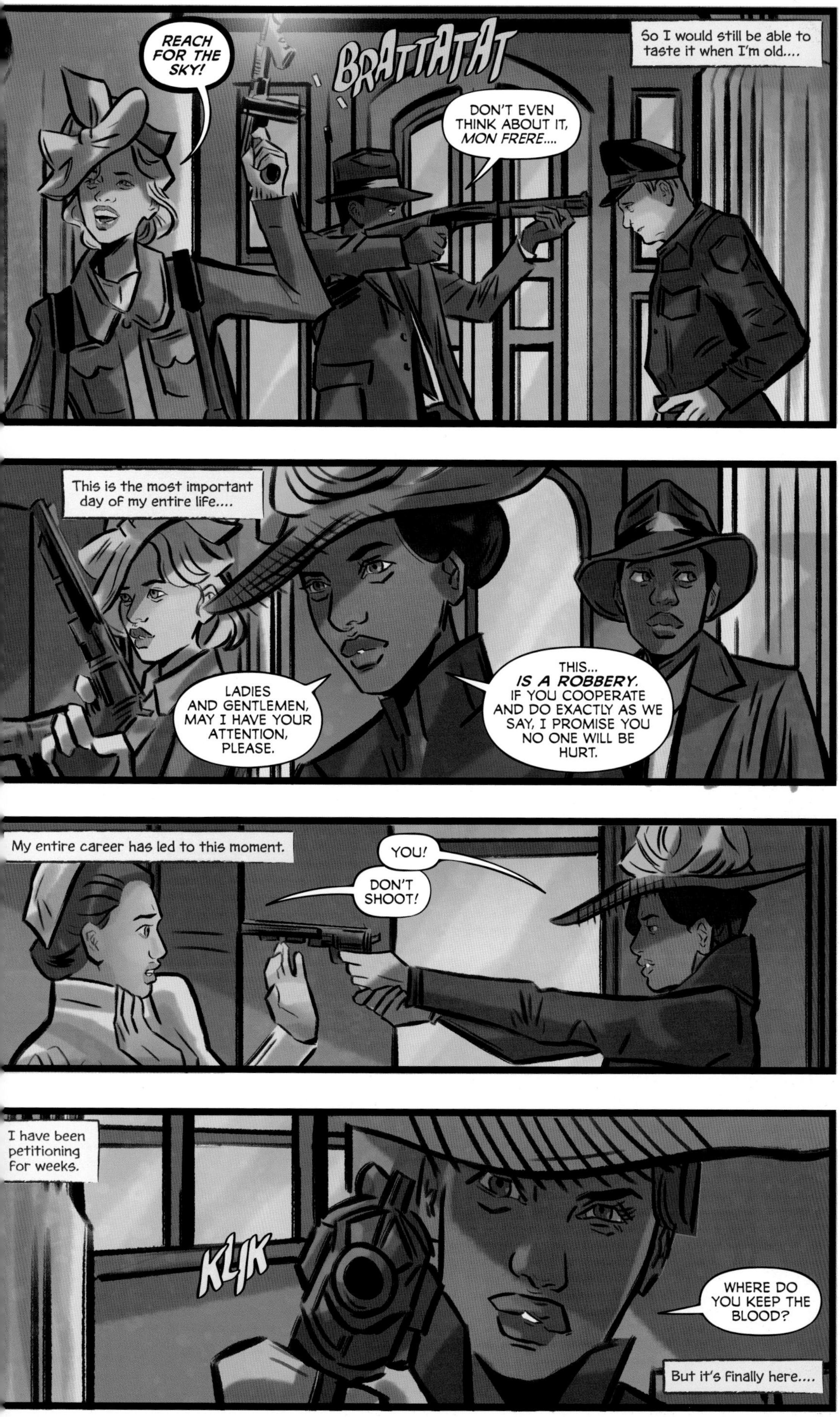
REACH FOR THE SKY!
BRATTATAT
So I would still be able to taste it when I'm old....
DON'T EVEN THINK ABOUT IT, *MON FRERE*....
This is the most important day of my entire life....
LADIES AND GENTLEMEN, MAY I HAVE YOUR ATTENTION, PLEASE.
THIS... ***IS A ROBBERY.*** IF YOU COOPERATE AND DO EXACTLY AS WE SAY, I PROMISE YOU NO ONE WILL BE HURT.
My entire career has led to this moment.
YOU!
DON'T SHOOT!
I have been petitioning for weeks.
KLIK
WHERE DO YOU KEEP THE BLOOD?
But it's finally here....

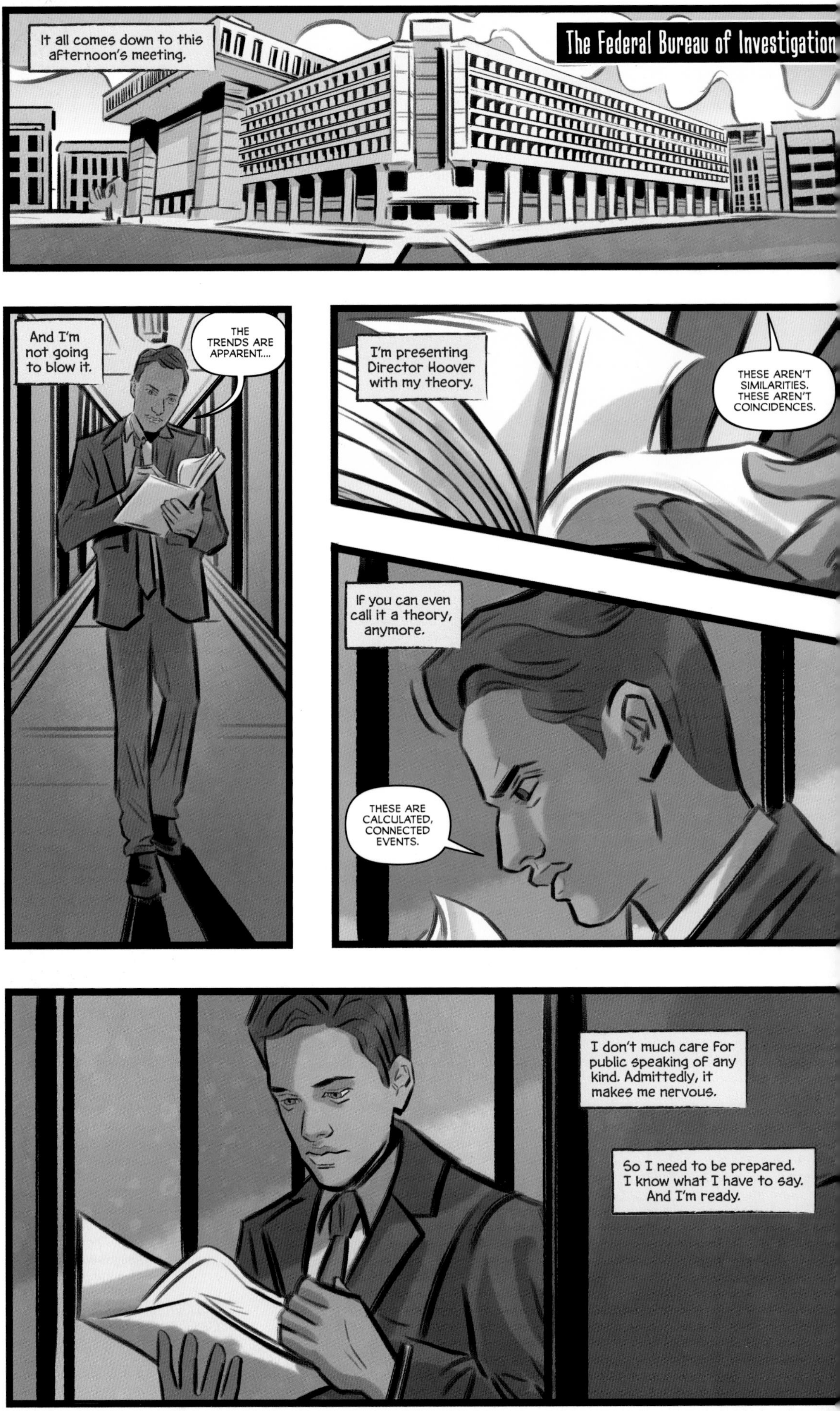
The Federal Bureau of Investigation
It all comes down to this afternoon's meeting.
And I'm not going to blow it.
THE TRENDS ARE APPARENT....
I'm presenting Director Hoover with my theory.
THESE AREN'T SIMILARITIES. THESE AREN'T COINCIDENCES.
If you can even call it a theory, anymore.
THESE ARE CALCULATED, CONNECTED EVENTS.
I don't much care for public speaking of any kind. Admittedly, it makes me nervous.
So I need to be prepared. I know what I have to say. And I'm ready.

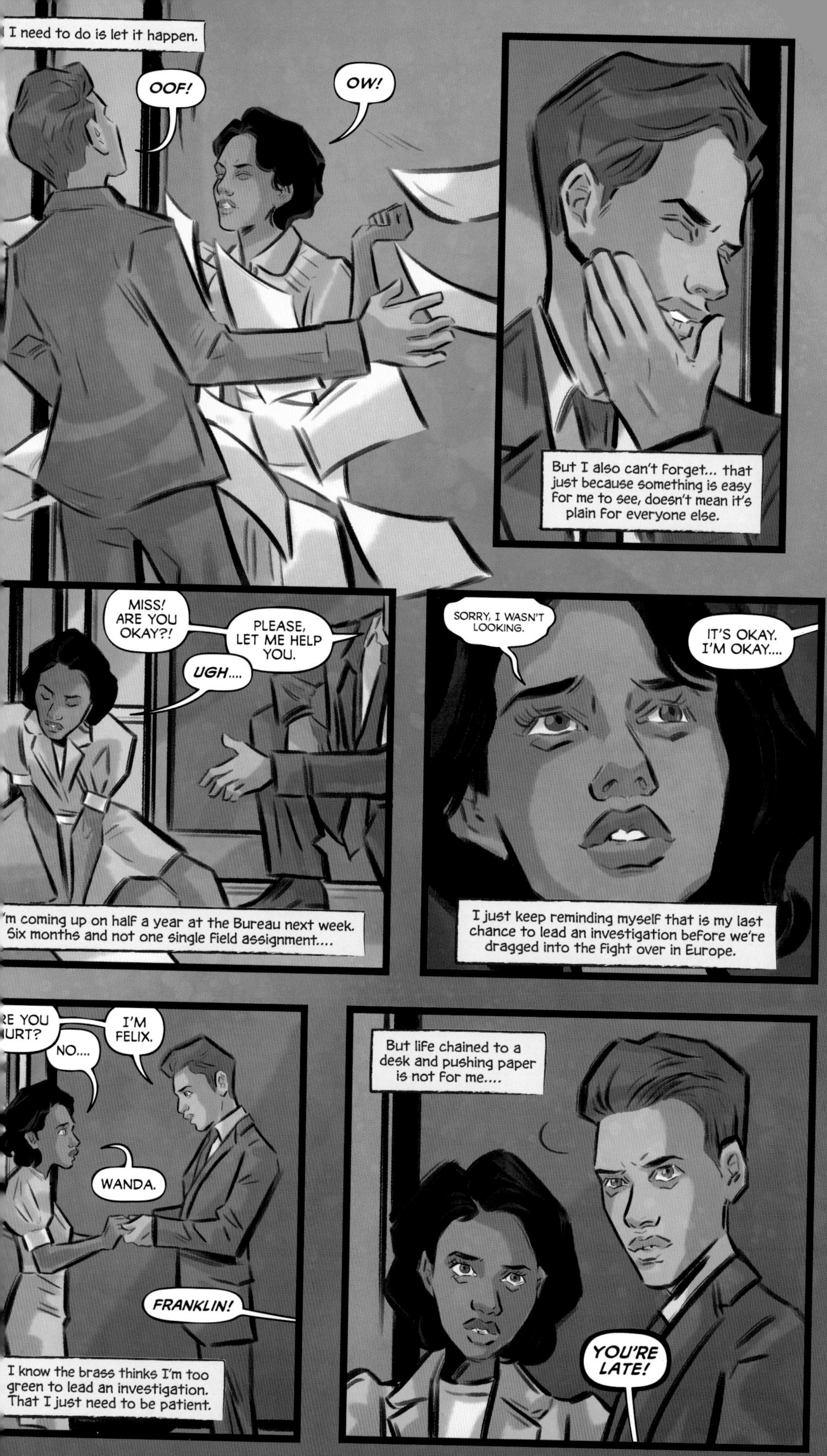
I need to do is let it happen.
OOF!
OW!
But I also can't forget... that just because something is easy for me to see, doesn't mean it's plain for everyone else.
MISS! ARE YOU OKAY?!
PLEASE, LET ME HELP YOU.
UGH....
'm coming up on half a year at the Bureau next week. Six months and not one single field assignment....
SORRY, I WASN'T LOOKING.
IT'S OKAY. I'M OKAY....
I just keep reminding myself that is my last chance to lead an investigation before we're dragged into the fight over in Europe.
RE YOU URT?
NO....
I'M FELIX.
WANDA.
FRANKLIN!
I know the brass thinks I'm too green to lead an investigation. That I just need to be patient.
But life chained to a desk and pushing paper is not for me....
YOU'RE LATE!

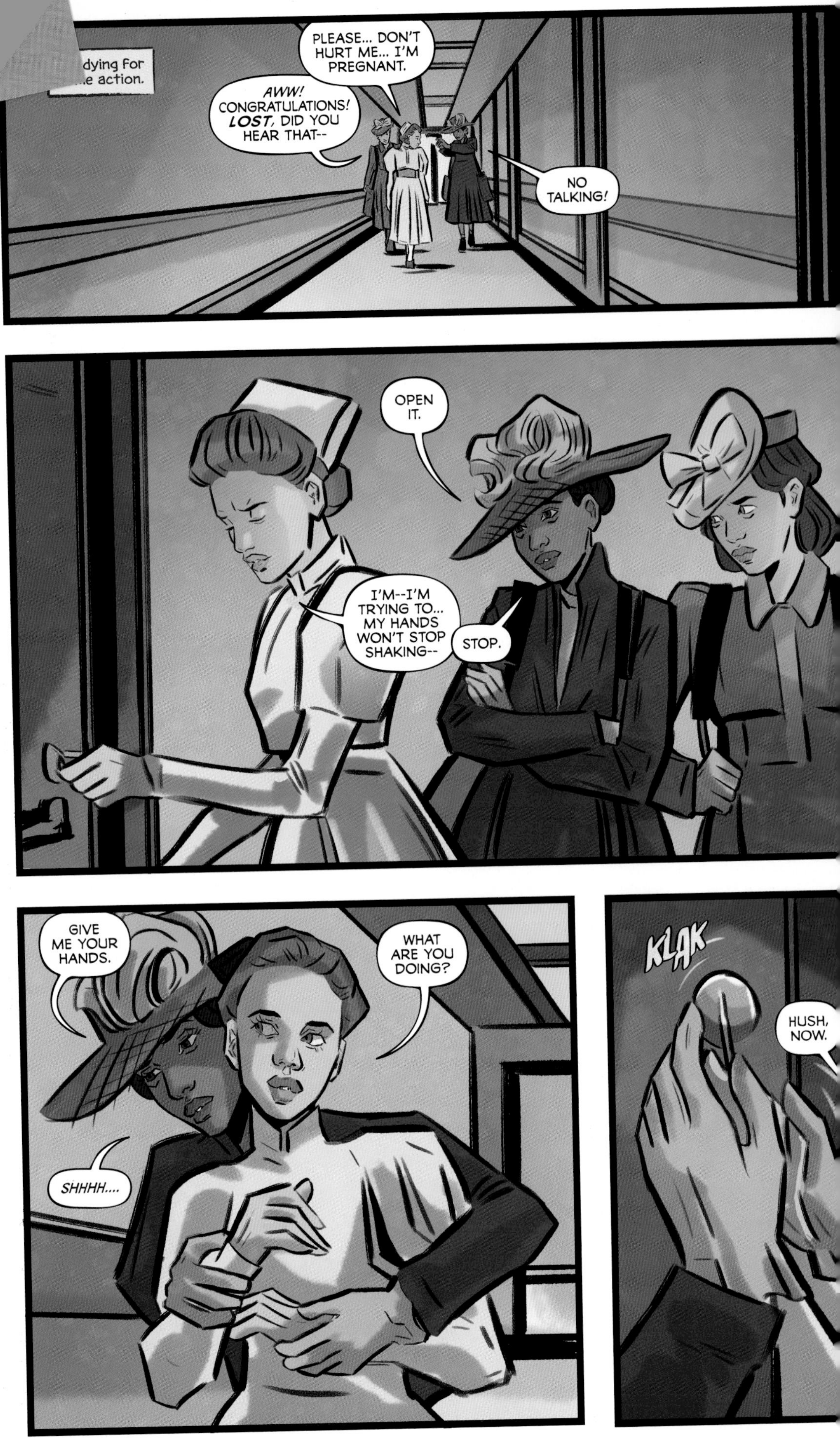
…dying for
…e action.
PLEASE... DON'T HURT ME... I'M PREGNANT.
AWW! CONGRATULATIONS! LOST, DID YOU HEAR THAT--
NO TALKING!
OPEN IT.
I'M--I'M TRYING TO... MY HANDS WON'T STOP SHAKING--
STOP.
GIVE ME YOUR HANDS.
WHAT ARE YOU DOING?
SHHHH....
KLAK
HUSH, NOW.

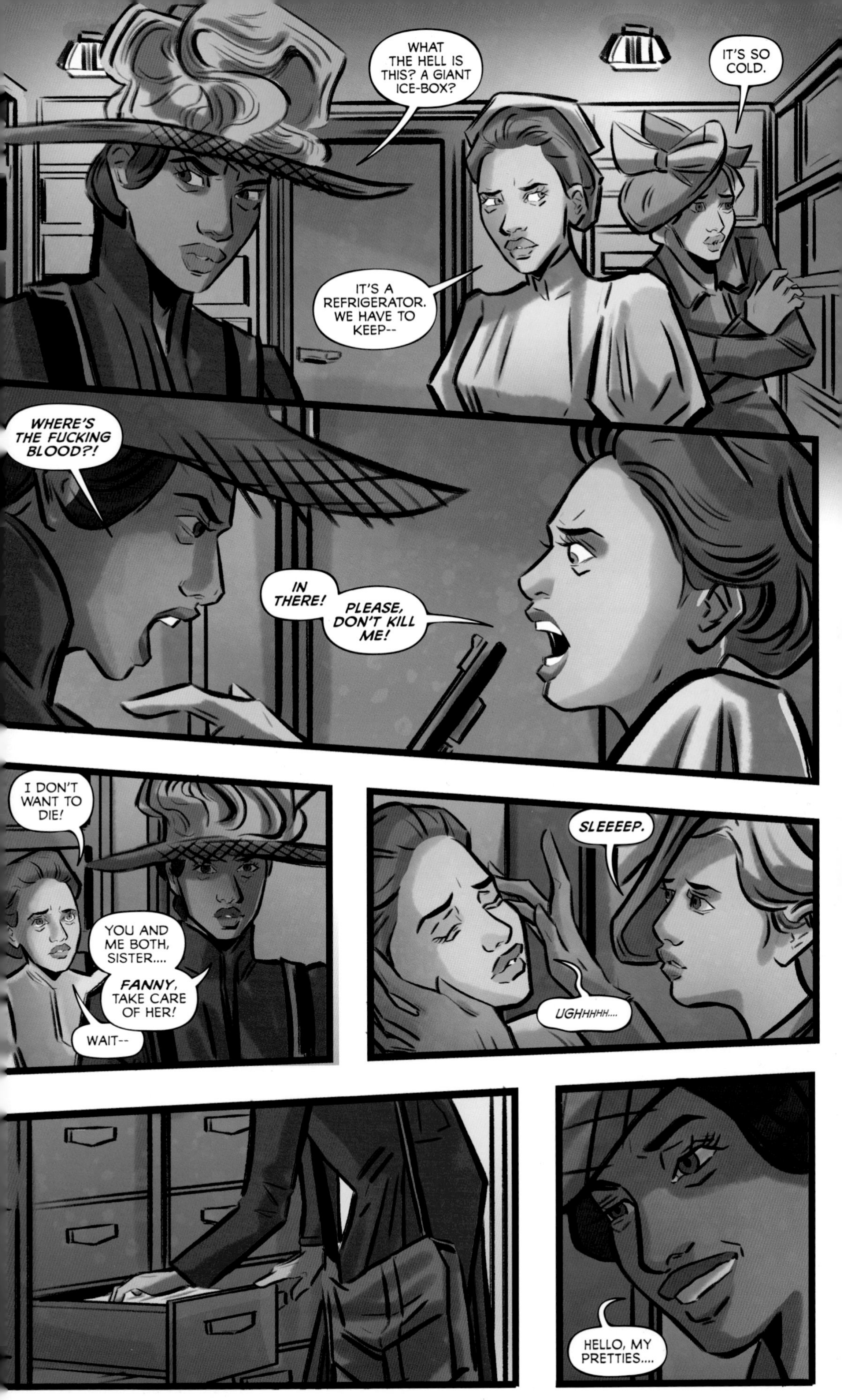

WHAT THE HELL IS THIS? A GIANT ICE-BOX?
IT'S SO COLD.
IT'S A REFRIGERATOR. WE HAVE TO KEEP--
WHERE'S THE FUCKING BLOOD?!
IN THERE!
PLEASE, DON'T KILL ME!
I DON'T WANT TO DIE!
YOU AND ME BOTH, SISTER....
FANNY, TAKE CARE OF HER!
WAIT--
SLEEEEP.
UGHHHHH....
HELLO, MY PRETTIES....

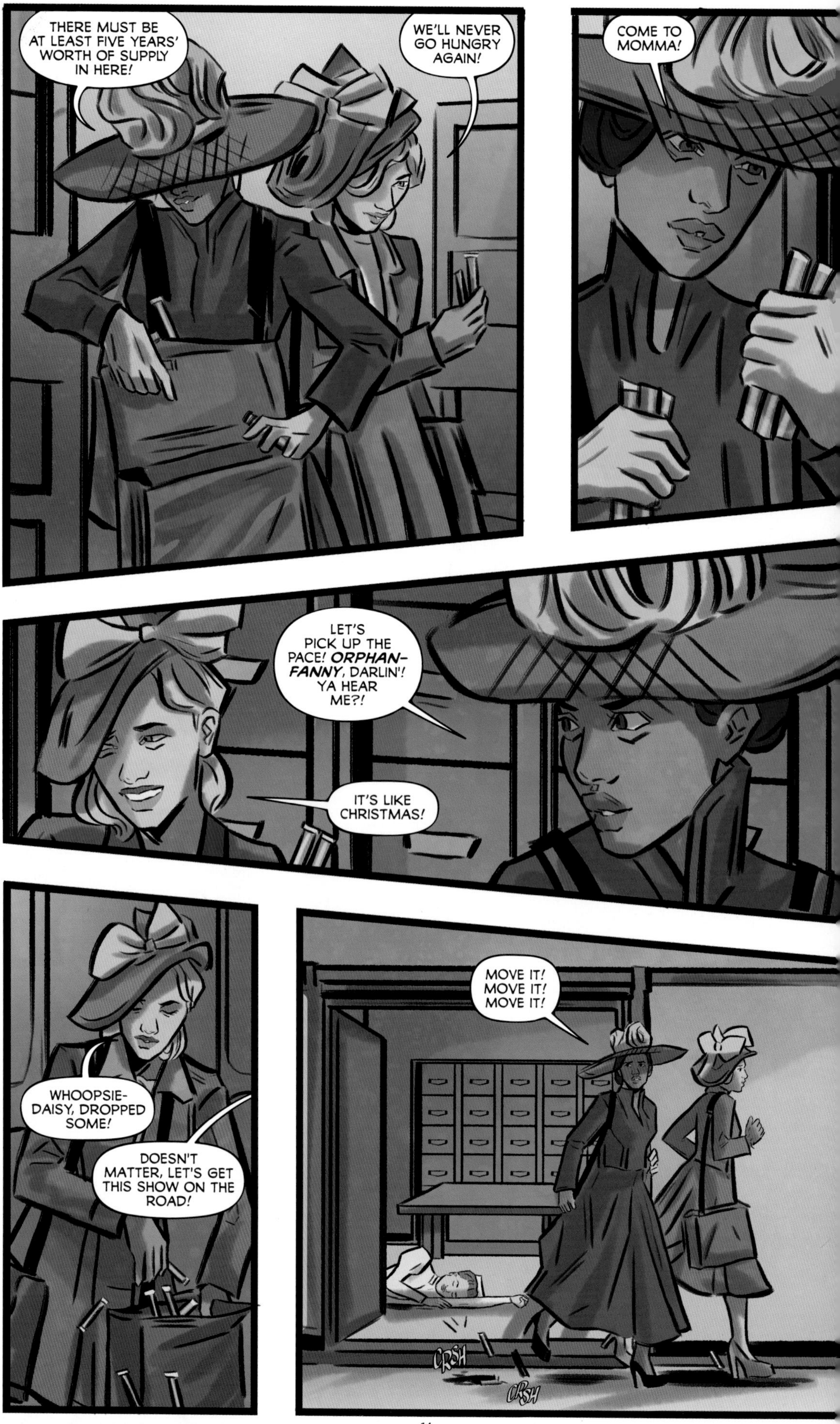
THERE MUST BE AT LEAST FIVE YEARS' WORTH OF SUPPLY IN HERE!
WE'LL NEVER GO HUNGRY AGAIN!
COME TO MOMMA!
LET'S PICK UP THE PACE! **ORPHAN-FANNY**, DARLIN'! YA HEAR ME?!
IT'S LIKE CHRISTMAS!
WHOOPSIE-DAISY, DROPPED SOME!
DOESN'T MATTER, LET'S GET THIS SHOW ON THE ROAD!
MOVE IT! MOVE IT! MOVE IT!
CRSH
CRSH

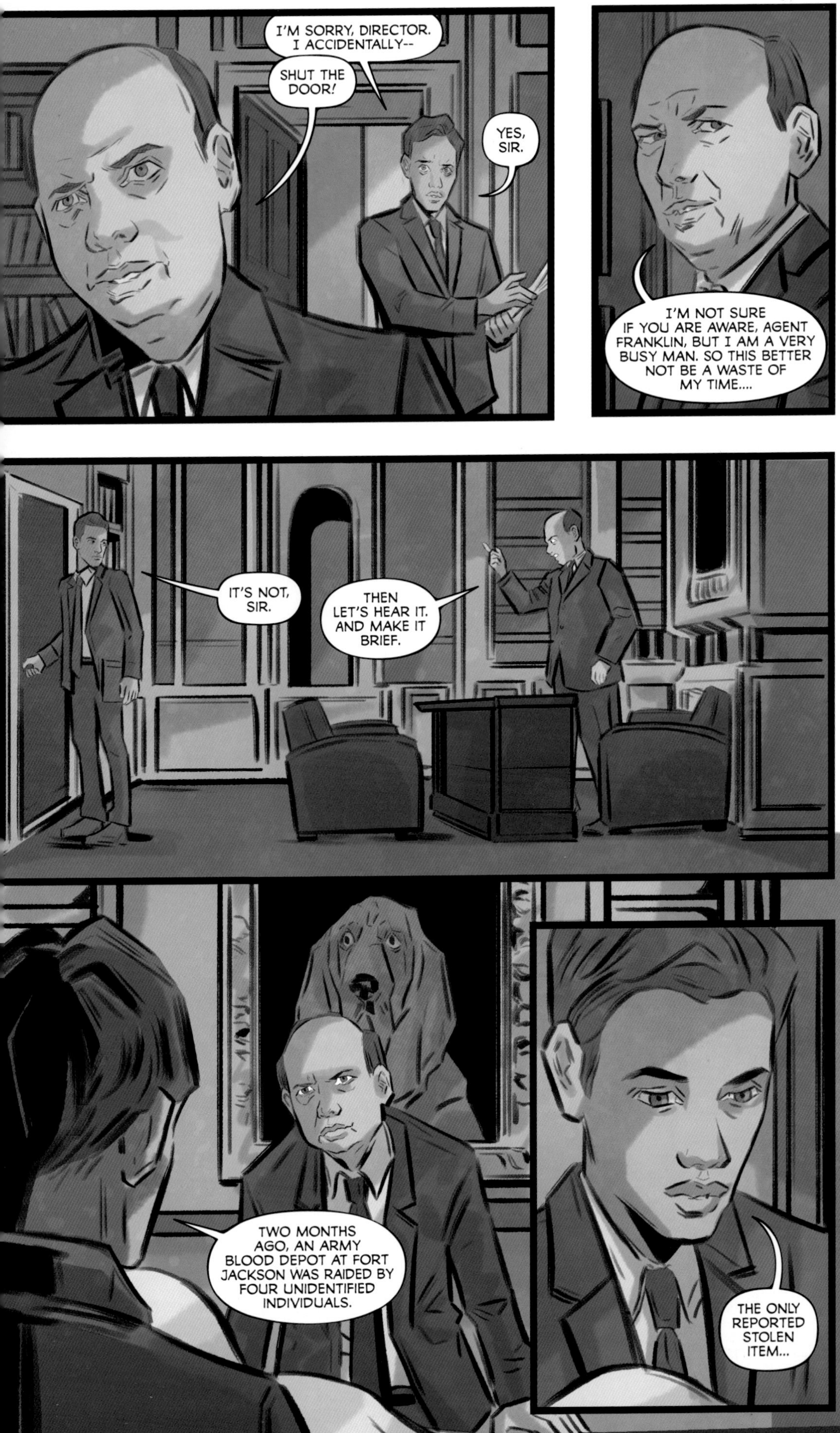
I'M SORRY, DIRECTOR. I ACCIDENTALLY--
SHUT THE DOOR!
YES, SIR.
I'M NOT SURE IF YOU ARE AWARE, AGENT FRANKLIN, BUT I AM A VERY BUSY MAN. SO THIS BETTER NOT BE A WASTE OF MY TIME....
IT'S NOT, SIR.
THEN LET'S HEAR IT. AND MAKE IT BRIEF.
TWO MONTHS AGO, AN ARMY BLOOD DEPOT AT FORT JACKSON WAS RAIDED BY FOUR UNIDENTIFIED INDIVIDUALS.
THE ONLY REPORTED STOLEN ITEM...

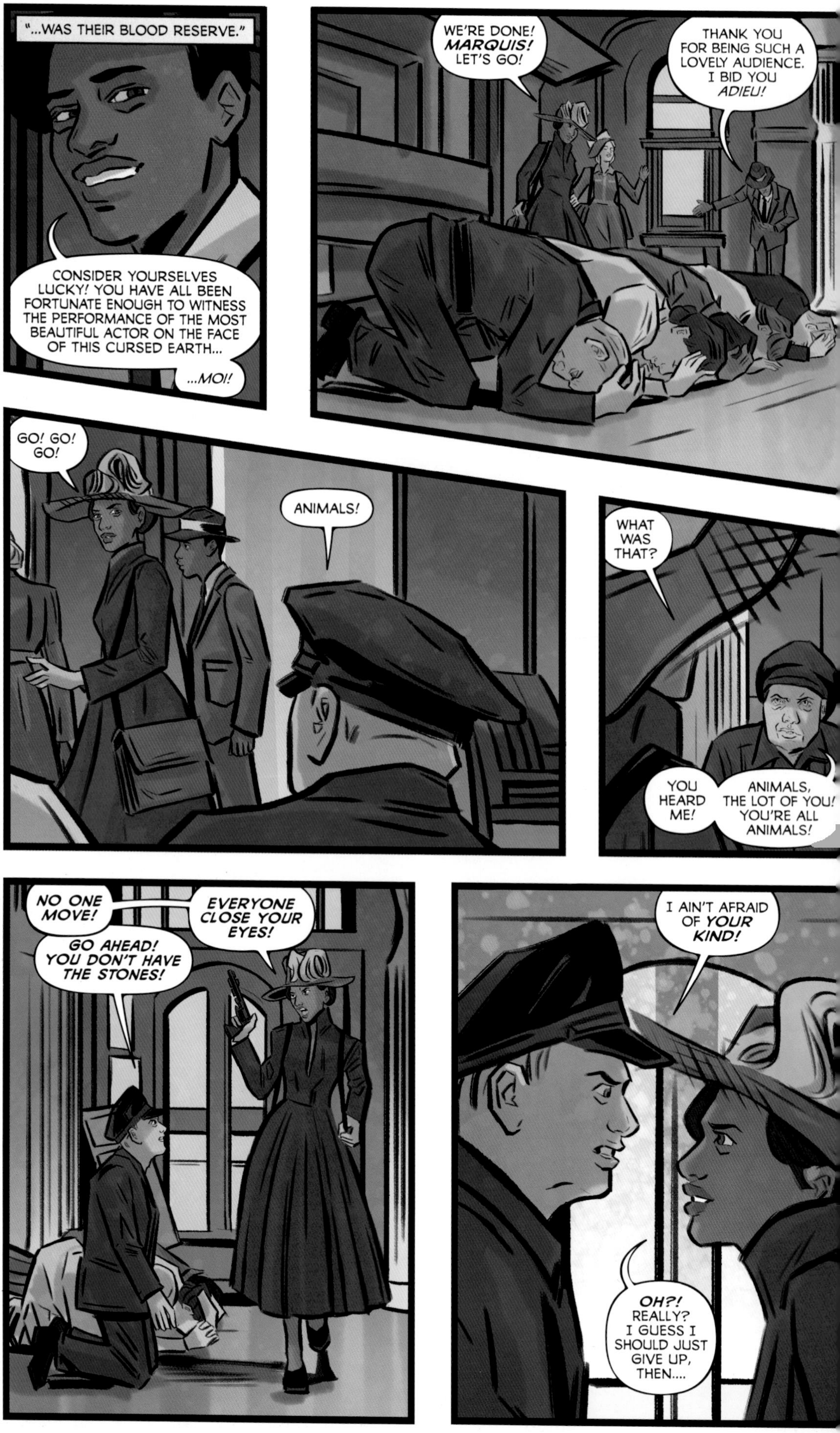
"...WAS THEIR BLOOD RESERVE."
CONSIDER YOURSELVES LUCKY! YOU HAVE ALL BEEN FORTUNATE ENOUGH TO WITNESS THE PERFORMANCE OF THE MOST BEAUTIFUL ACTOR ON THE FACE OF THIS CURSED EARTH...
...MOI!
WE'RE DONE! MARQUIS! LET'S GO!
THANK YOU FOR BEING SUCH A LOVELY AUDIENCE. I BID YOU ADIEU!
GO! GO! GO!
ANIMALS!
WHAT WAS THAT?
YOU HEARD ME!
ANIMALS, THE LOT OF YOU! YOU'RE ALL ANIMALS!
NO ONE MOVE!
EVERYONE CLOSE YOUR EYES!
GO AHEAD! YOU DON'T HAVE THE STONES!
I AIN'T AFRAID OF YOUR KIND!
OH?! REALLY? I GUESS I SHOULD JUST GIVE UP, THEN....

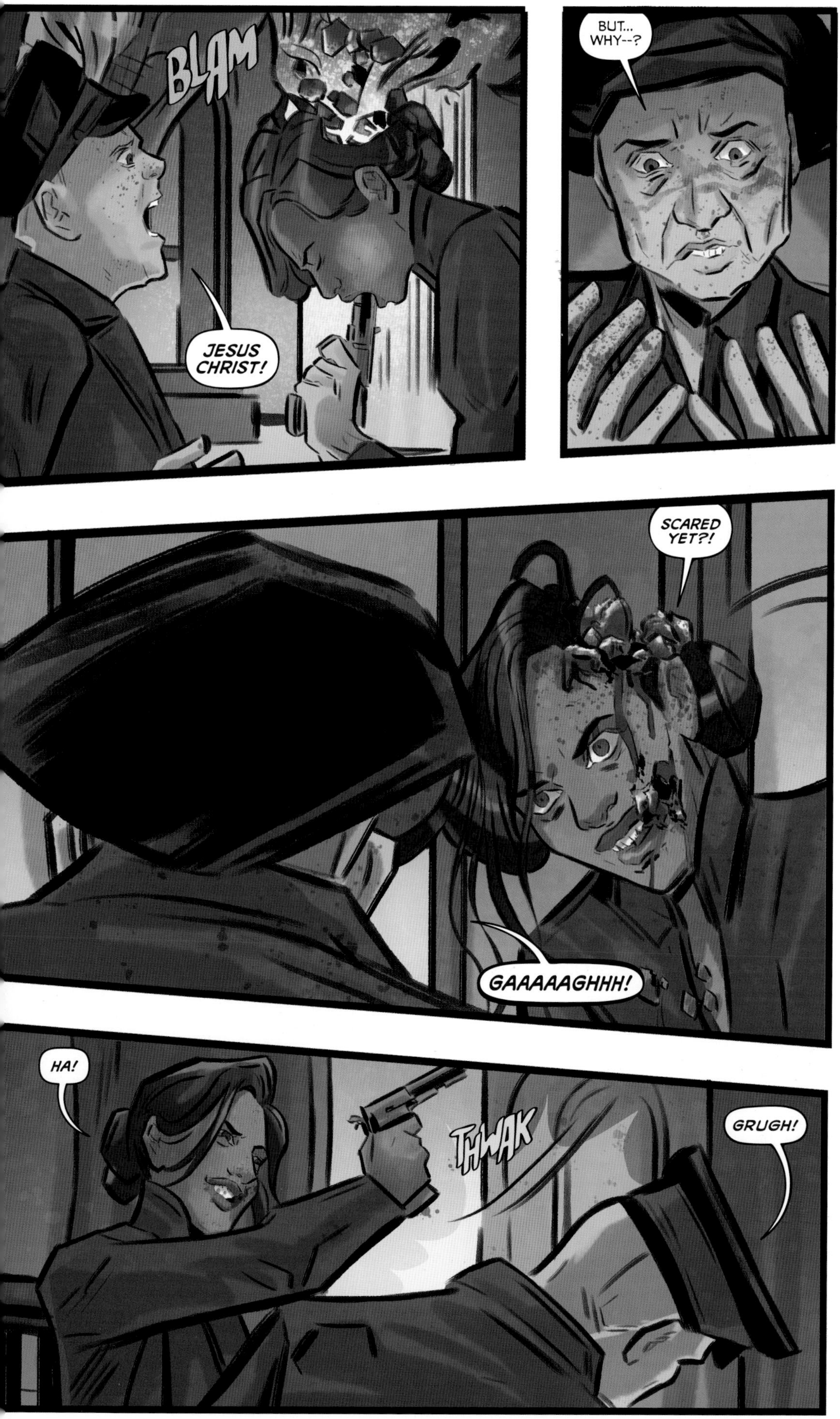
BLAM
JESUS CHRIST!
BUT... WHY--?
SCARED YET?!
GAAAAAGHHH!
HA!
THWAK
GRUGH!

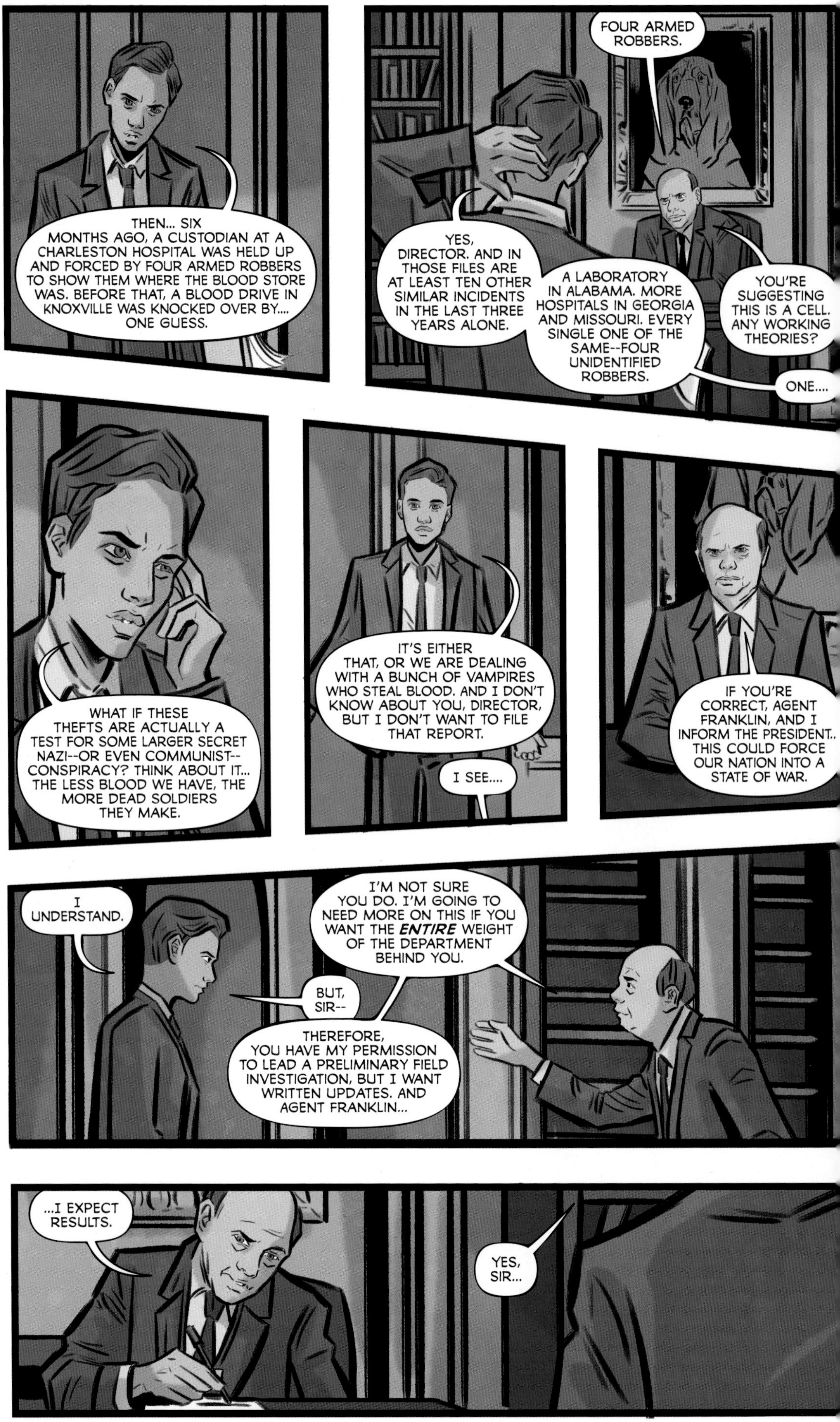
THEN... SIX MONTHS AGO, A CUSTODIAN AT A CHARLESTON HOSPITAL WAS HELD UP AND FORCED BY FOUR ARMED ROBBERS TO SHOW THEM WHERE THE BLOOD STORE WAS. BEFORE THAT, A BLOOD DRIVE IN KNOXVILLE WAS KNOCKED OVER BY.... ONE GUESS.
FOUR ARMED ROBBERS.
YES, DIRECTOR. AND IN THOSE FILES ARE AT LEAST TEN OTHER SIMILAR INCIDENTS IN THE LAST THREE YEARS ALONE.
A LABORATORY IN ALABAMA. MORE HOSPITALS IN GEORGIA AND MISSOURI. EVERY SINGLE ONE OF THE SAME--FOUR UNIDENTIFIED ROBBERS.
YOU'RE SUGGESTING THIS IS A CELL. ANY WORKING THEORIES?
ONE....
WHAT IF THESE THEFTS ARE ACTUALLY A TEST FOR SOME LARGER SECRET NAZI--OR EVEN COMMUNIST--CONSPIRACY? THINK ABOUT IT... THE LESS BLOOD WE HAVE, THE MORE DEAD SOLDIERS THEY MAKE.
IT'S EITHER THAT, OR WE ARE DEALING WITH A BUNCH OF VAMPIRES WHO STEAL BLOOD. AND I DON'T KNOW ABOUT YOU, DIRECTOR, BUT I DON'T WANT TO FILE THAT REPORT.
I SEE....
IF YOU'RE CORRECT, AGENT FRANKLIN, AND I INFORM THE PRESIDENT.. THIS COULD FORCE OUR NATION INTO A STATE OF WAR.
I UNDERSTAND.
I'M NOT SURE YOU DO. I'M GOING TO NEED MORE ON THIS IF YOU WANT THE *ENTIRE* WEIGHT OF THE DEPARTMENT BEHIND YOU.
BUT, SIR--
THEREFORE, YOU HAVE MY PERMISSION TO LEAD A PRELIMINARY FIELD INVESTIGATION, BUT I WANT WRITTEN UPDATES. AND AGENT FRANKLIN...
...I EXPECT RESULTS.
YES, SIR...

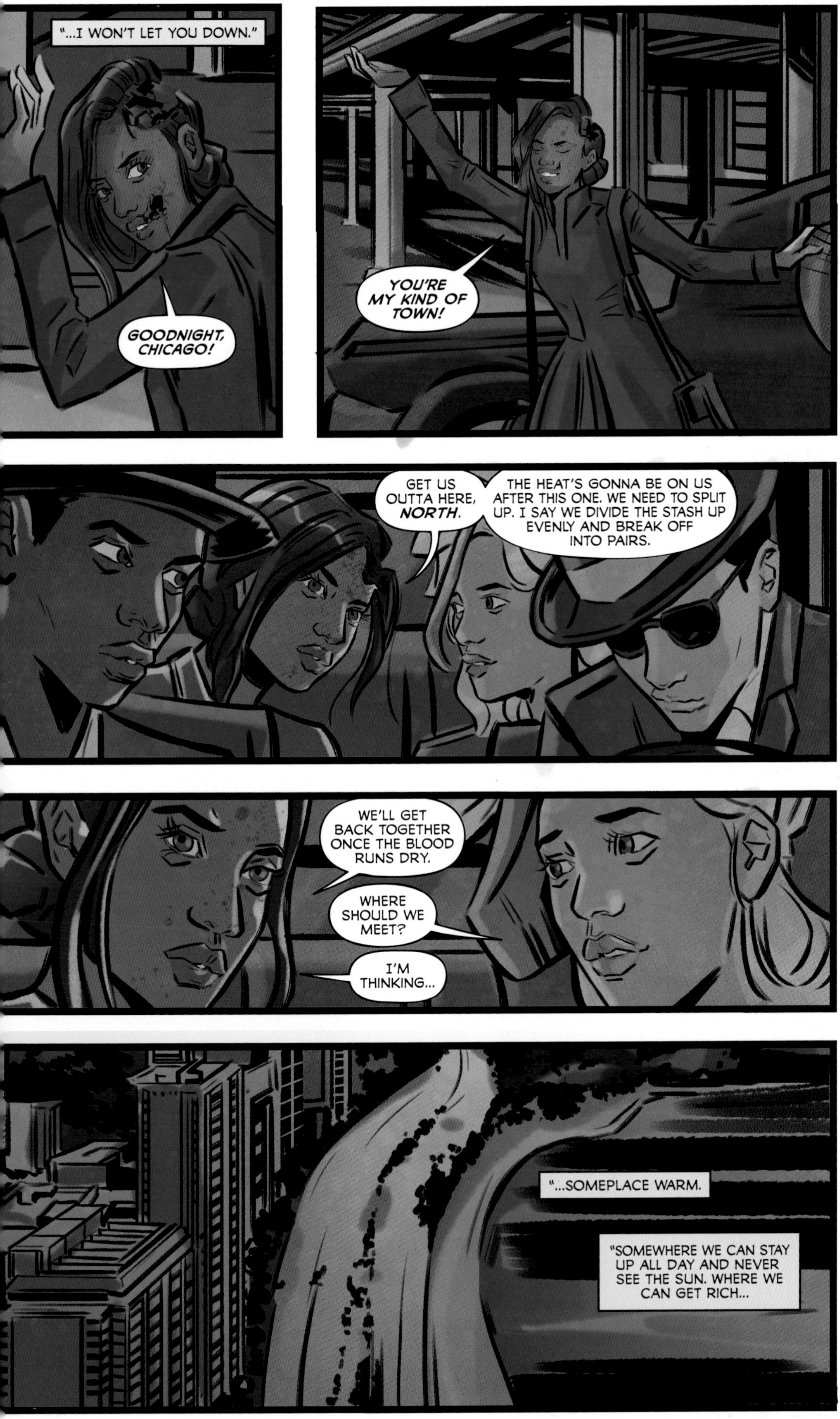
"...I WON'T LET YOU DOWN."
GOODNIGHT, CHICAGO!
YOU'RE MY KIND OF TOWN!
GET US OUTTA HERE, NORTH.
THE HEAT'S GONNA BE ON US AFTER THIS ONE. WE NEED TO SPLIT UP. I SAY WE DIVIDE THE STASH UP EVENLY AND BREAK OFF INTO PAIRS.
WE'LL GET BACK TOGETHER ONCE THE BLOOD RUNS DRY.
WHERE SHOULD WE MEET?
I'M THINKING...
"...SOMEPLACE WARM.
"SOMEWHERE WE CAN STAY UP ALL DAY AND NEVER SEE THE SUN. WHERE WE CAN GET RICH...

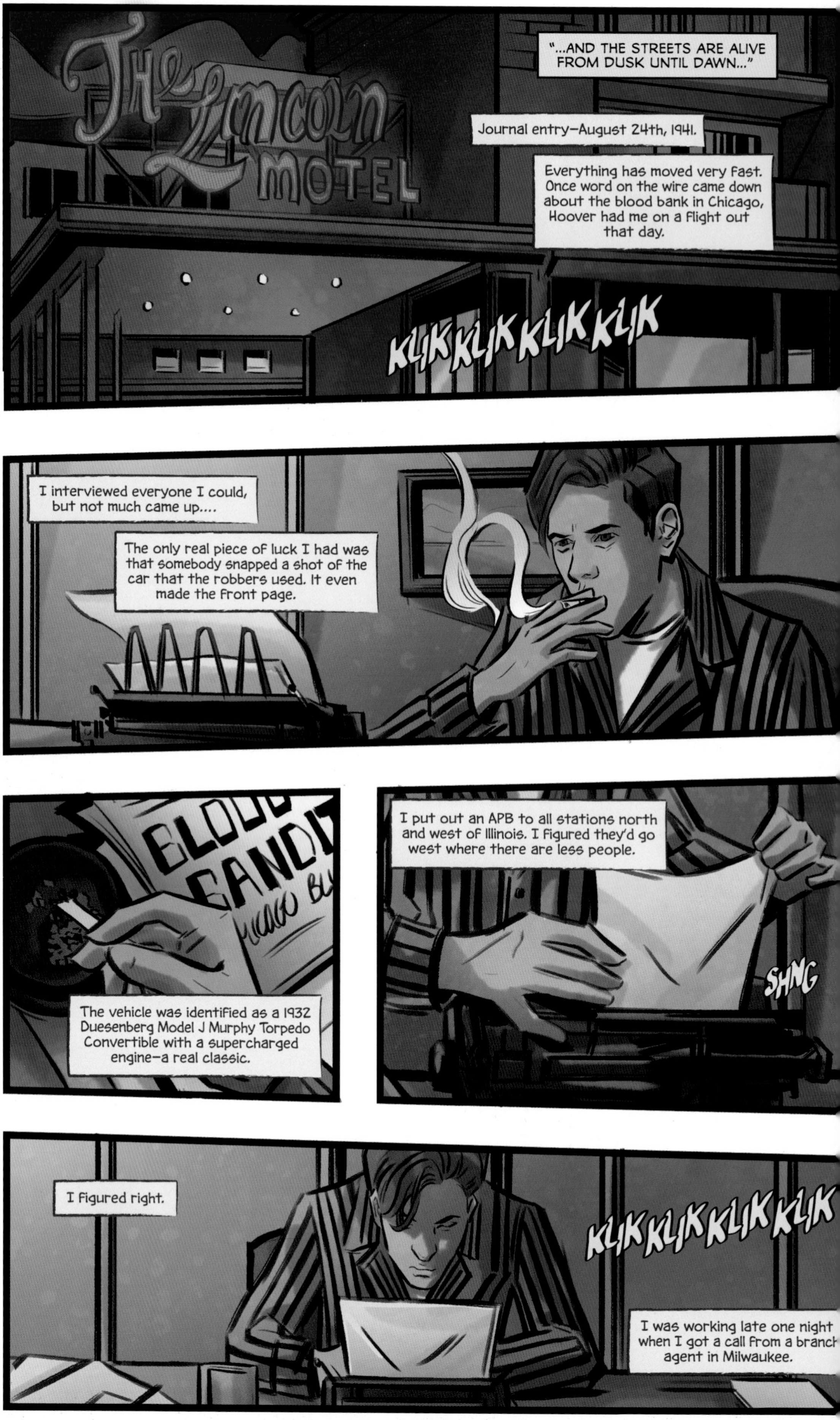
The Lincoln Motel
"...AND THE STREETS ARE ALIVE FROM DUSK UNTIL DAWN..."
Journal entry—August 24th, 1941.
Everything has moved very fast. Once word on the wire came down about the blood bank in Chicago, Hoover had me on a flight out that day.
KLIK KLIK KLIK KLIK
I interviewed everyone I could, but not much came up....
The only real piece of luck I had was that somebody snapped a shot of the car that the robbers used. It even made the front page.
The vehicle was identified as a 1932 Duesenberg Model J Murphy Torpedo Convertible with a supercharged engine—a real classic.
I put out an APB to all stations north and west of Illinois. I figured they'd go west where there are less people.
SHNG
I figured right.
KLIK KLIK KLIK KLIK
I was working late one night when I got a call from a branch agent in Milwaukee.

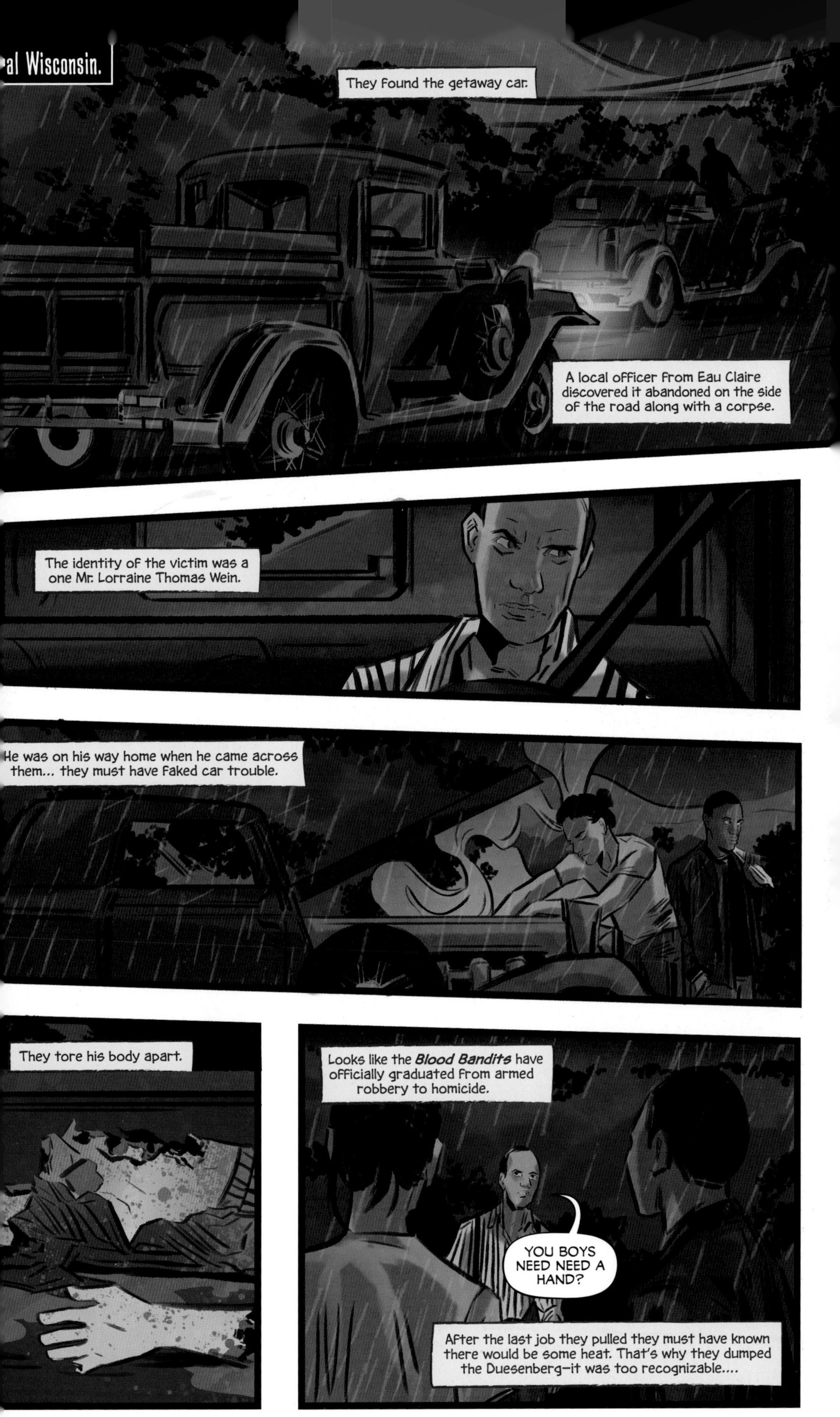
al Wisconsin.
They found the getaway car.
A local officer from Eau Claire discovered it abandoned on the side of the road along with a corpse.
The identity of the victim was a one Mr. Lorraine Thomas Wein.
He was on his way home when he came across them... they must have faked car trouble.
They tore his body apart.
Looks like the *Blood Bandits* have officially graduated from armed robbery to homicide.
YOU BOYS NEED NEED A HAND?
After the last job they pulled they must have known there would be some heat. That's why they dumped the Duesenberg—it was too recognizable....

LET ME GO GET A PART FROM MY TRUCK....

I updated Director Hoover on the situation, and now the Bureau has eyes in every state looking for Wein's stolen vehicle.

But why didn't they just steal Wein's car? Why did they have to kill him? Why did they need to... escalate it?

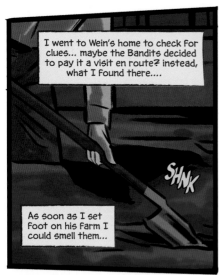

I went to Wein's home to check for clues... maybe the Bandits decided to pay it a visit en route? instead, what I found there....

SHNK

As soon as I set foot on his farm I could smell them...

...the bodies he had buried in his barnyard.

A private graveyard filled with his own personal collection of victims.

The man was a psychopathic killer. A bloodthirsty monster.

HANDS UP!

And if they hadn't have murdered him no one might have ever found out....

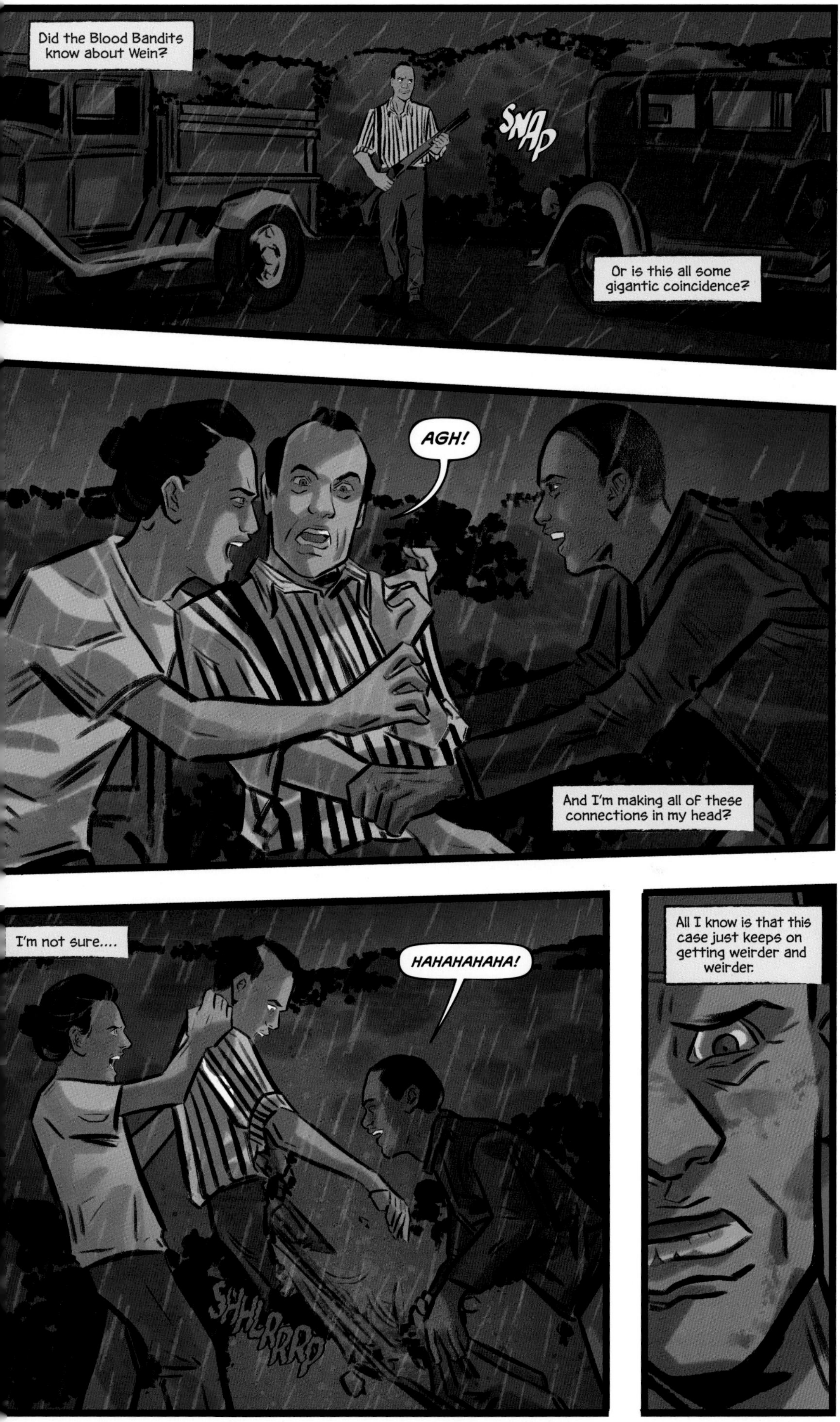

Did the Blood Bandits know about Wein?
SNAP
Or is this all some gigantic coincidence?
AGH!
And I'm making all of these connections in my head?
I'm not sure....
HAHAHAHAHA!
SHHLRRRP
All I know is that this case just keeps on getting weirder and weirder.

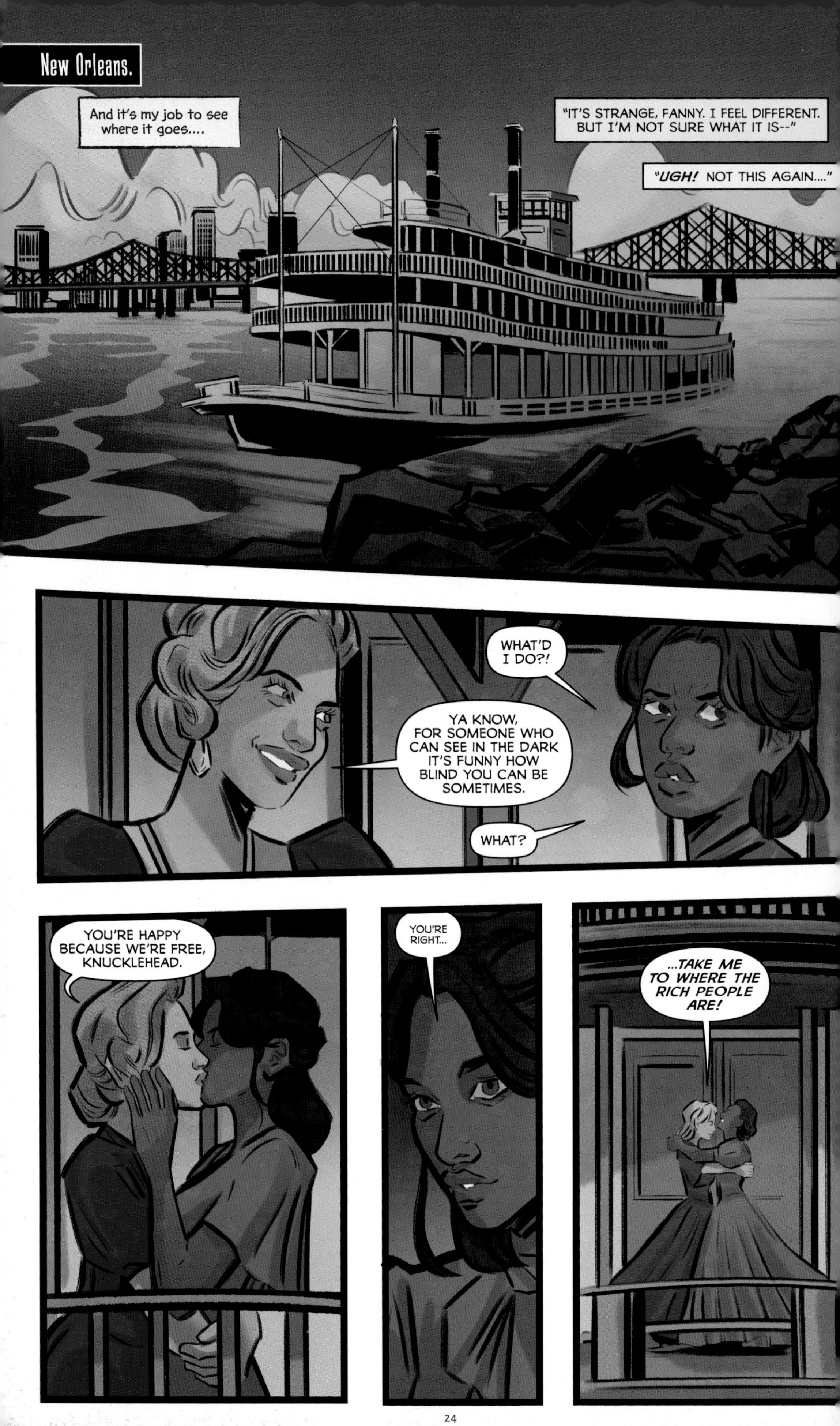
New Orleans.
And it's my job to see where it goes....
"IT'S STRANGE, FANNY. I FEEL DIFFERENT. BUT I'M NOT SURE WHAT IT IS--"
"UGH! NOT THIS AGAIN...."
WHAT'D I DO?!
YA KNOW, FOR SOMEONE WHO CAN SEE IN THE DARK IT'S FUNNY HOW BLIND YOU CAN BE SOMETIMES.
WHAT?
YOU'RE HAPPY BECAUSE WE'RE FREE, KNUCKLEHEAD.
YOU'RE RIGHT...
...TAKE ME TO WHERE THE RICH PEOPLE ARE!

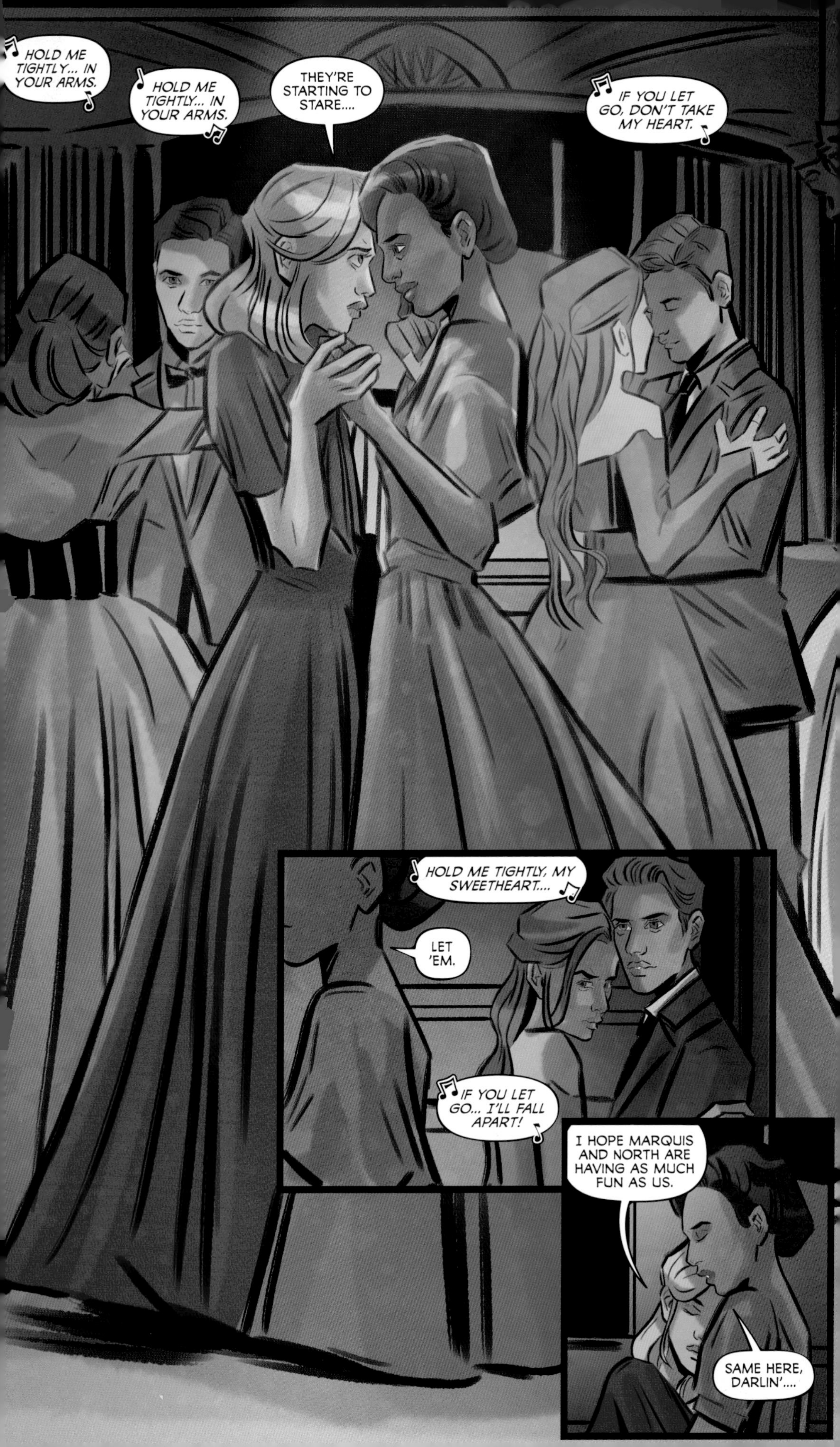
HOLD ME TIGHTLY... IN YOUR ARMS.
HOLD ME TIGHTLY... IN YOUR ARMS.
THEY'RE STARTING TO STARE....
IF YOU LET GO, DON'T TAKE MY HEART.
HOLD ME TIGHTLY, MY SWEETHEART....
LET 'EM.
IF YOU LET GO... I'LL FALL APART!
I HOPE MARQUIS AND NORTH ARE HAVING AS MUCH FUN AS US.
SAME HERE, DARLIN'....

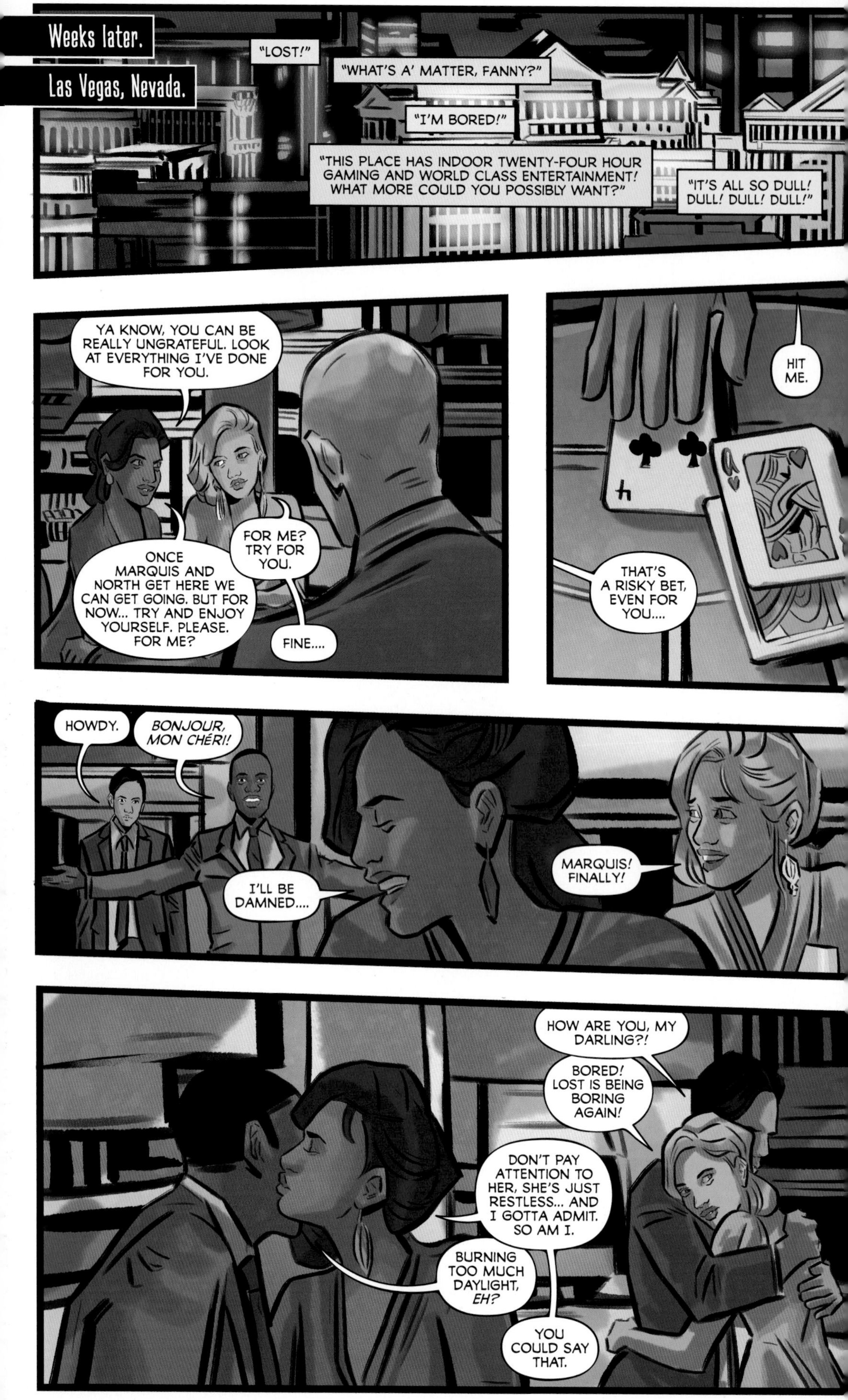

Weeks later.
Las Vegas, Nevada.
"LOST!"
"WHAT'S A' MATTER, FANNY?"
"I'M BORED!"
"THIS PLACE HAS INDOOR TWENTY-FOUR HOUR GAMING AND WORLD CLASS ENTERTAINMENT! WHAT MORE COULD YOU POSSIBLY WANT?"
"IT'S ALL SO DULL! DULL! DULL! DULL!"
YA KNOW, YOU CAN BE REALLY UNGRATEFUL. LOOK AT EVERYTHING I'VE DONE FOR YOU.
FOR ME? TRY FOR YOU.
ONCE MARQUIS AND NORTH GET HERE WE CAN GET GOING. BUT FOR NOW... TRY AND ENJOY YOURSELF. PLEASE. FOR ME?
FINE....
HIT ME.
THAT'S A RISKY BET, EVEN FOR YOU....
HOWDY.
BONJOUR, MON CHÉRI!
I'LL BE DAMNED....
MARQUIS! FINALLY!
HOW ARE YOU, MY DARLING?!
BORED! LOST IS BEING BORING AGAIN!
DON'T PAY ATTENTION TO HER, SHE'S JUST RESTLESS... AND I GOTTA ADMIT. SO AM I.
BURNING TOO MUCH DAYLIGHT, *EH?*
YOU COULD SAY THAT.

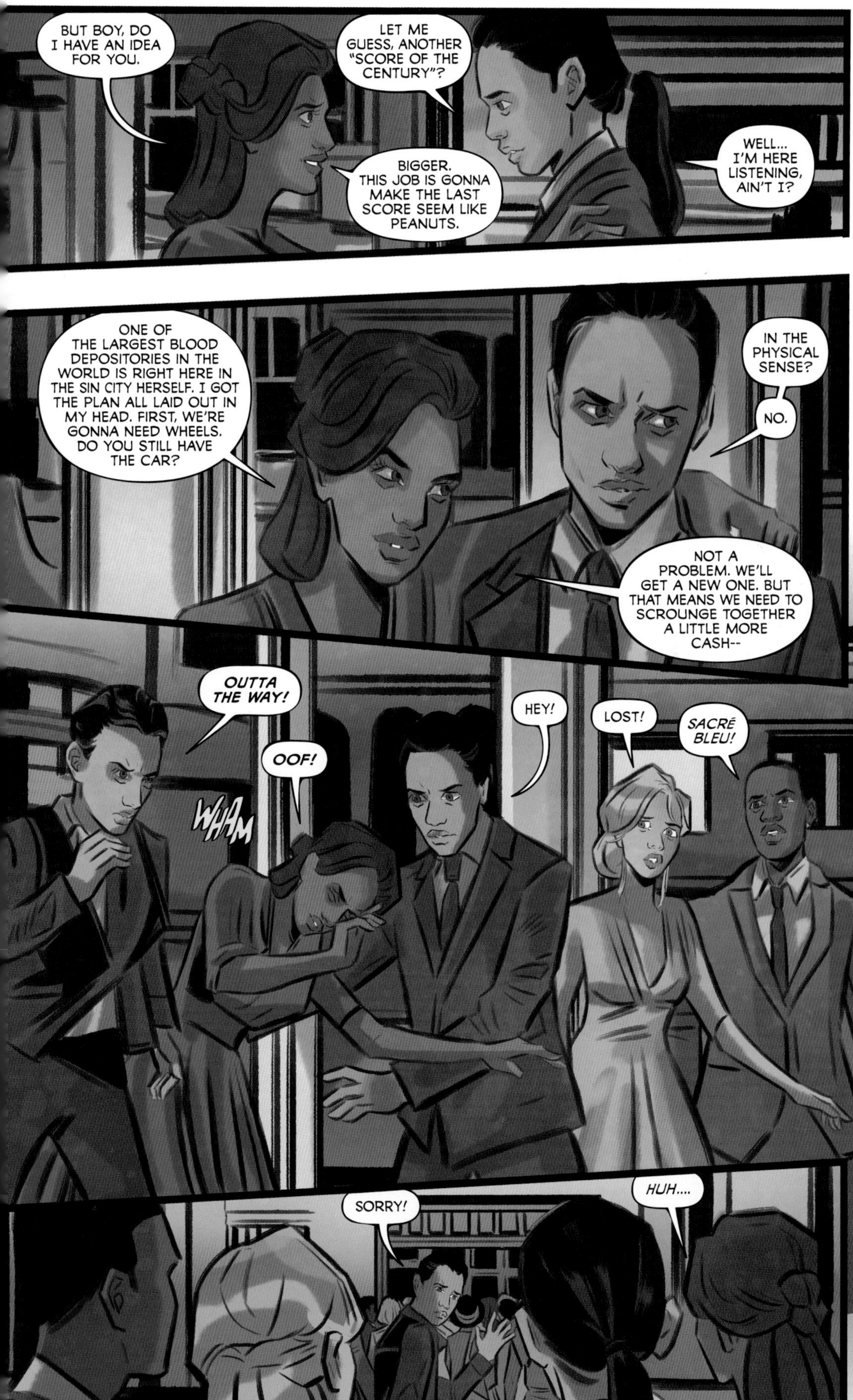
BUT BOY, DO I HAVE AN IDEA FOR YOU.
LET ME GUESS, ANOTHER "SCORE OF THE CENTURY"?
BIGGER. THIS JOB IS GONNA MAKE THE LAST SCORE SEEM LIKE PEANUTS.
WELL... I'M HERE LISTENING, AIN'T I?
ONE OF THE LARGEST BLOOD DEPOSITORIES IN THE WORLD IS RIGHT HERE IN THE SIN CITY HERSELF. I GOT THE PLAN ALL LAID OUT IN MY HEAD. FIRST, WE'RE GONNA NEED WHEELS. DO YOU STILL HAVE THE CAR?
IN THE PHYSICAL SENSE?
NO.
NOT A PROBLEM. WE'LL GET A NEW ONE. BUT THAT MEANS WE NEED TO SCROUNGE TOGETHER A LITTLE MORE CASH--
OUTTA THE WAY!
WHAM
OOF!
HEY!
LOST!
SACRÉ BLEU!
SORRY!
HUH....

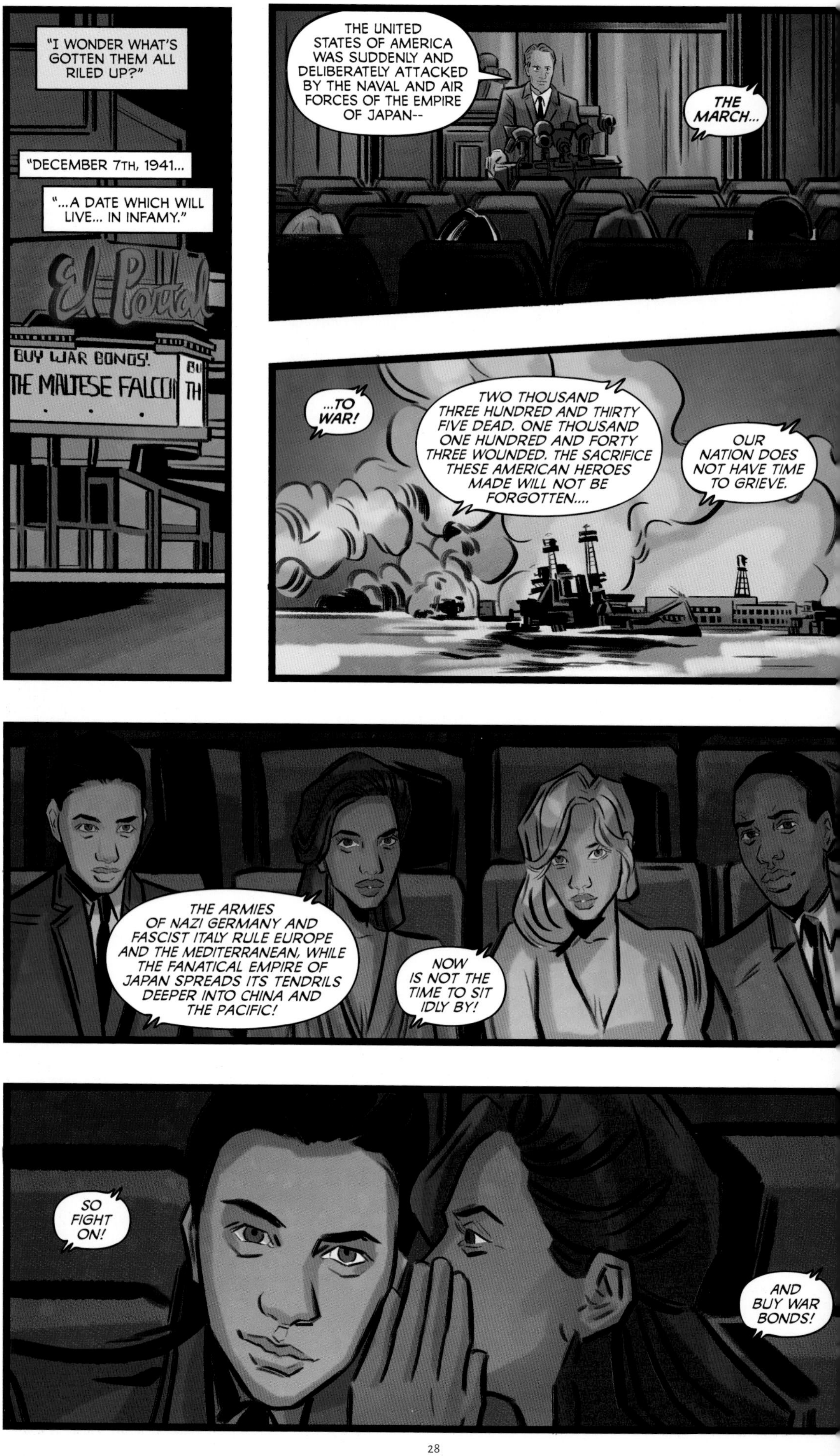
"I WONDER WHAT'S GOTTEN THEM ALL RILED UP?"
"DECEMBER 7TH, 1941...
"...A DATE WHICH WILL LIVE... IN INFAMY."
BUY WAR BONDS!
THE UNITED STATES OF AMERICA WAS SUDDENLY AND DELIBERATELY ATTACKED BY THE NAVAL AND AIR FORCES OF THE EMPIRE OF JAPAN--
THE MARCH...
...TO WAR!
TWO THOUSAND THREE HUNDRED AND THIRTY FIVE DEAD. ONE THOUSAND ONE HUNDRED AND FORTY THREE WOUNDED. THE SACRIFICE THESE AMERICAN HEROES MADE WILL NOT BE FORGOTTEN....
OUR NATION DOES NOT HAVE TIME TO GRIEVE.
THE ARMIES OF NAZI GERMANY AND FASCIST ITALY RULE EUROPE AND THE MEDITERRANEAN, WHILE THE FANATICAL EMPIRE OF JAPAN SPREADS ITS TENDRILS DEEPER INTO CHINA AND THE PACIFIC!
NOW IS NOT THE TIME TO SIT IDLY BY!
SO FIGHT ON!
AND BUY WAR BONDS!

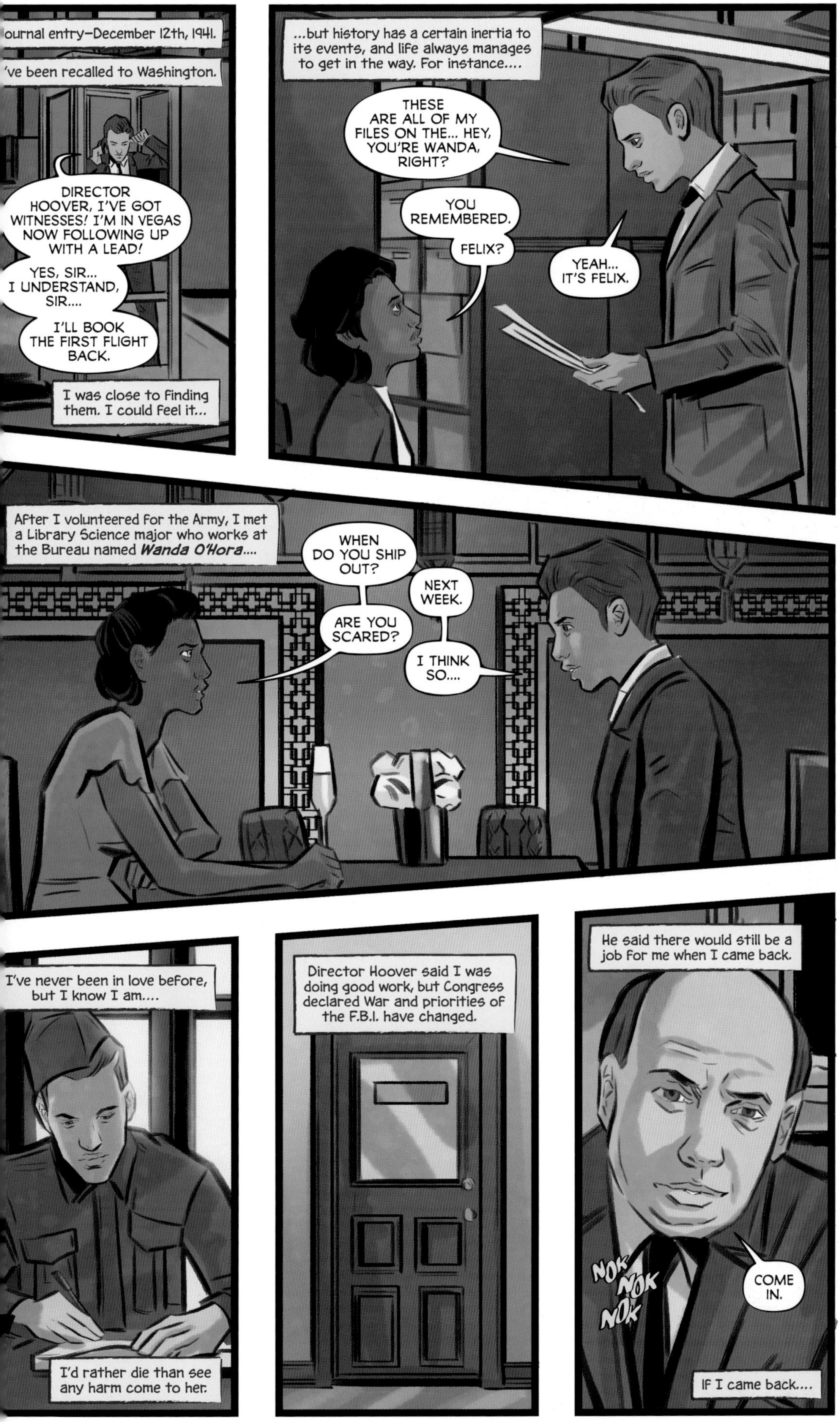

ournal entry—December 12th, 1941.
've been recalled to Washington.
DIRECTOR HOOVER, I'VE GOT WITNESSES! I'M IN VEGAS NOW FOLLOWING UP WITH A LEAD!
YES, SIR... I UNDERSTAND, SIR....
I'LL BOOK THE FIRST FLIGHT BACK.
I was close to finding them. I could feel it...
...but history has a certain inertia to its events, and life always manages to get in the way. For instance....
THESE ARE ALL OF MY FILES ON THE... HEY, YOU'RE WANDA, RIGHT?
YOU REMEMBERED.
FELIX?
YEAH... IT'S FELIX.
After I volunteered for the Army, I met a Library Science major who works at the Bureau named *Wanda O'Hora*....
WHEN DO YOU SHIP OUT?
NEXT WEEK.
ARE YOU SCARED?
I THINK SO....
I've never been in love before, but I know I am....
I'd rather die than see any harm come to her.
Director Hoover said I was doing good work, but Congress declared War and priorities of the F.B.I. have changed.
He said there would still be a job for me when I came back.
NOK NOK NOK
COME IN.
If I came back....

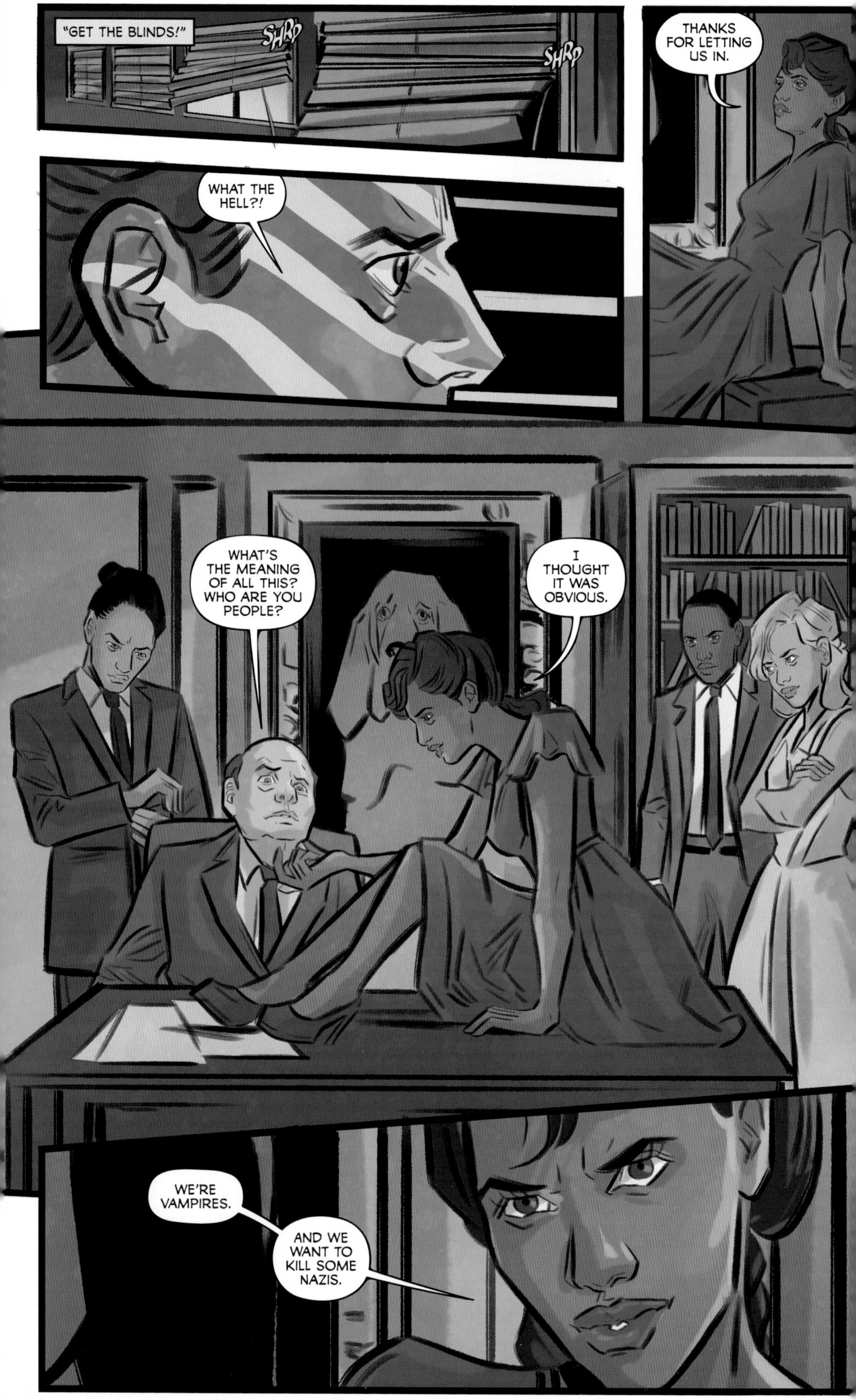
"GET THE BLINDS!"
SHRP
SHRP
THANKS FOR LETTING US IN.
WHAT THE HELL?!
WHAT'S THE MEANING OF ALL THIS? WHO ARE YOU PEOPLE?
I THOUGHT IT WAS OBVIOUS.
WE'RE VAMPIRES.
AND WE WANT TO KILL SOME NAZIS.

CHAPTER

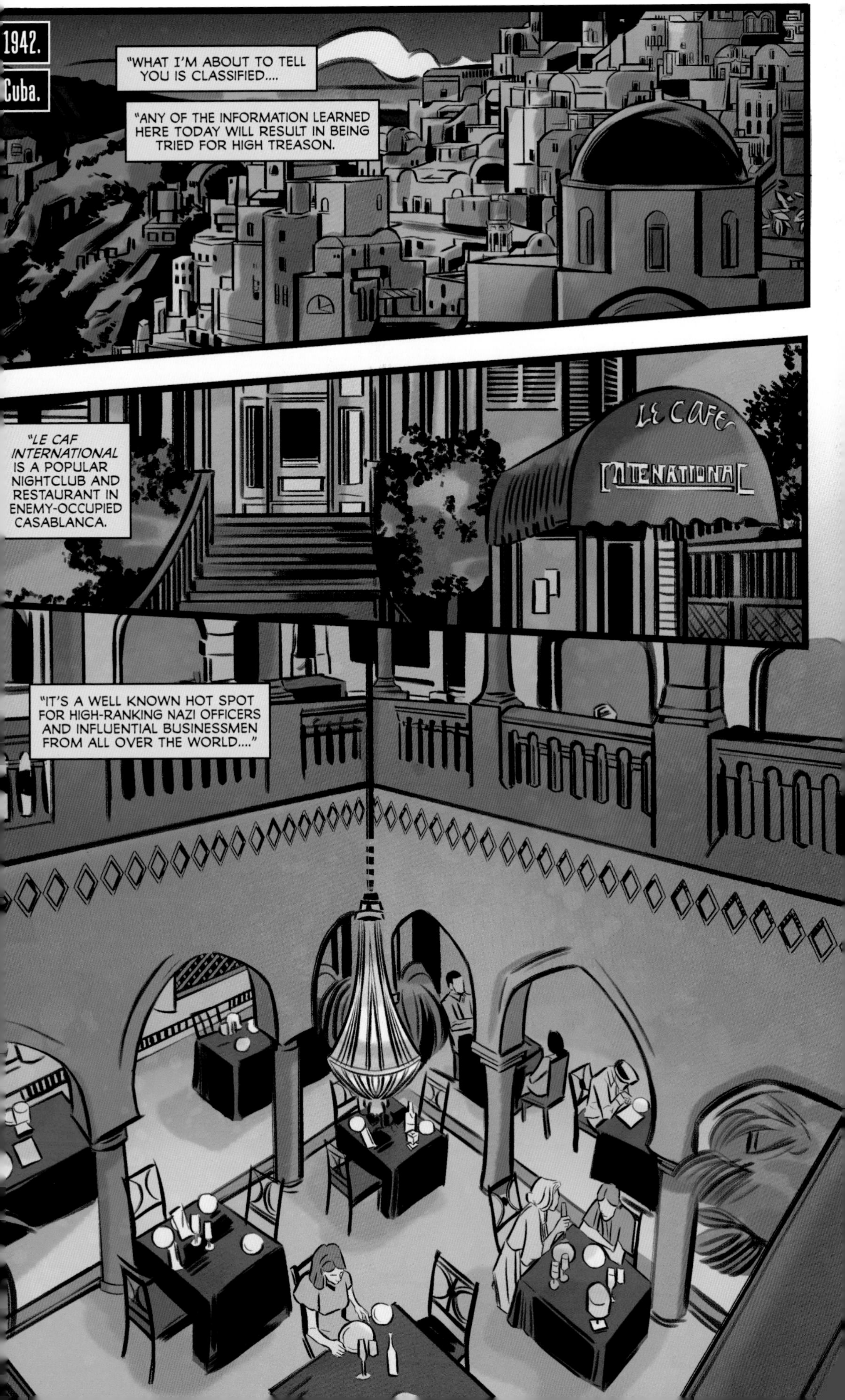
1942.
Cuba.
"WHAT I'M ABOUT TO TELL YOU IS CLASSIFIED....
"ANY OF THE INFORMATION LEARNED HERE TODAY WILL RESULT IN BEING TRIED FOR HIGH TREASON.
"LE CAF INTERNATIONAL IS A POPULAR NIGHTCLUB AND RESTAURANT IN ENEMY-OCCUPIED CASABLANCA.
LE CAFE
"IT'S A WELL KNOWN HOT SPOT FOR HIGH-RANKING NAZI OFFICERS AND INFLUENTIAL BUSINESSMEN FROM ALL OVER THE WORLD...."

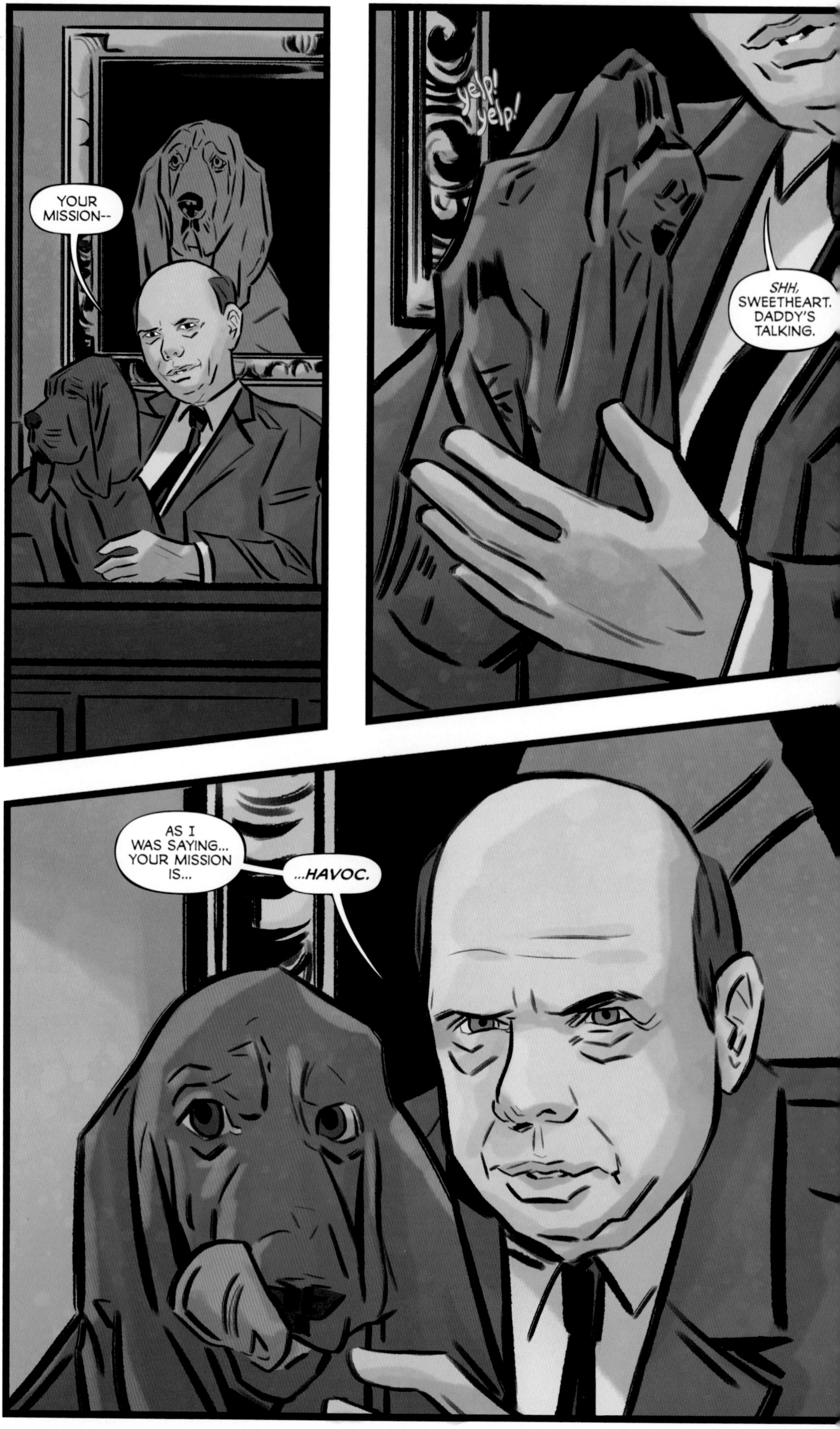
YOUR MISSION--
yelp! yelp!
SHH, SWEETHEART. DADDY'S TALKING.
AS I WAS SAYING... YOUR MISSION IS...
...HAVOC.

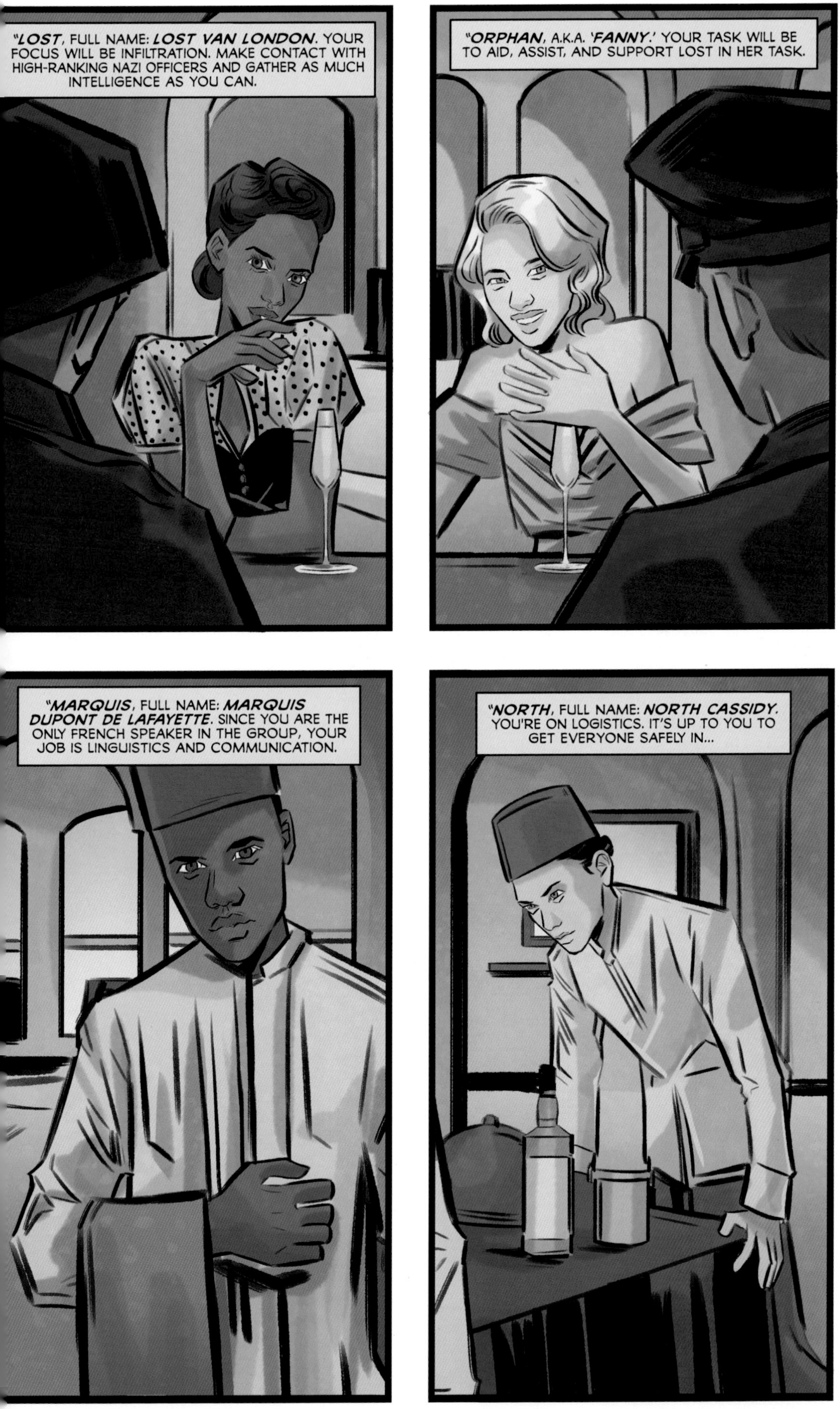
"LOST, FULL NAME: LOST VAN LONDON. YOUR FOCUS WILL BE INFILTRATION. MAKE CONTACT WITH HIGH-RANKING NAZI OFFICERS AND GATHER AS MUCH INTELLIGENCE AS YOU CAN.
"ORPHAN, A.K.A. 'FANNY.' YOUR TASK WILL BE TO AID, ASSIST, AND SUPPORT LOST IN HER TASK.
"MARQUIS, FULL NAME: MARQUIS DUPONT DE LAFAYETTE. SINCE YOU ARE THE ONLY FRENCH SPEAKER IN THE GROUP, YOUR JOB IS LINGUISTICS AND COMMUNICATION.
"NORTH, FULL NAME: NORTH CASSIDY. YOU'RE ON LOGISTICS. IT'S UP TO YOU TO GET EVERYONE SAFELY IN...

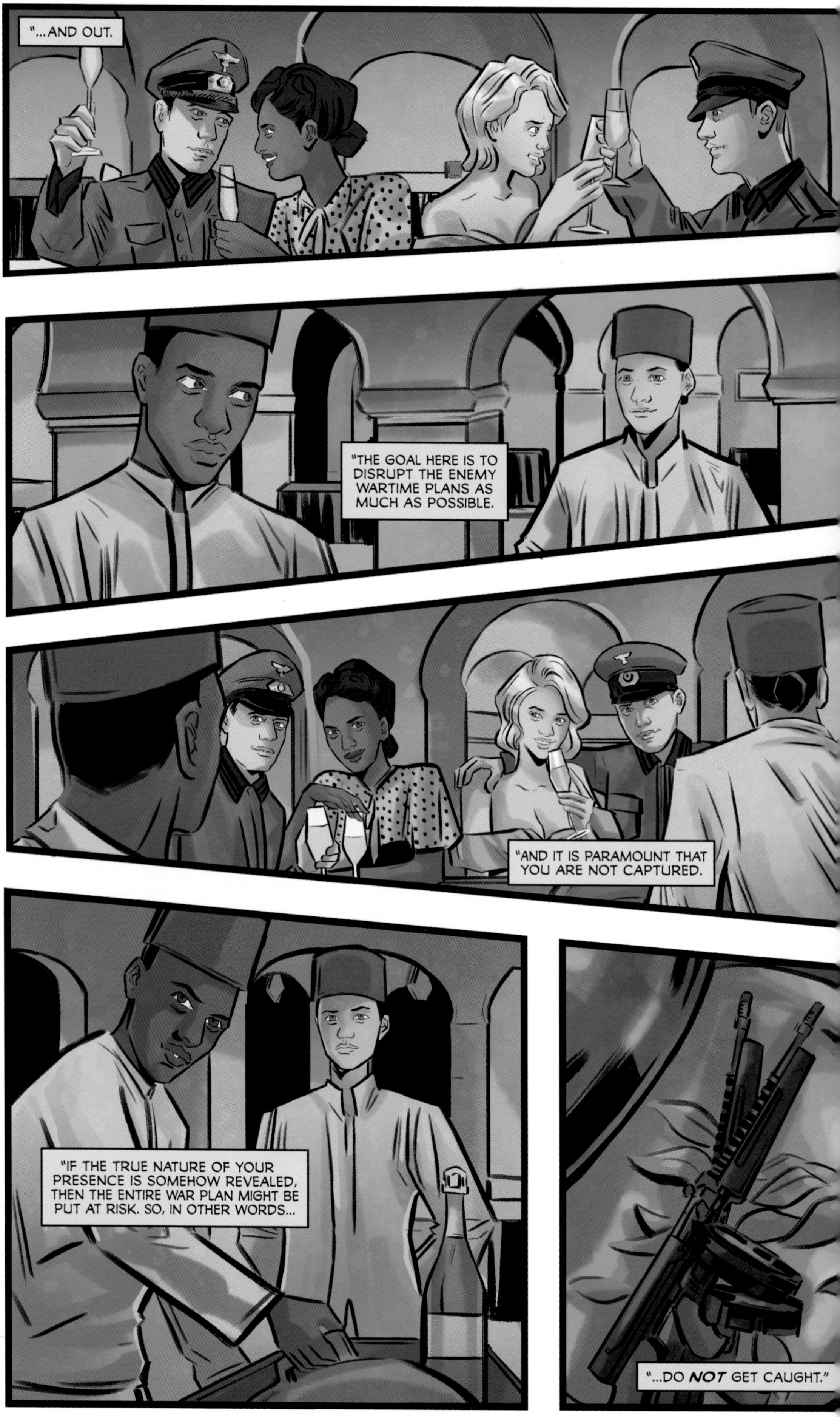
"...AND OUT.
"THE GOAL HERE IS TO DISRUPT THE ENEMY WARTIME PLANS AS MUCH AS POSSIBLE.
"AND IT IS PARAMOUNT THAT YOU ARE NOT CAPTURED.
"IF THE TRUE NATURE OF YOUR PRESENCE IS SOMEHOW REVEALED, THEN THE ENTIRE WAR PLAN MIGHT BE PUT AT RISK. SO, IN OTHER WORDS...
"...DO *NOT* GET CAUGHT."

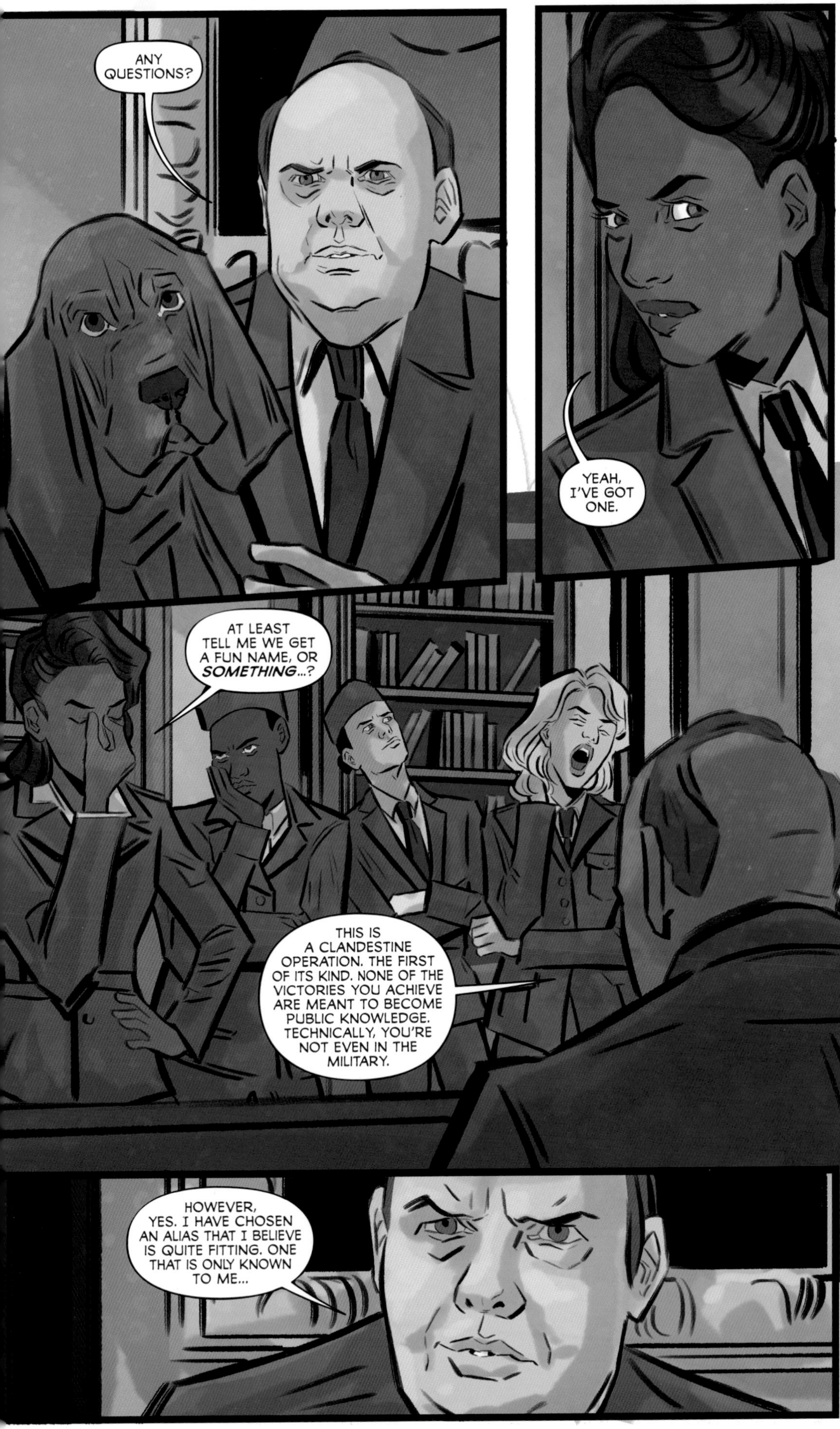
ANY QUESTIONS?
YEAH, I'VE GOT ONE.
AT LEAST TELL ME WE GET A FUN NAME, OR *SOMETHING*...?
THIS IS A CLANDESTINE OPERATION. THE FIRST OF ITS KIND. NONE OF THE VICTORIES YOU ACHIEVE ARE MEANT TO BECOME PUBLIC KNOWLEDGE. TECHNICALLY, YOU'RE NOT EVEN IN THE MILITARY.
HOWEVER, YES. I HAVE CHOSEN AN ALIAS THAT I BELIEVE IS QUITE FITTING. ONE THAT IS ONLY KNOWN TO ME...

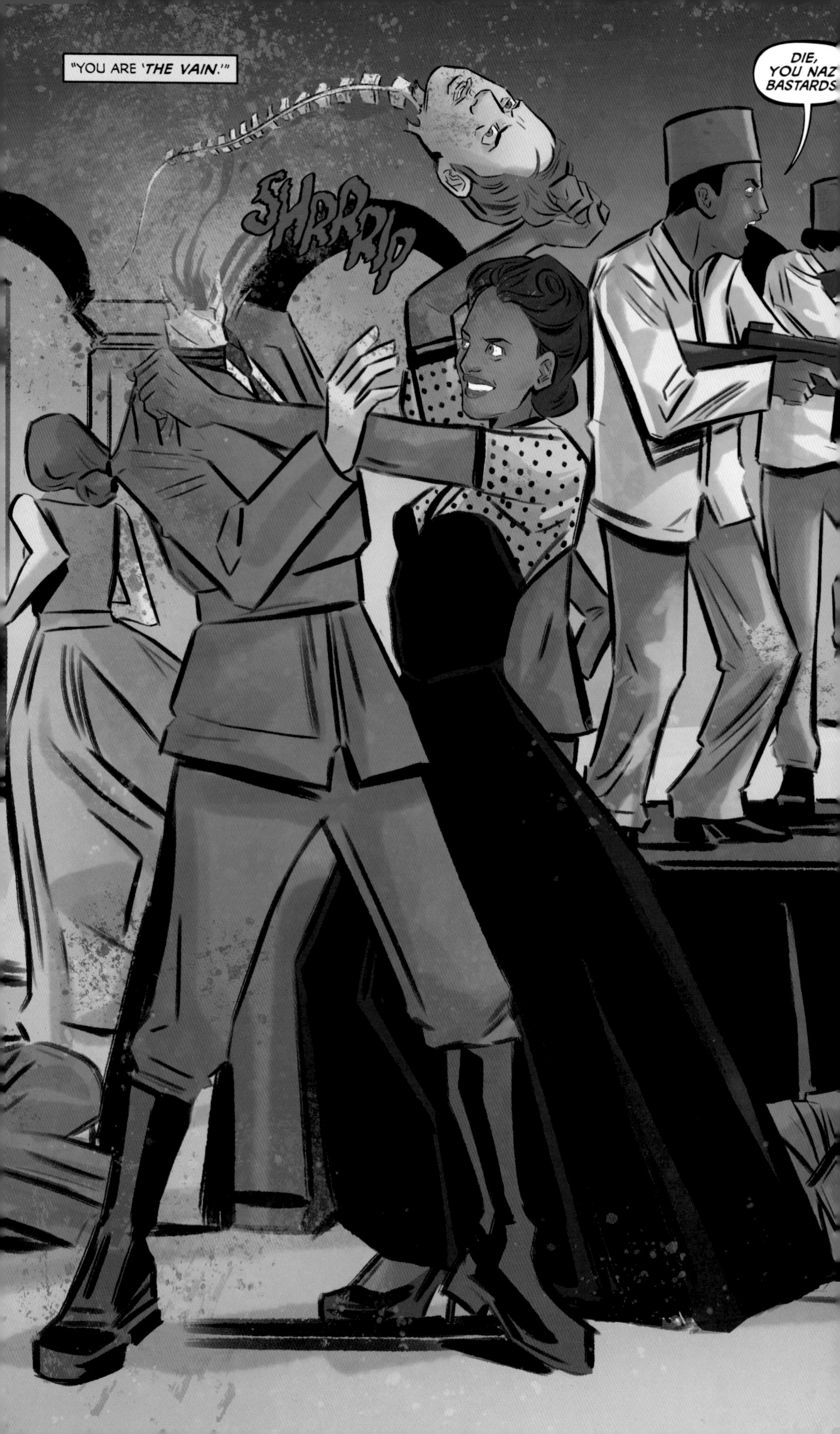
"YOU ARE '*THE VAIN*.'"
SHRRRIP
DIE, YOU NAZ BASTARDS

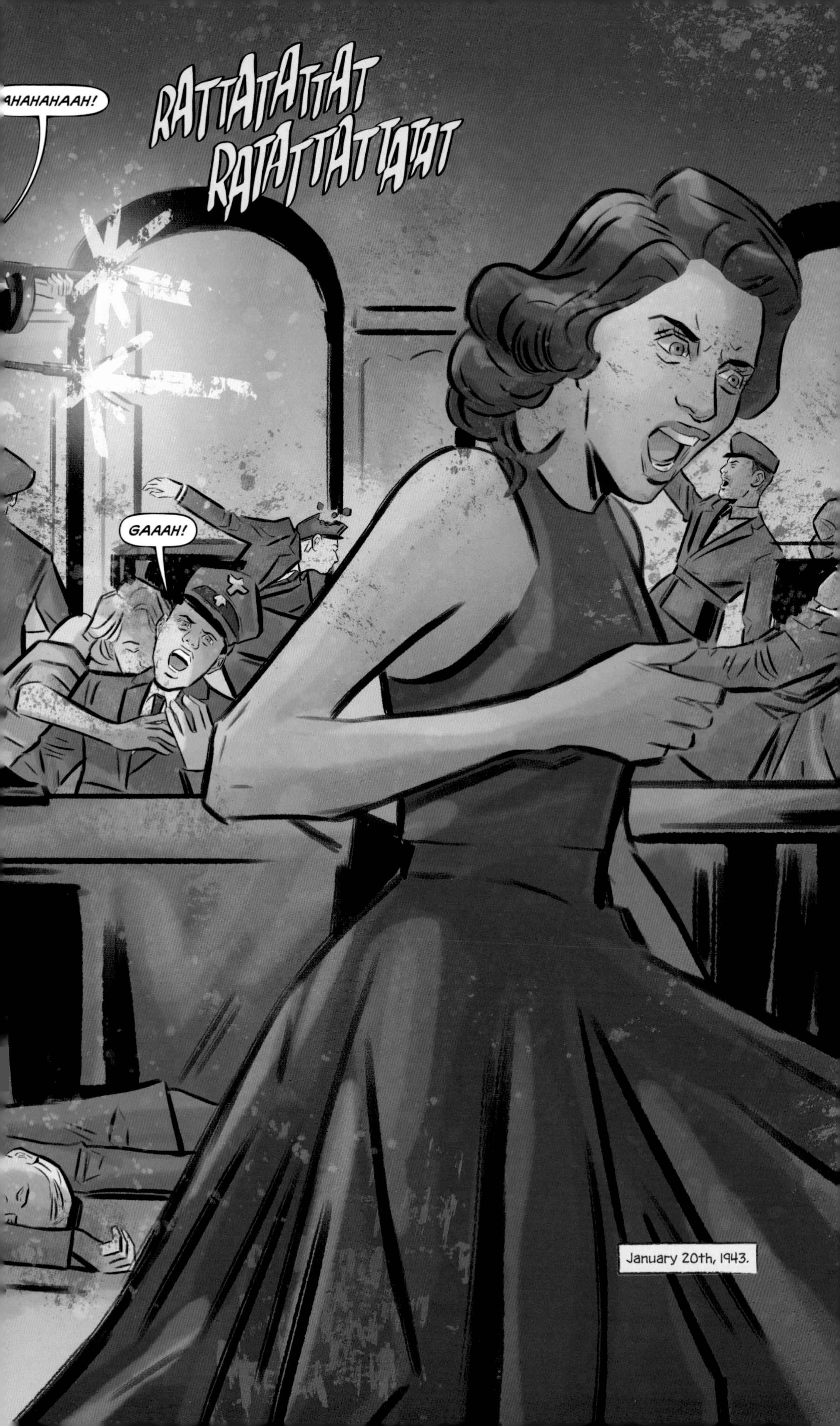
AHAHAHAAH!
RATTATATTAT
RATATTATTATAT
GAAAH!
January 20th, 1943.

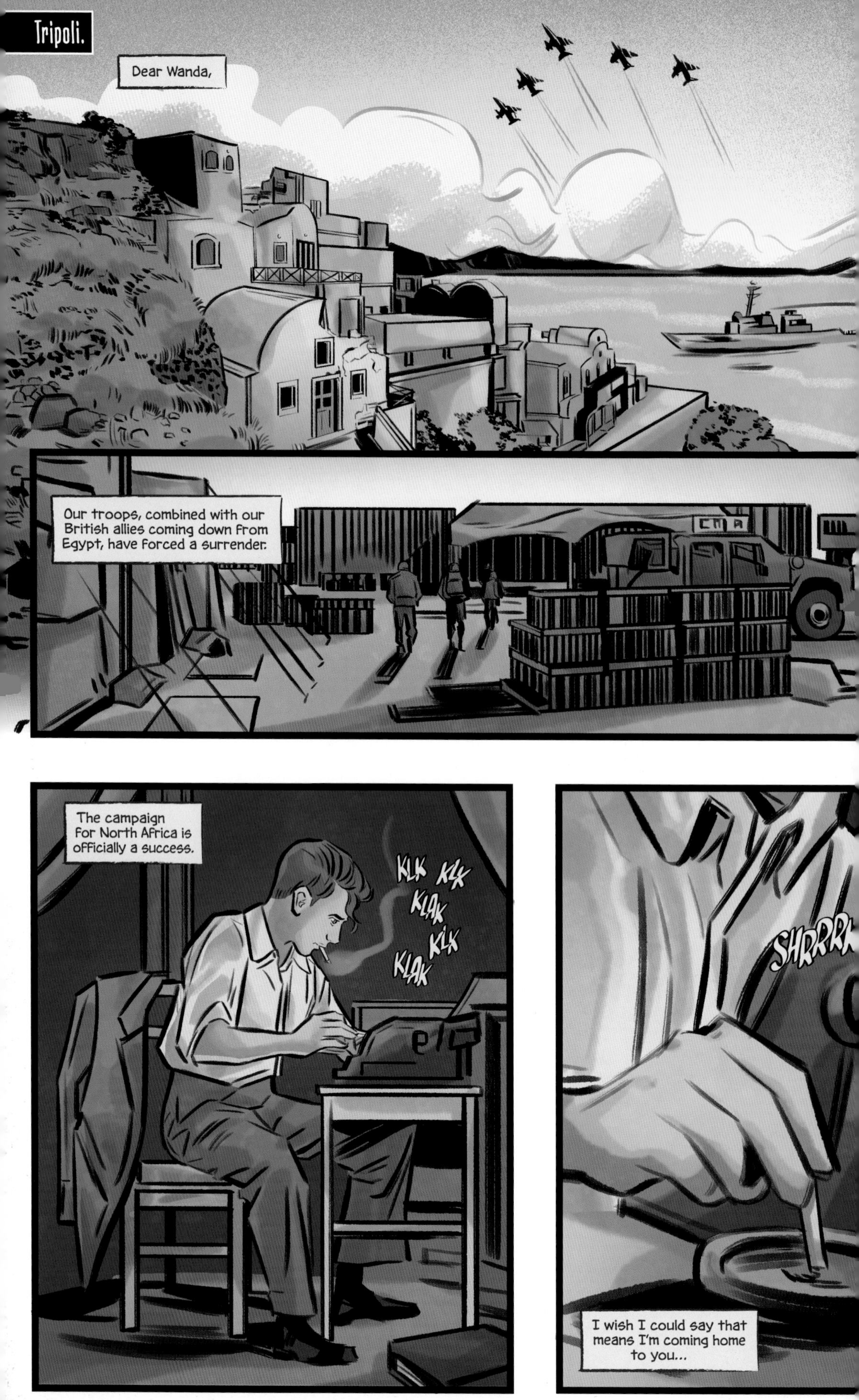

Tripoli.
Dear Wanda,
Our troops, combined with our British allies coming down from Egypt, have forced a surrender.
The campaign for North Africa is officially a success.
KLK KLK KLAK KLK KLAK
SHRRRK
I wish I could say that means I'm coming home to you...

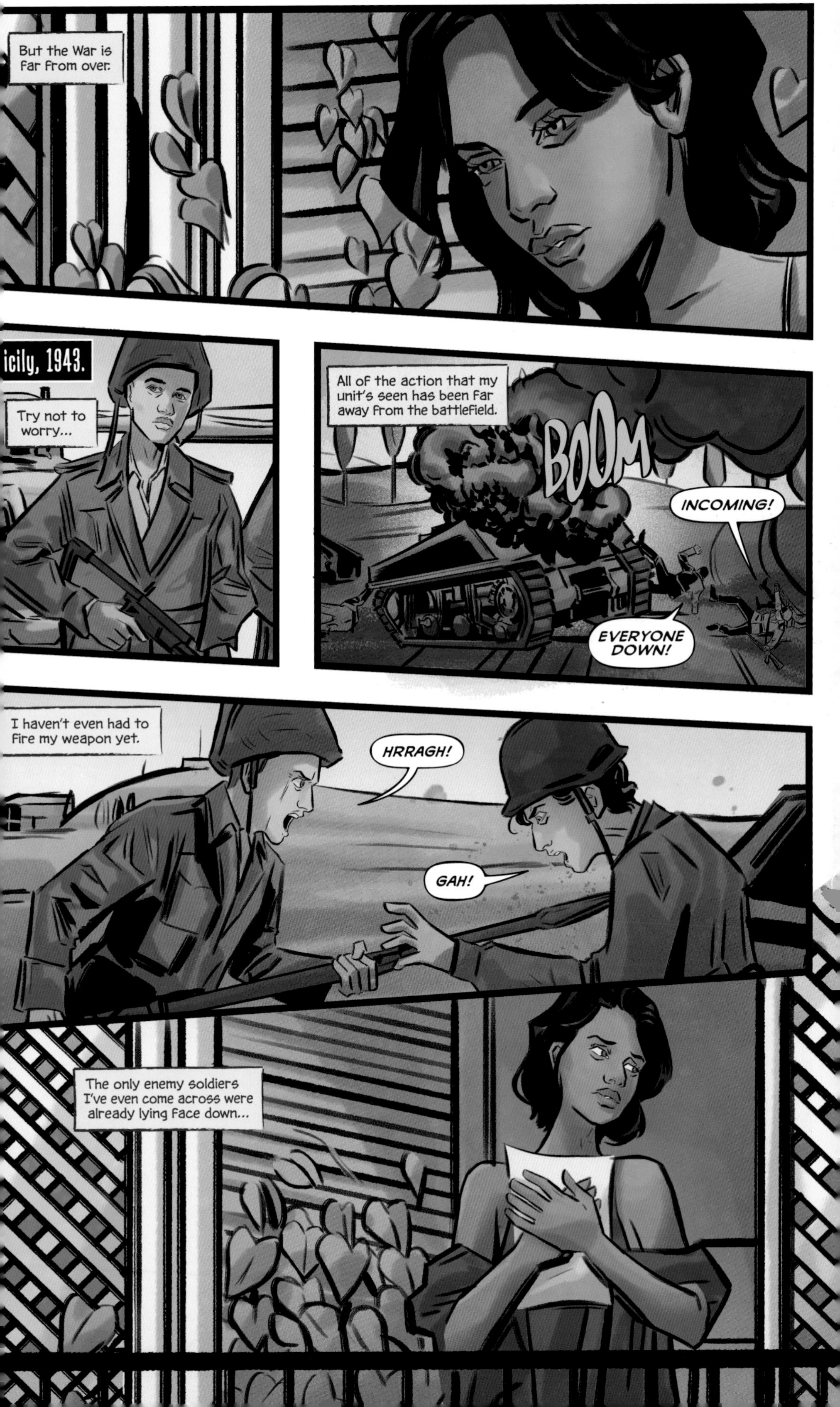

But the War is far from over.
icily, 1943.
Try not to worry...
All of the action that my unit's seen has been far away from the battlefield.
BOOM
INCOMING!
EVERYONE DOWN!
I haven't even had to fire my weapon yet.
HRRAGH!
GAH!
The only enemy soldiers I've even come across were already lying face down...

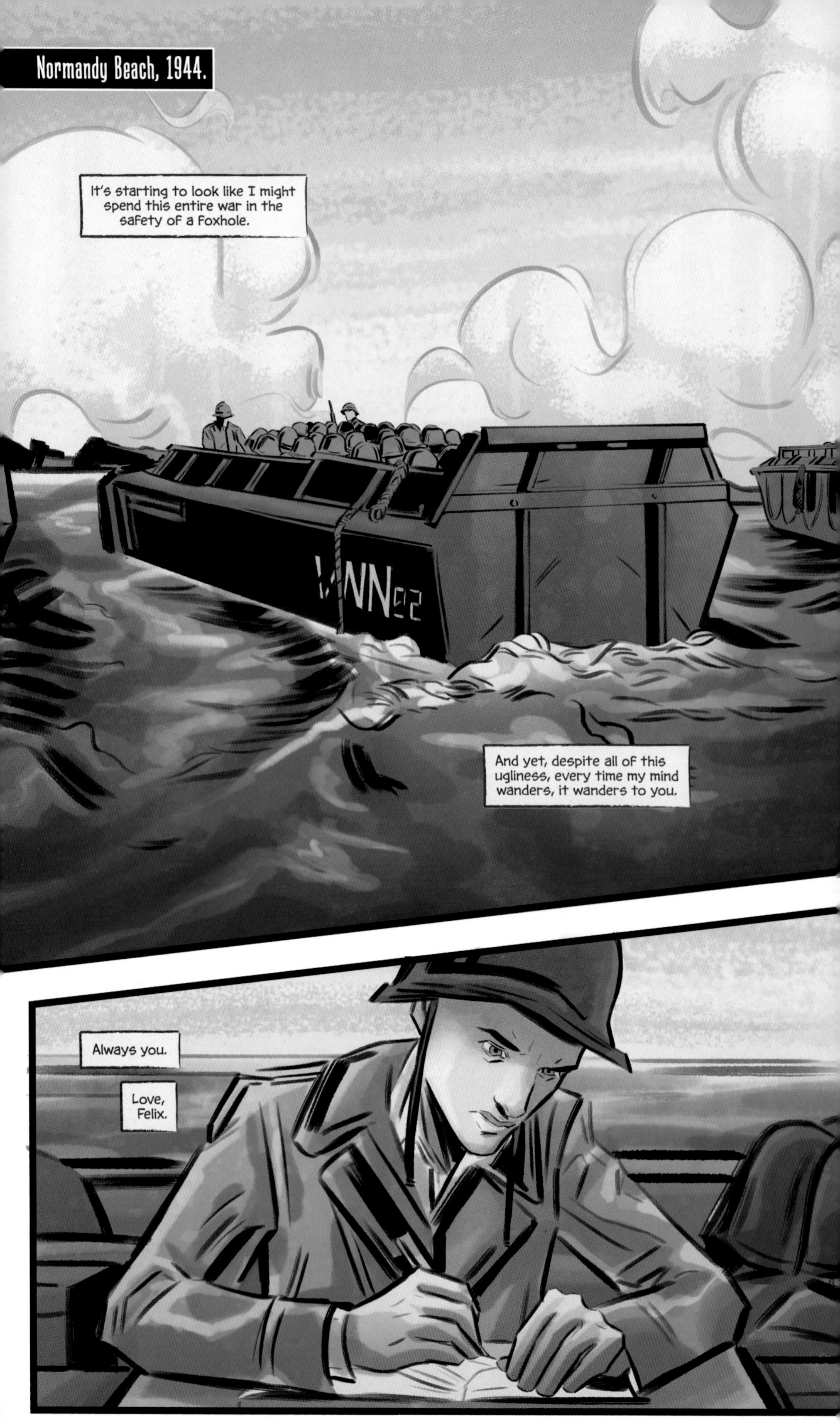

Normandy Beach, 1944.
It's starting to look like I might spend this entire war in the safety of a foxhole.
And yet, despite all of this ugliness, every time my mind wanders, it wanders to you.
Always you.
Love, Felix.

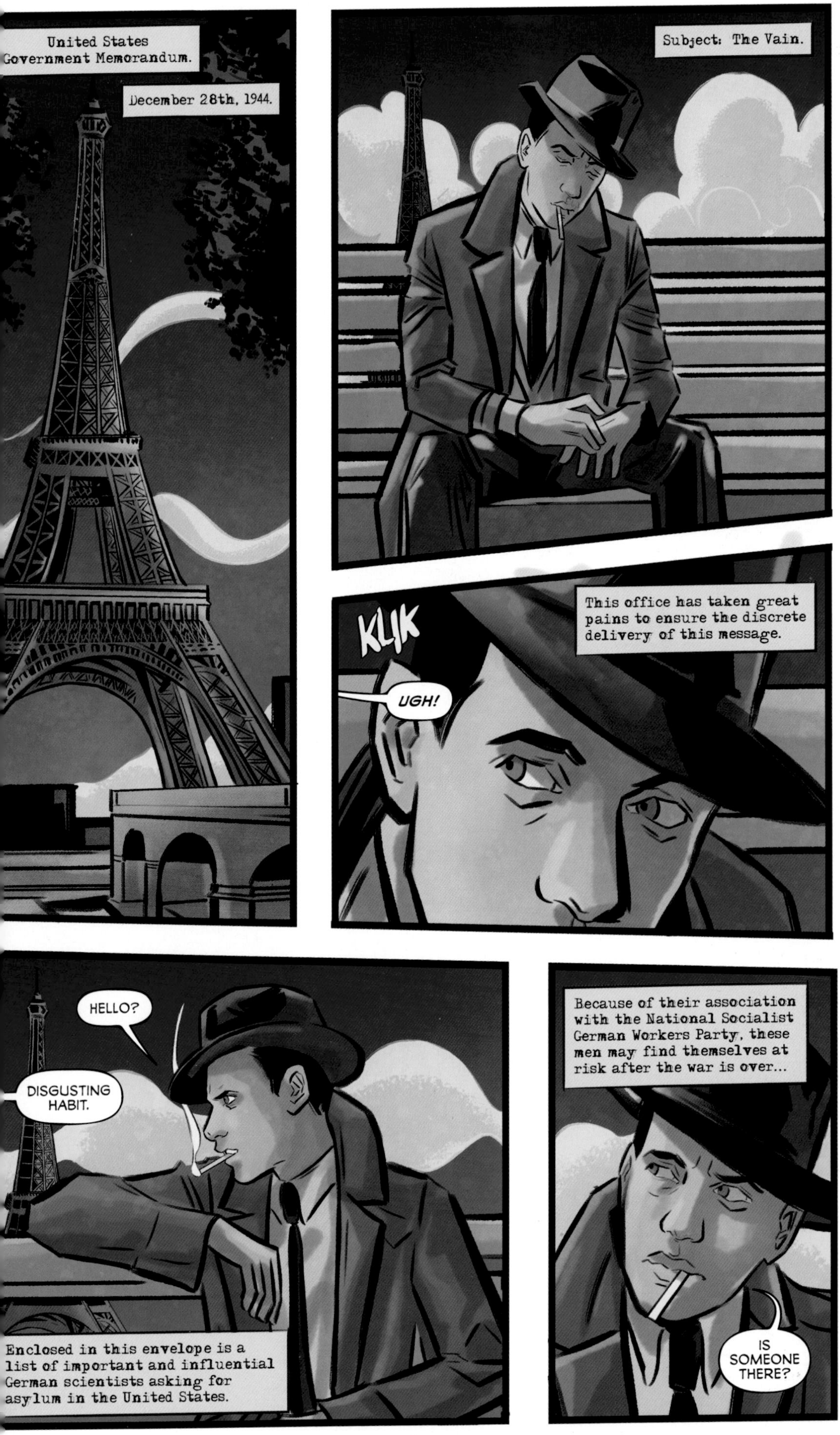
United States Government Memorandum.
December 28th, 1944.
Subject: The Vain.
KLIK
This office has taken great pains to ensure the discrete delivery of this message.
UGH!
HELLO?
DISGUSTING HABIT.
Enclosed in this envelope is a list of important and influential German scientists asking for asylum in the United States.
Because of their association with the National Socialist German Workers Party, these men may find themselves at risk after the war is over...
IS SOMEONE THERE?

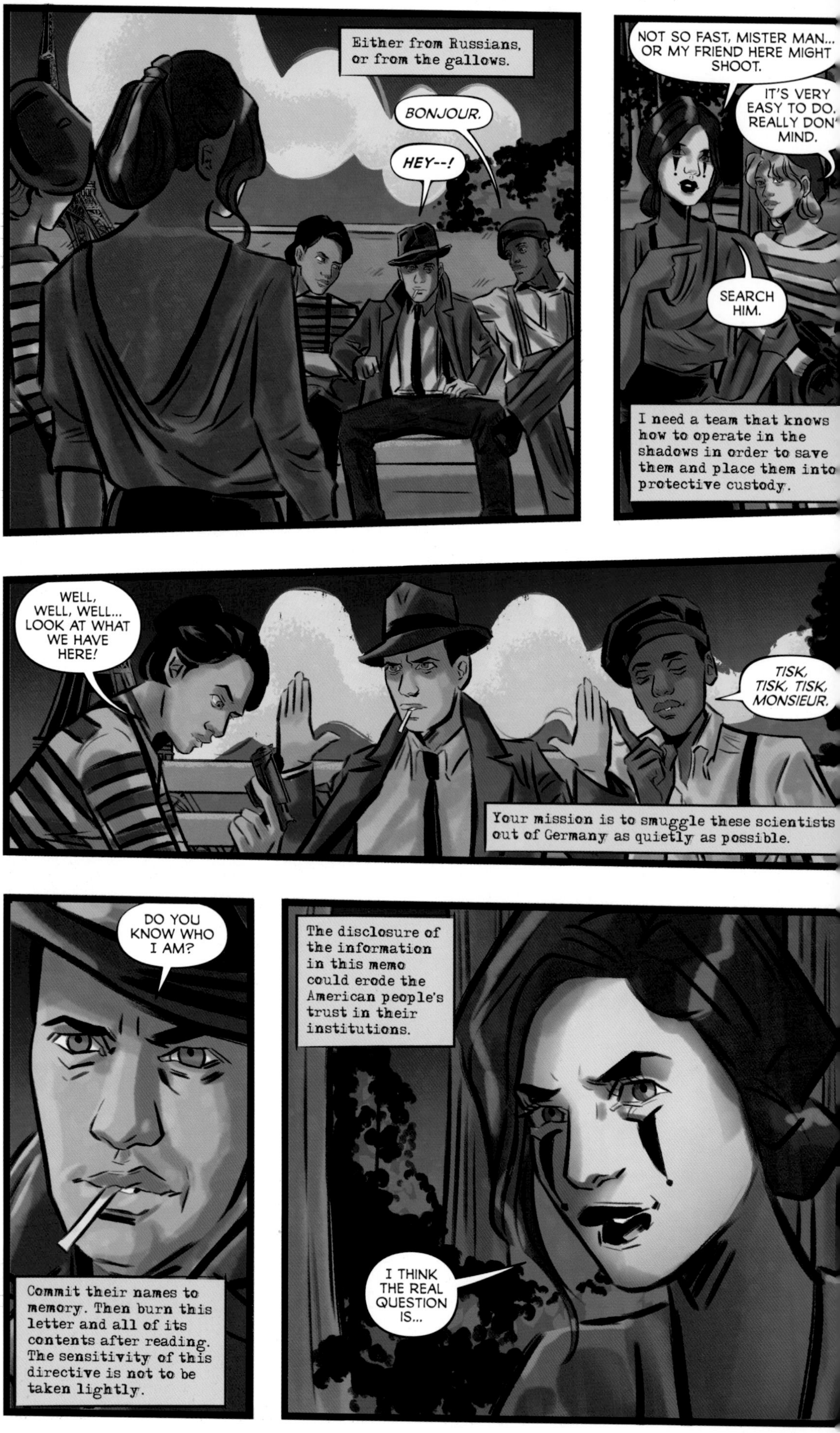
Either from Russians, or from the gallows.
BONJOUR.
HEY--!
NOT SO FAST, MISTER MAN... OR MY FRIEND HERE MIGHT SHOOT.
IT'S VERY EASY TO DO. REALLY DON' MIND.
SEARCH HIM.
I need a team that knows how to operate in the shadows in order to save them and place them into protective custody.
WELL, WELL, WELL... LOOK AT WHAT WE HAVE HERE!
TISK, TISK, TISK, MONSIEUR.
Your mission is to smuggle these scientists out of Germany as quietly as possible.
DO YOU KNOW WHO I AM?
Commit their names to memory. Then burn this letter and all of its contents after reading. The sensitivity of this directive is not to be taken lightly.
The disclosure of the information in this memo could erode the American people's trust in their institutions.
I THINK THE REAL QUESTION IS...

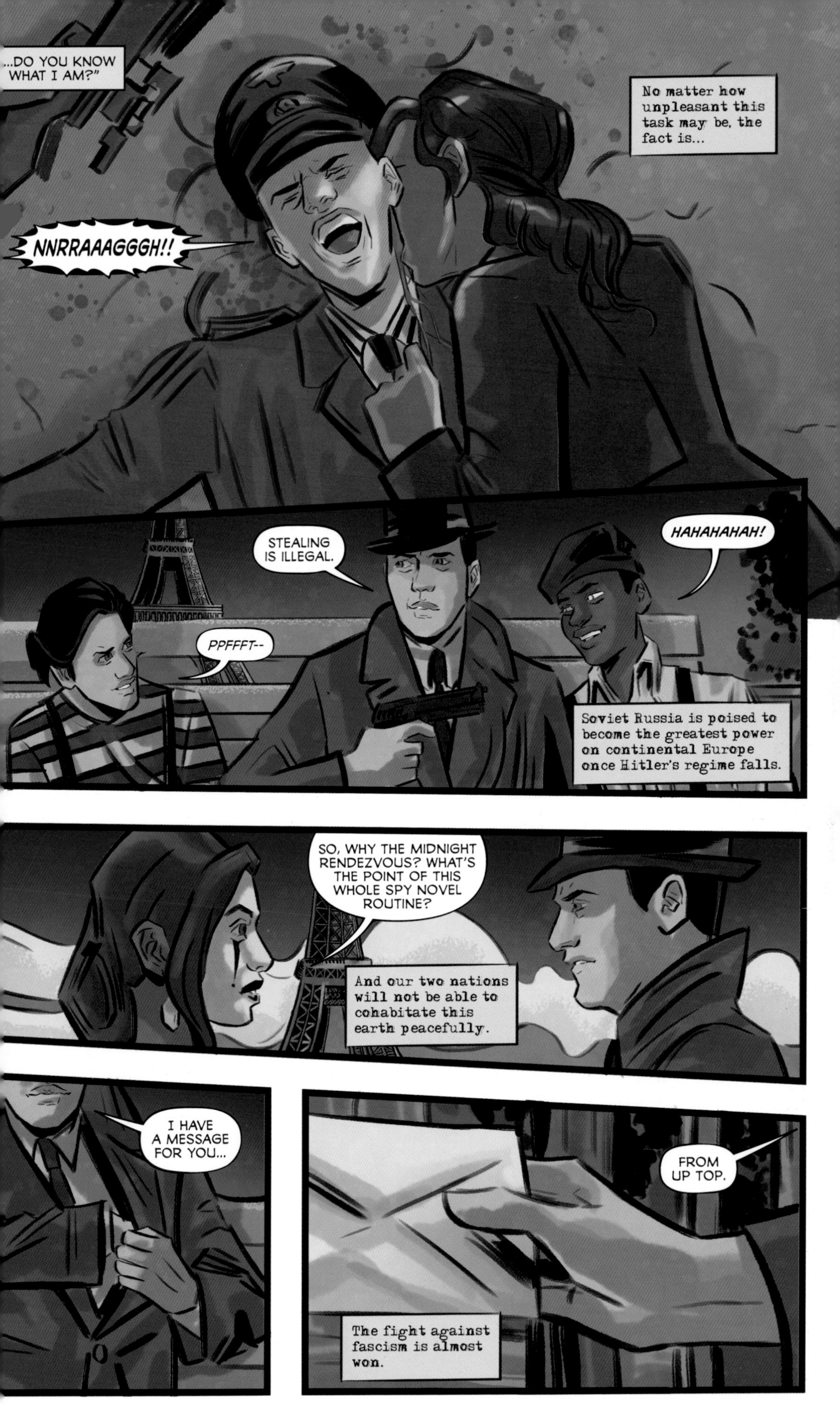
...DO YOU KNOW WHAT I AM?"
No matter how unpleasant this task may be, the fact is...
NNRRAAAGGGH!!
STEALING IS ILLEGAL.
HAHAHAHAH!
PPFFFT--
Soviet Russia is poised to become the greatest power on continental Europe once Hitler's regime falls.
SO, WHY THE MIDNIGHT RENDEZVOUS? WHAT'S THE POINT OF THIS WHOLE SPY NOVEL ROUTINE?
And our two nations will not be able to cohabitate this earth peacefully.
I HAVE A MESSAGE FOR YOU...
FROM UP TOP.
The fight against fascism is almost won.

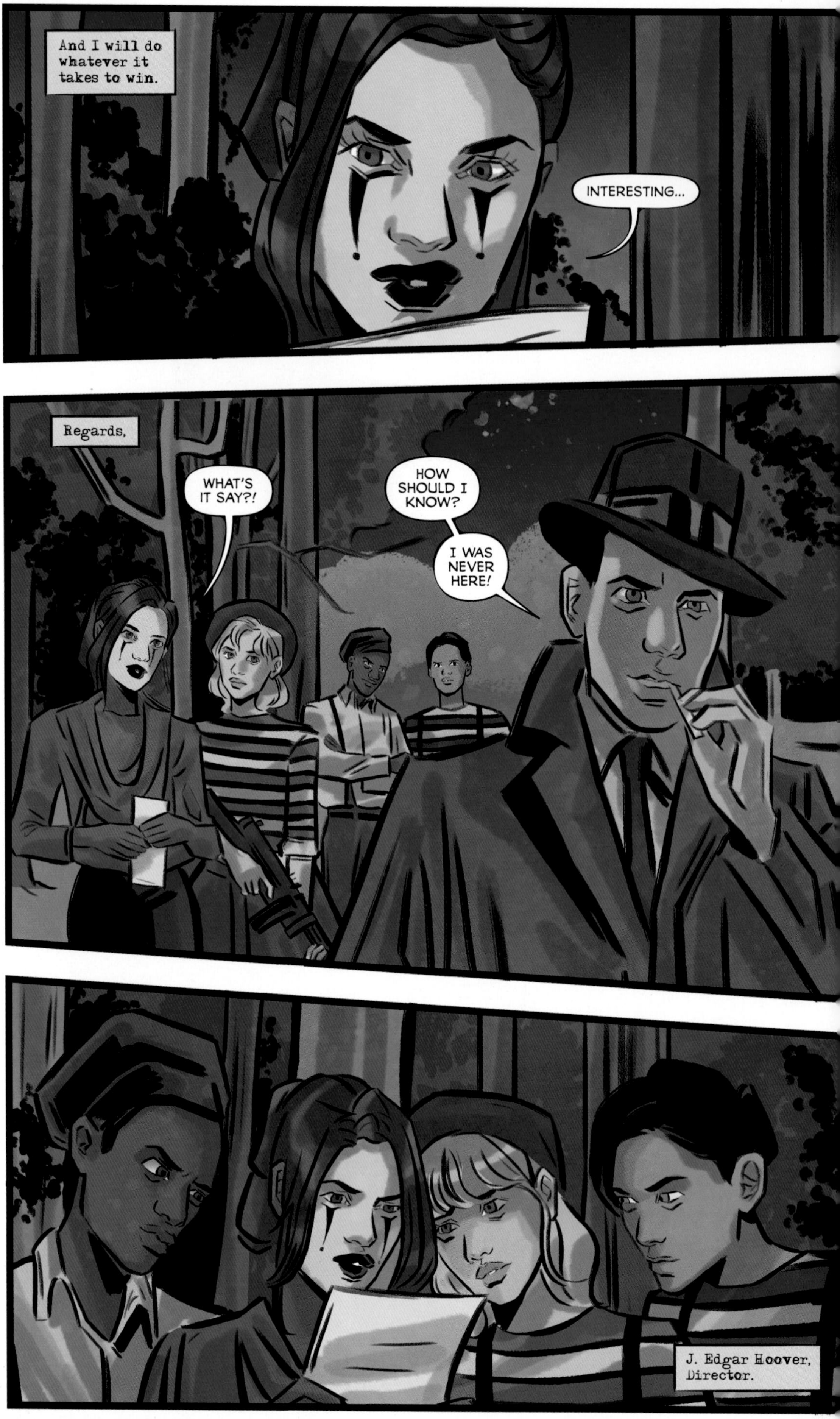
And I will do whatever it takes to win.
INTERESTING...
Regards,
WHAT'S IT SAY?!
HOW SHOULD I KNOW?
I WAS NEVER HERE!
J. Edgar Hoover, Director.

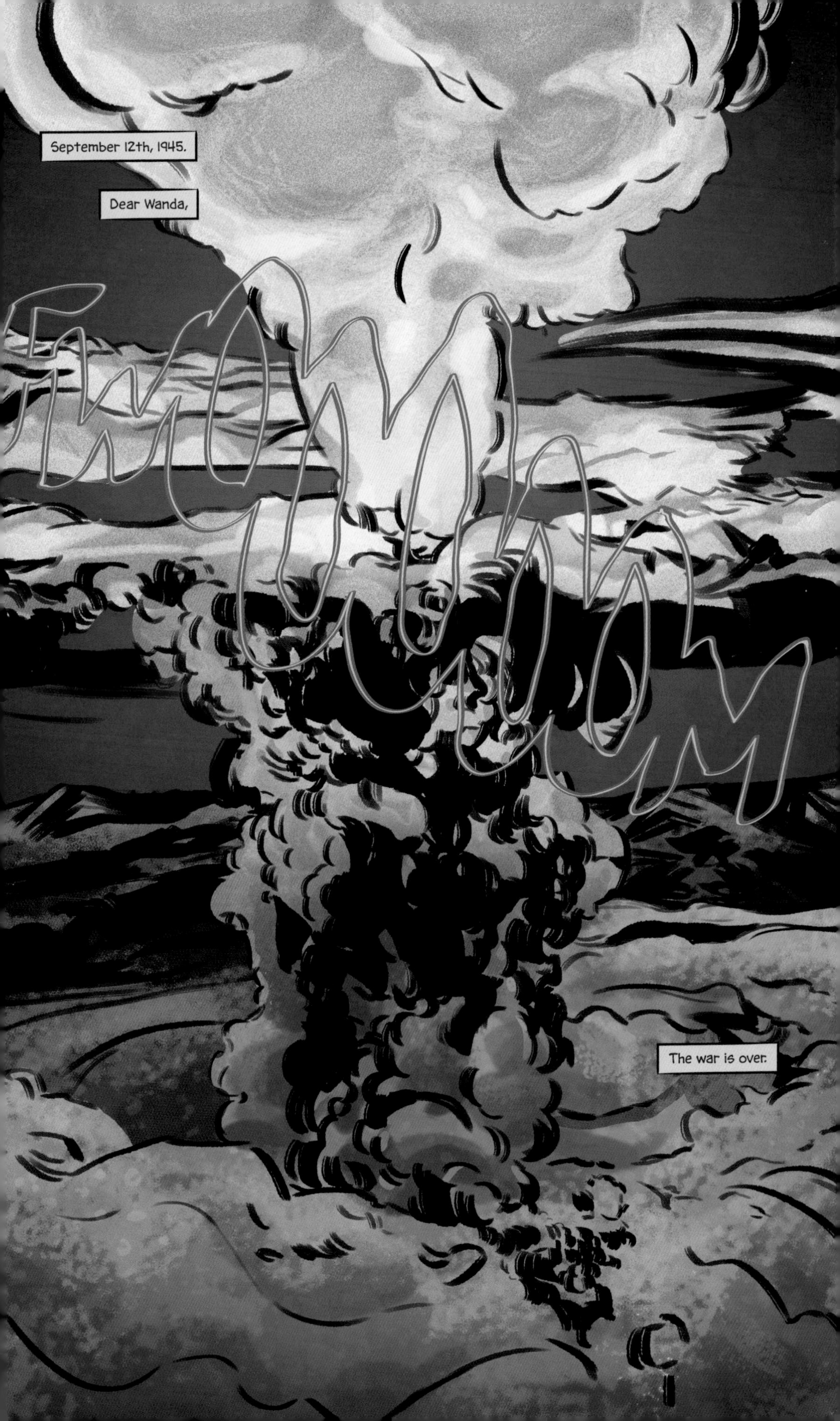
September 12th, 1945.
Dear Wanda,
FWOOOOOM
The war is over.

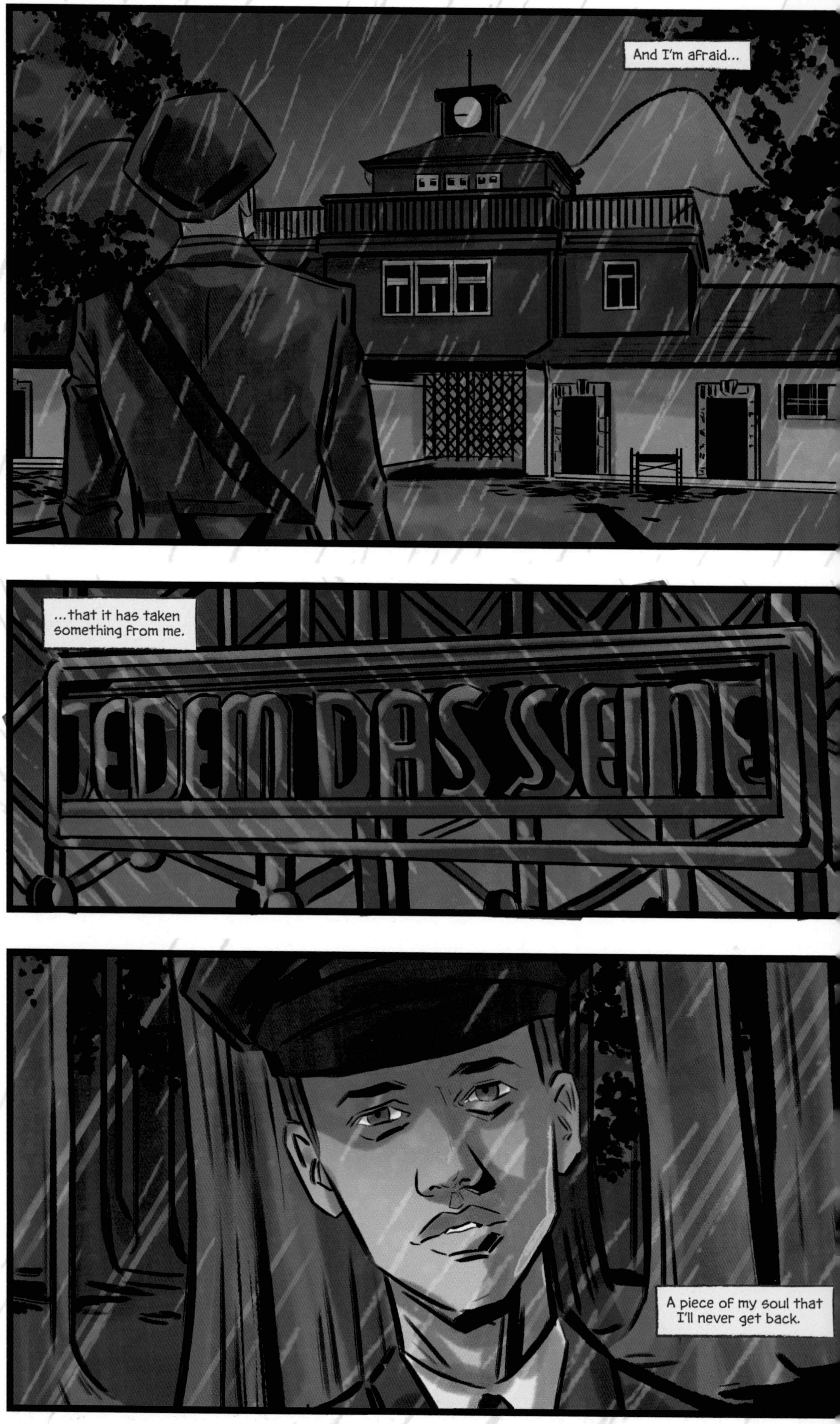
And I'm afraid...
...that it has taken something from me.
JEDEM DAS SEINE
A piece of my soul that I'll never get back.

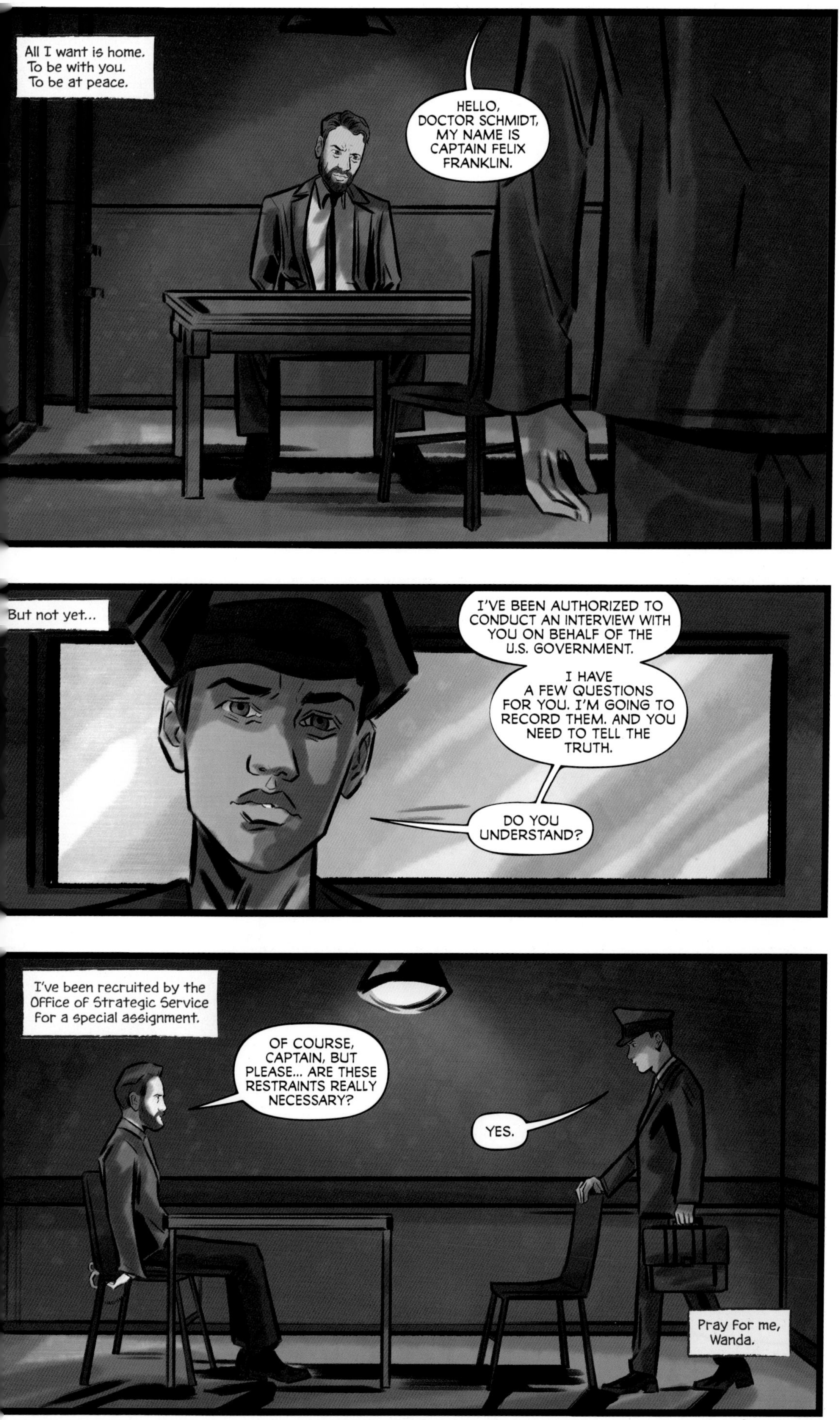
All I want is home. To be with you. To be at peace.
HELLO, DOCTOR SCHMIDT, MY NAME IS CAPTAIN FELIX FRANKLIN.
But not yet...
I'VE BEEN AUTHORIZED TO CONDUCT AN INTERVIEW WITH YOU ON BEHALF OF THE U.S. GOVERNMENT.
I HAVE A FEW QUESTIONS FOR YOU. I'M GOING TO RECORD THEM. AND YOU NEED TO TELL THE TRUTH.
DO YOU UNDERSTAND?
I've been recruited by the Office of Strategic Service for a special assignment.
OF COURSE, CAPTAIN, BUT PLEASE... ARE THESE RESTRAINTS REALLY NECESSARY?
YES.
Pray for me, Wanda.

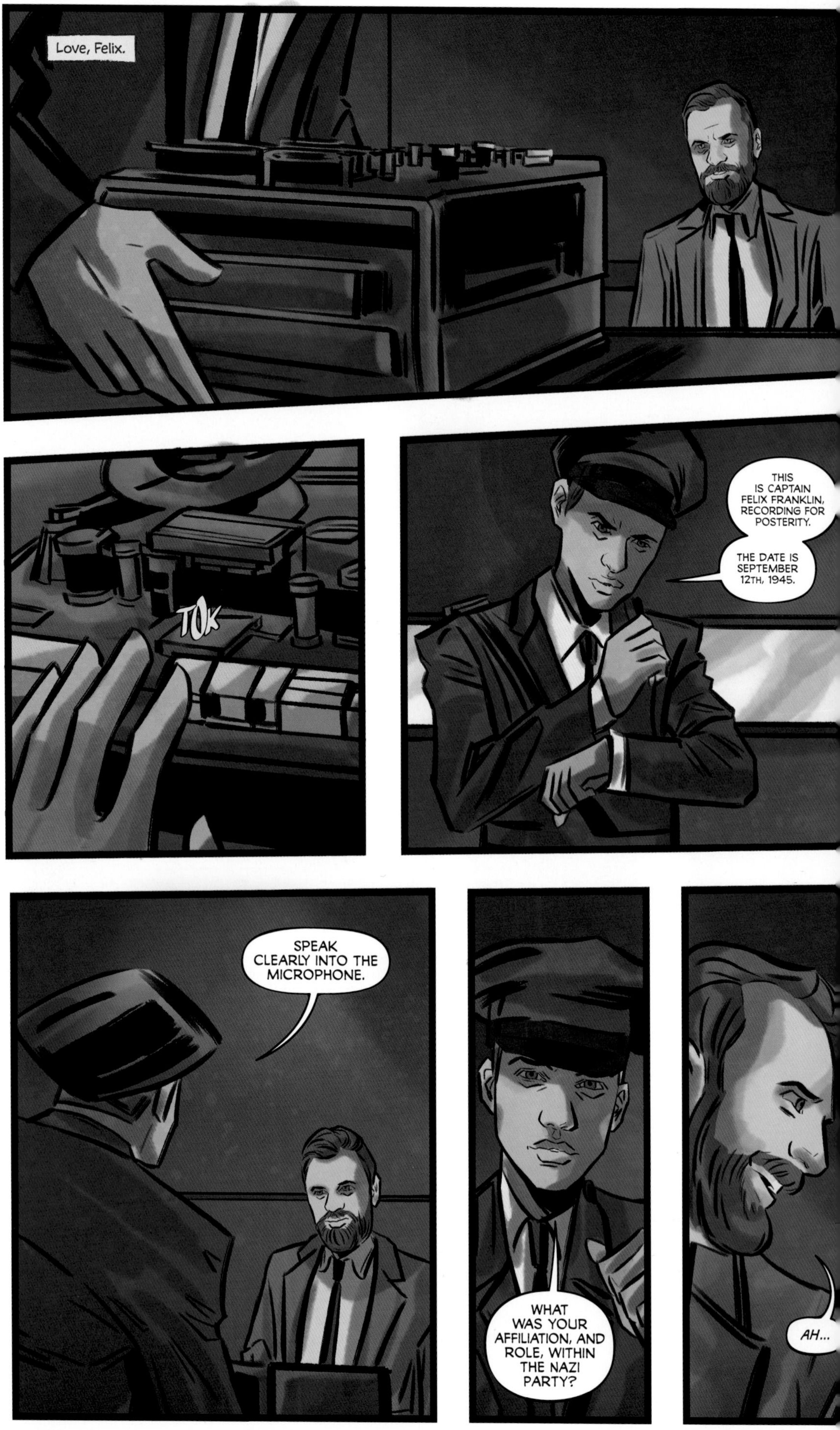
Love, Felix.
TOK
THIS IS CAPTAIN FELIX FRANKLIN, RECORDING FOR POSTERITY.
THE DATE IS SEPTEMBER 12TH, 1945.
SPEAK CLEARLY INTO THE MICROPHONE.
WHAT WAS YOUR AFFILIATION, AND ROLE, WITHIN THE NAZI PARTY?
AH...

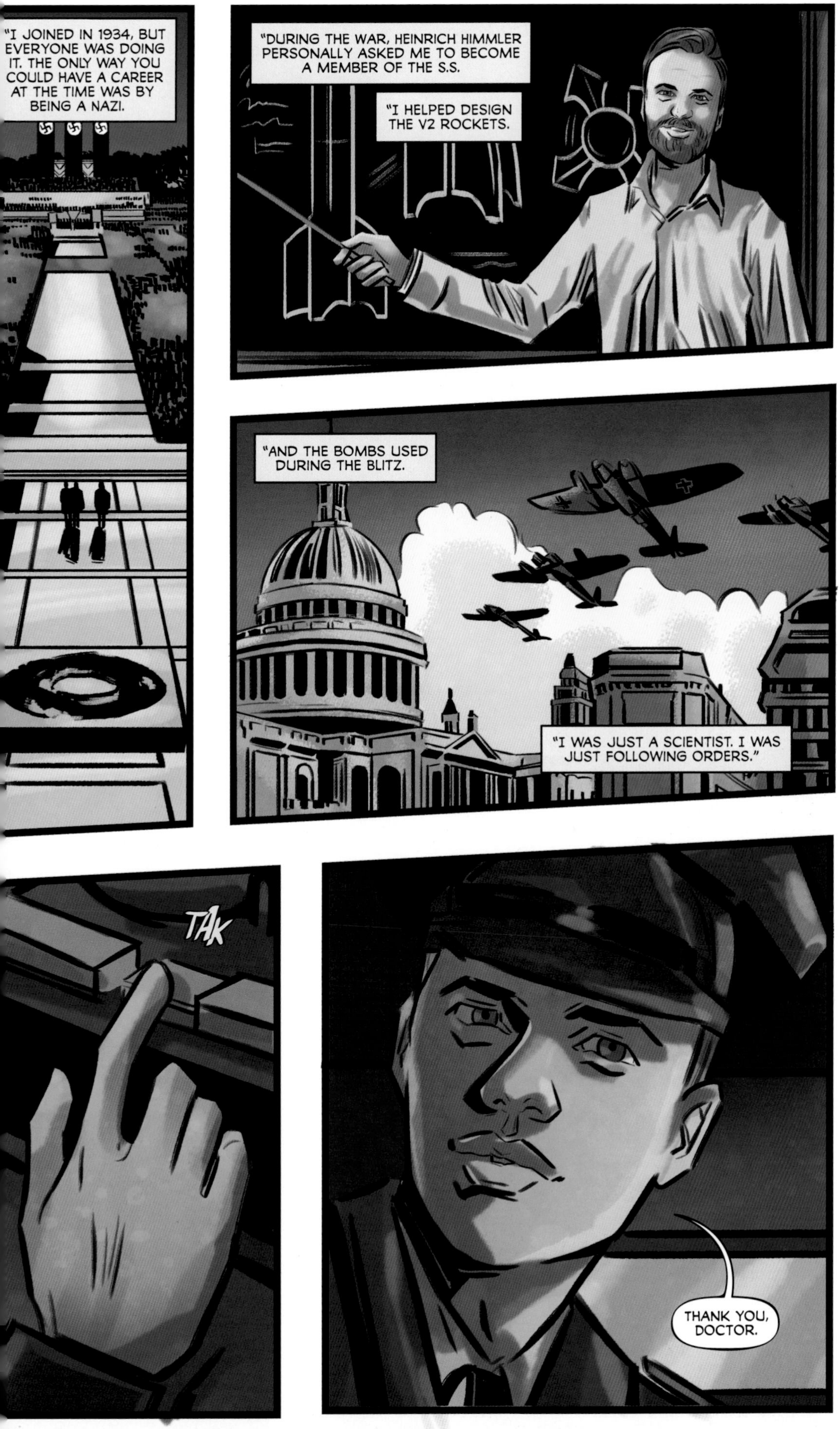
"I JOINED IN 1934, BUT EVERYONE WAS DOING IT. THE ONLY WAY YOU COULD HAVE A CAREER AT THE TIME WAS BY BEING A NAZI.
"DURING THE WAR, HEINRICH HIMMLER PERSONALLY ASKED ME TO BECOME A MEMBER OF THE S.S.
"I HELPED DESIGN THE V2 ROCKETS.
"AND THE BOMBS USED DURING THE BLITZ.
"I WAS JUST A SCIENTIST. I WAS JUST FOLLOWING ORDERS."
TAK
THANK YOU, DOCTOR.

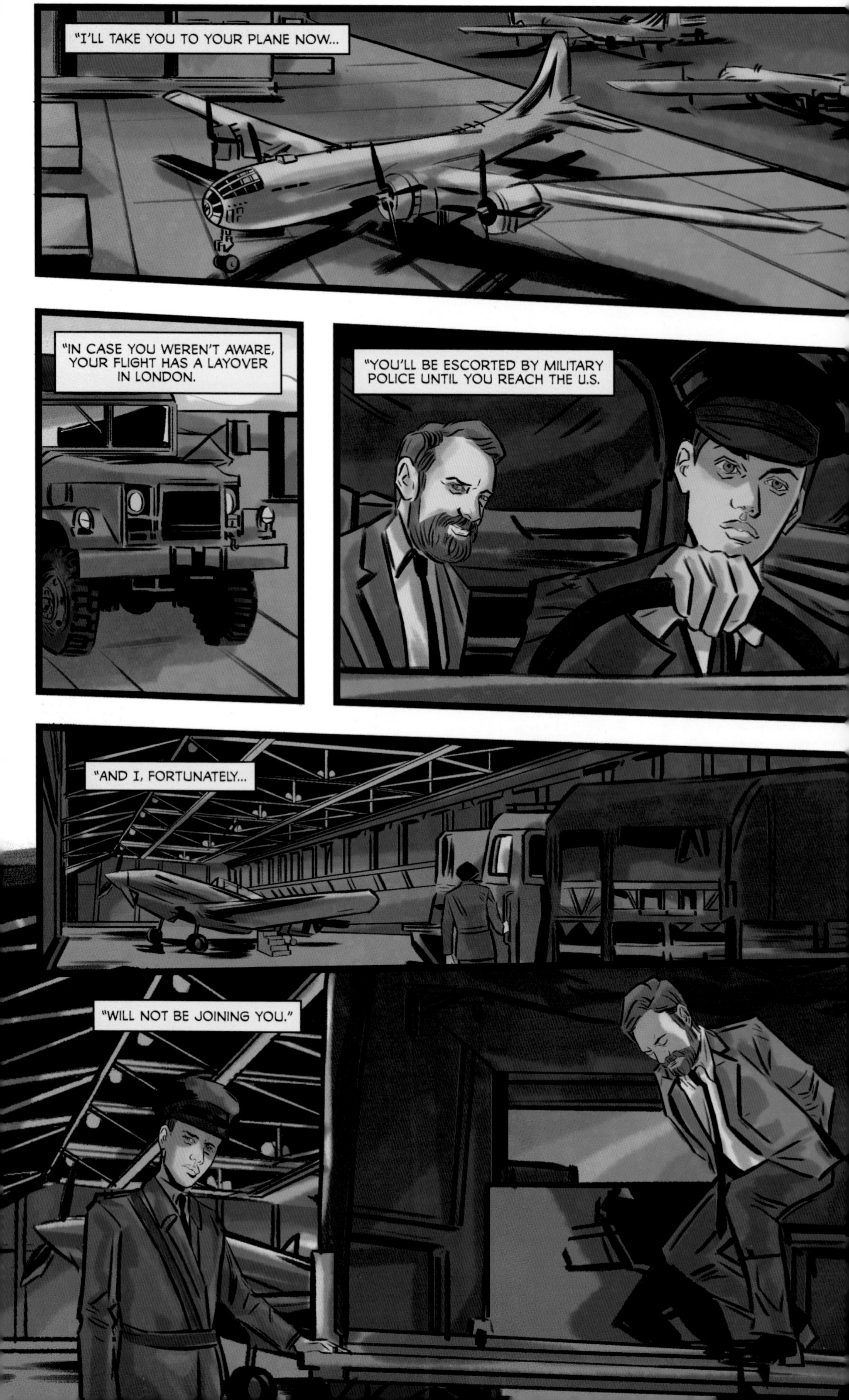
"I'LL TAKE YOU TO YOUR PLANE NOW...
"IN CASE YOU WEREN'T AWARE, YOUR FLIGHT HAS A LAYOVER IN LONDON.
"YOU'LL BE ESCORTED BY MILITARY POLICE UNTIL YOU REACH THE U.S.
"AND I, FORTUNATELY...
"WILL NOT BE JOINING YOU."

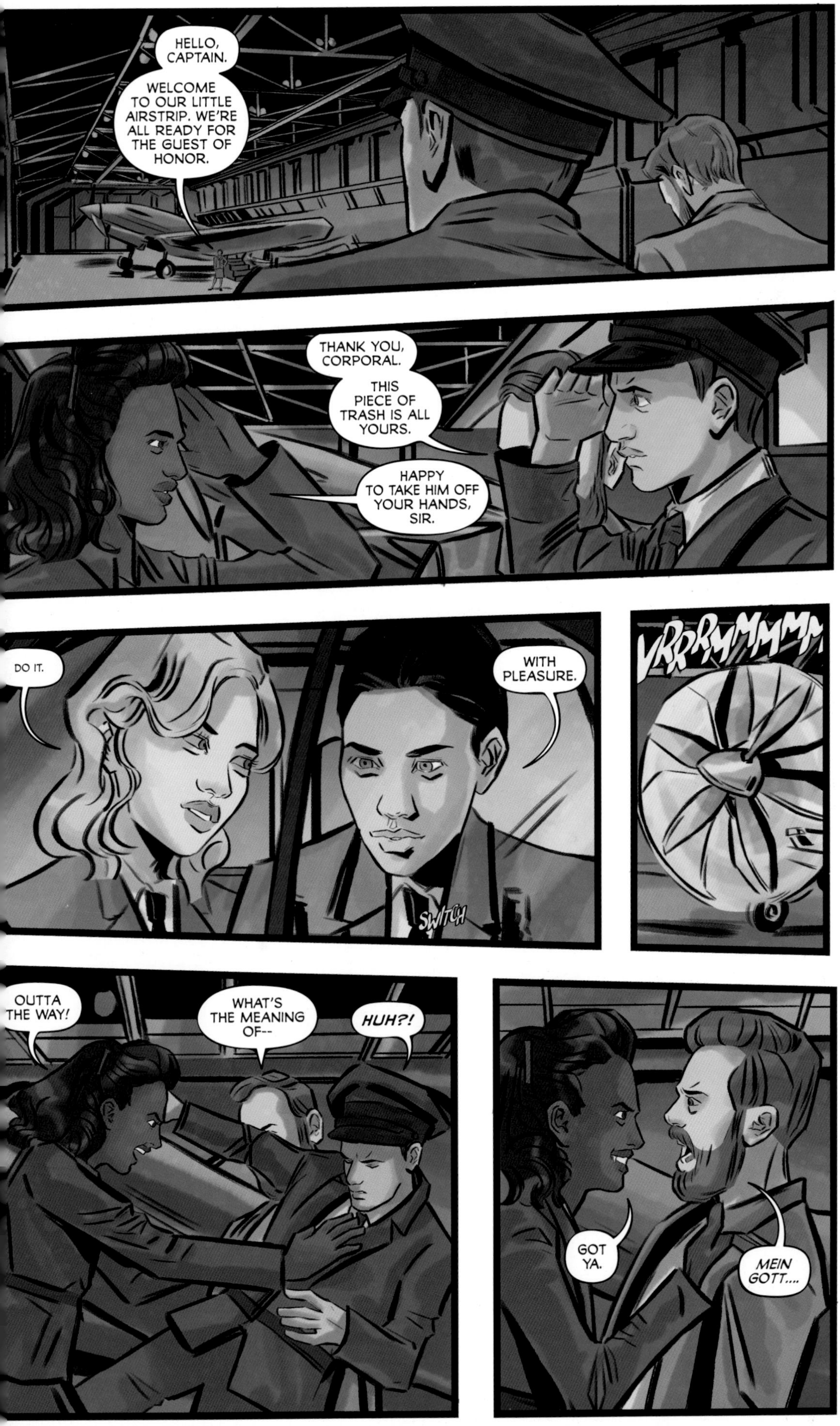
HELLO, CAPTAIN.
WELCOME TO OUR LITTLE AIRSTRIP. WE'RE ALL READY FOR THE GUEST OF HONOR.
THANK YOU, CORPORAL.
THIS PIECE OF TRASH IS ALL YOURS.
HAPPY TO TAKE HIM OFF YOUR HANDS, SIR.
DO IT.
WITH PLEASURE.
SWITCH
VRRRMMMMM
OUTTA THE WAY!
WHAT'S THE MEANING OF--
HUH?!
GOT YA.
MEIN GOTT....

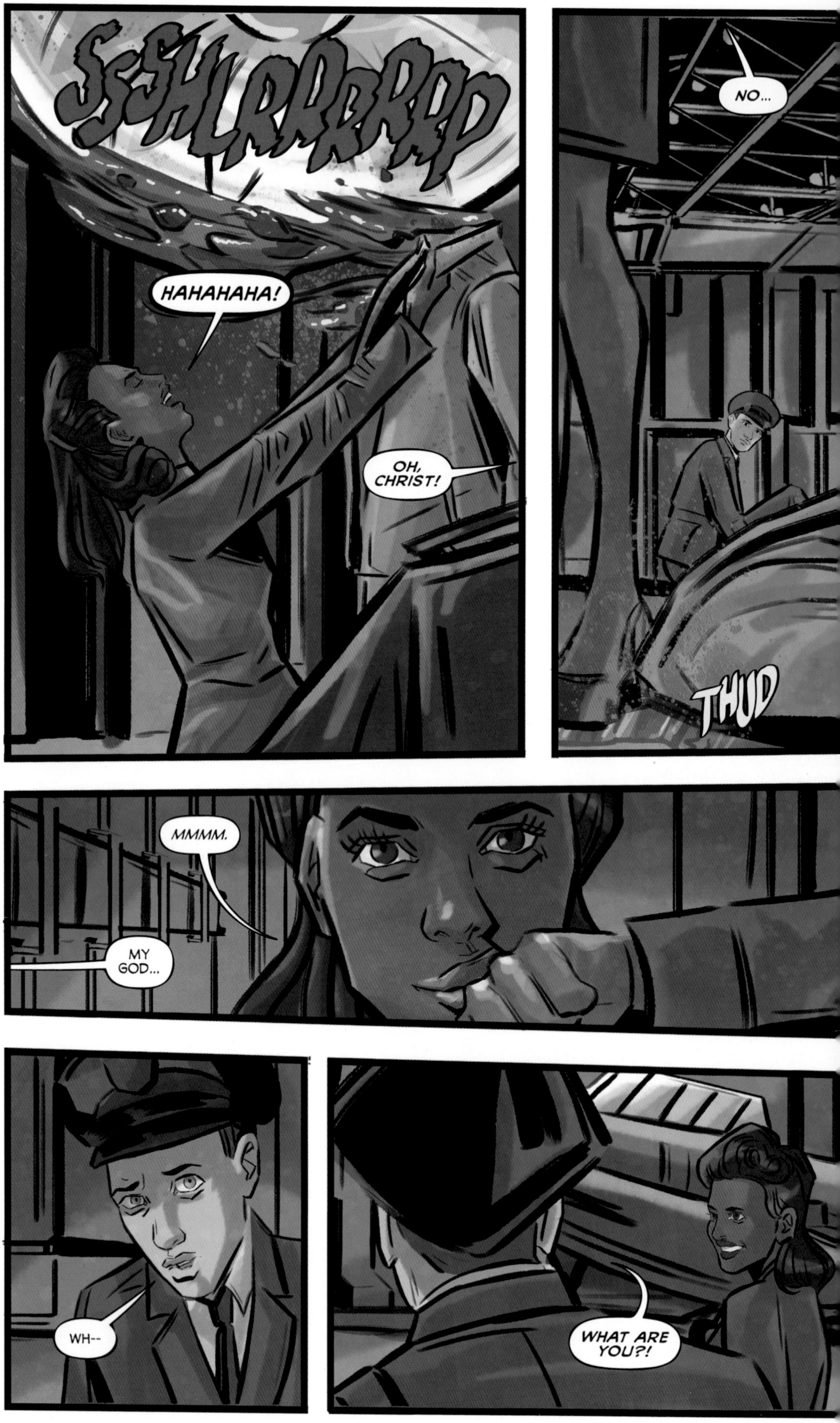
SSSHLRRRRRAP
HAHAHAHA!
OH, CHRIST!
NO...
THUD
MMMM.
MY GOD...
WH--
WHAT ARE YOU?!

CHAPTER 3

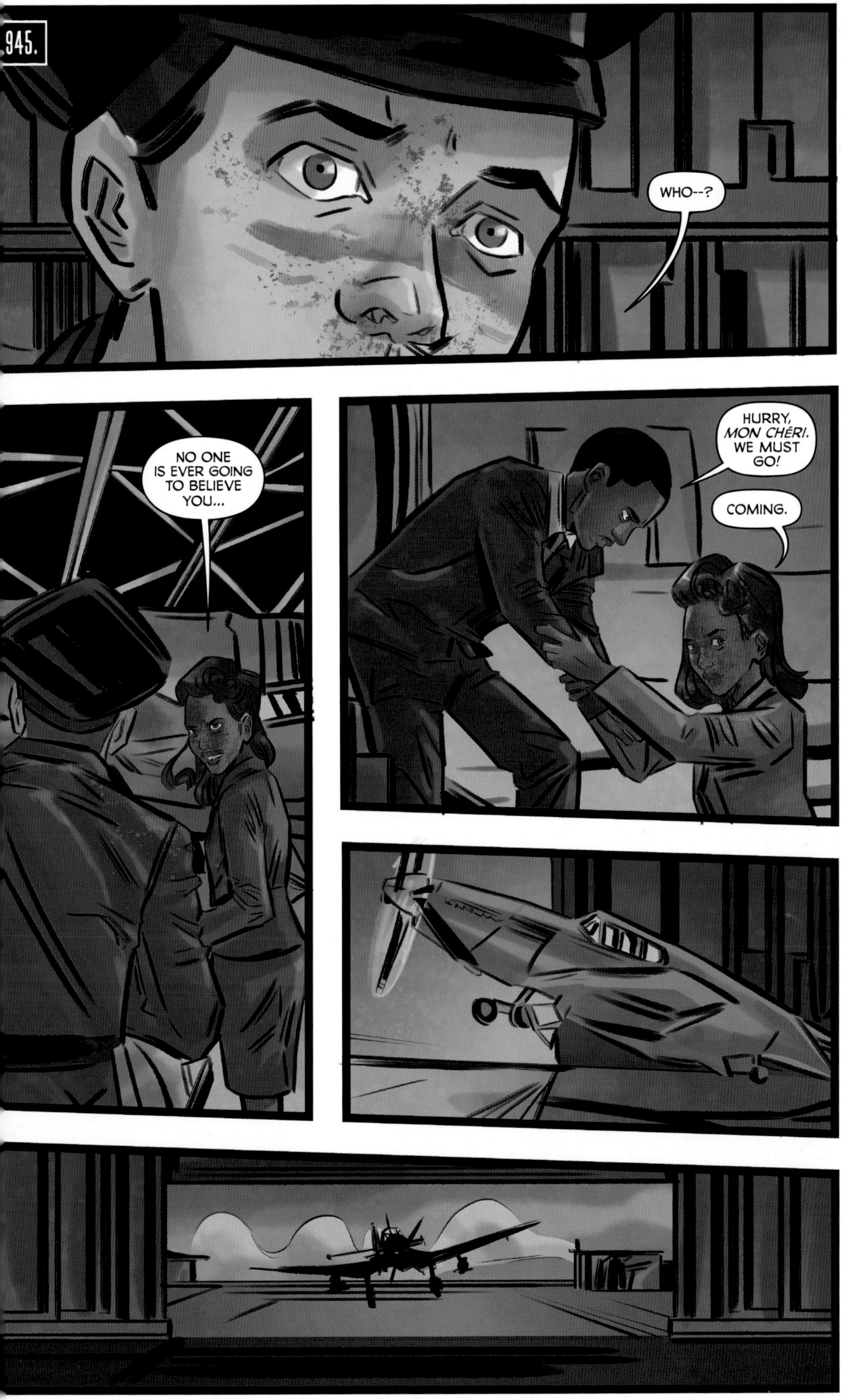

945.
WHO--?
NO ONE IS EVER GOING TO BELIEVE YOU...
HURRY, *MON CHÉRI*. WE MUST GO!
COMING.

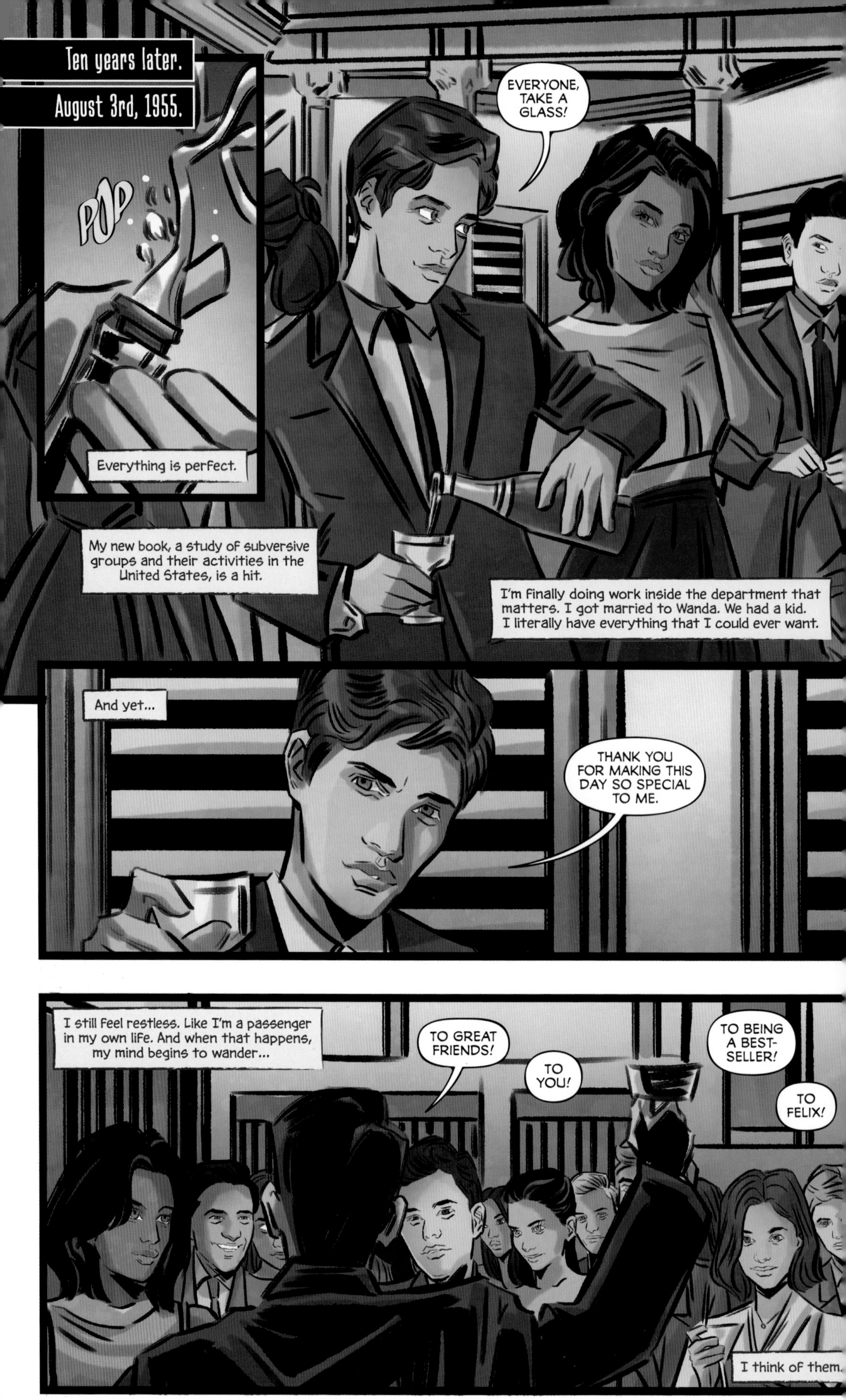
Ten years later.
August 3rd, 1955.
POP
Everything is perfect.
EVERYONE, TAKE A GLASS!
My new book, a study of subversive groups and their activities in the United States, is a hit.
I'm finally doing work inside the department that matters. I got married to Wanda. We had a kid. I literally have everything that I could ever want.
And yet...
THANK YOU FOR MAKING THIS DAY SO SPECIAL TO ME.
I still feel restless. Like I'm a passenger in my own life. And when that happens, my mind begins to wander...
TO GREAT FRIENDS!
TO YOU!
TO BEING A BEST-SELLER!
TO FELIX!
I think of them.

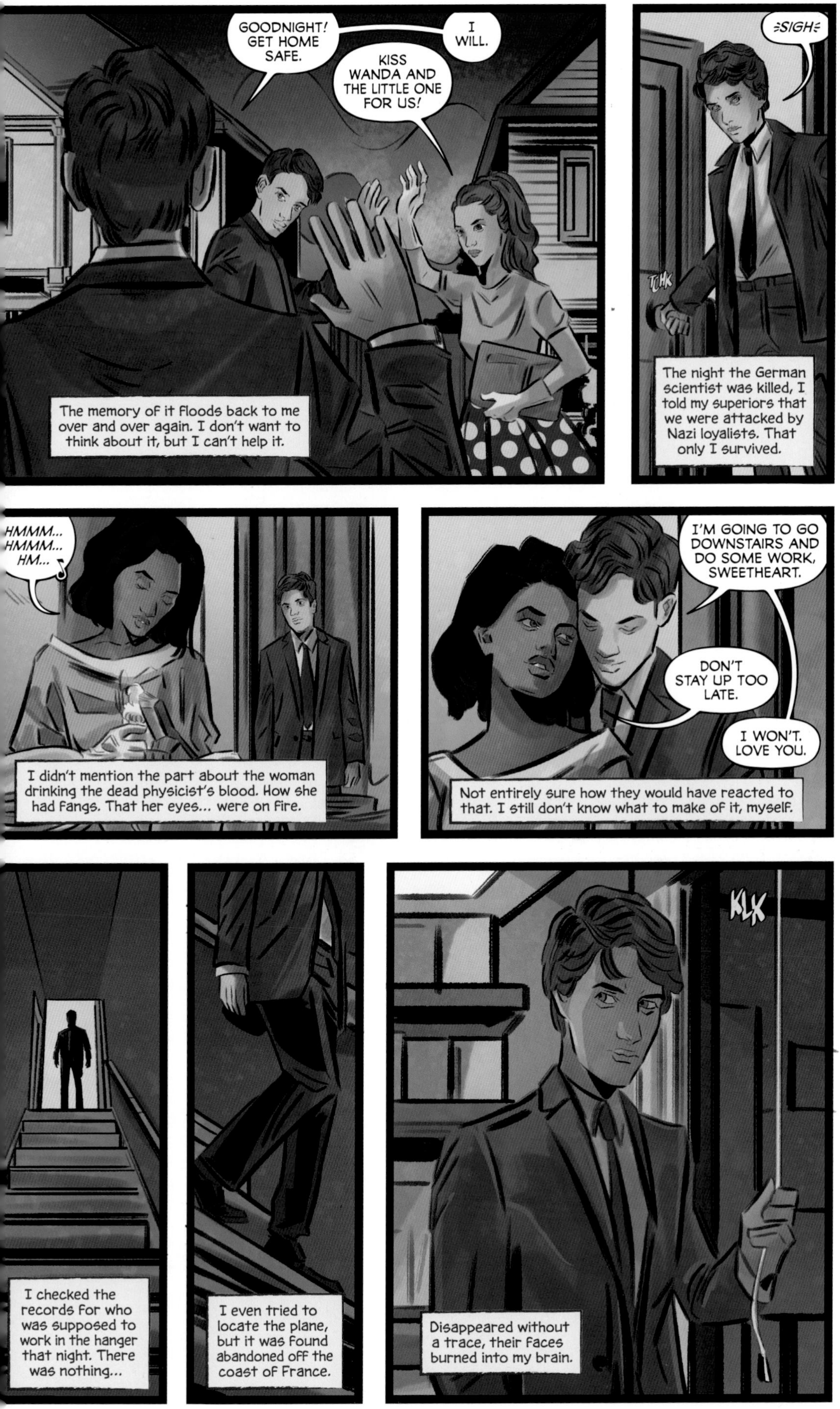
GOODNIGHT! GET HOME SAFE.
I WILL.
KISS WANDA AND THE LITTLE ONE FOR US!
The memory of it floods back to me over and over again. I don't want to think about it, but I can't help it.
SIGH
TCHK
The night the German scientist was killed, I told my superiors that we were attacked by Nazi loyalists. That only I survived.
HMMM... HMMM... HM...
I didn't mention the part about the woman drinking the dead physicist's blood. How she had fangs. That her eyes... were on fire.
I'M GOING TO GO DOWNSTAIRS AND DO SOME WORK, SWEETHEART.
DON'T STAY UP TOO LATE.
I WON'T. LOVE YOU.
Not entirely sure how they would have reacted to that. I still don't know what to make of it, myself.
I checked the records for who was supposed to work in the hanger that night. There was nothing...
I even tried to locate the plane, but it was found abandoned off the coast of France.
KLIK
Disappeared without a trace, their faces burned into my brain.

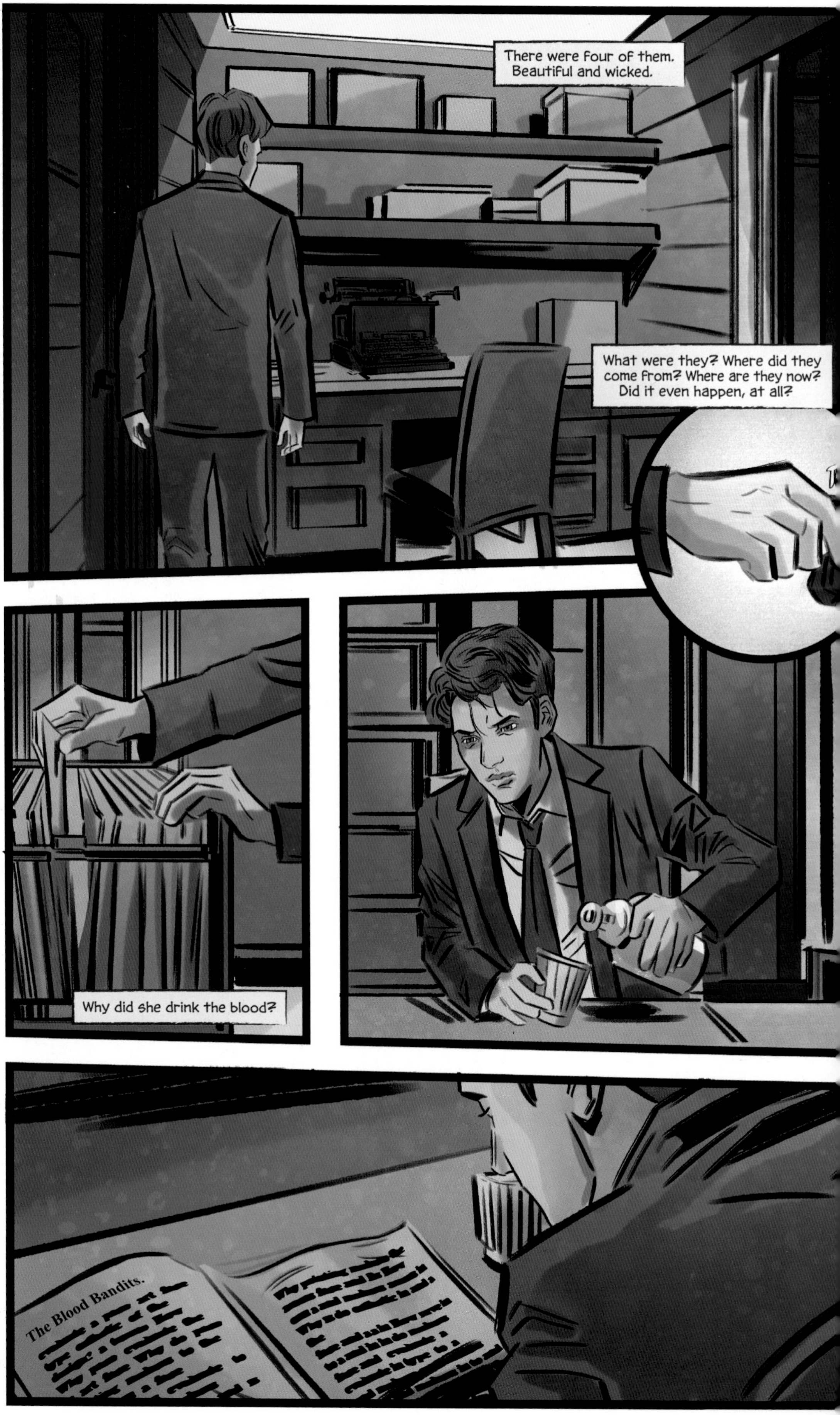
There were four of them. Beautiful and wicked.
What were they? Where did they come from? Where are they now? Did it even happen, at all?
Why did she drink the blood?
The Blood Bandits.

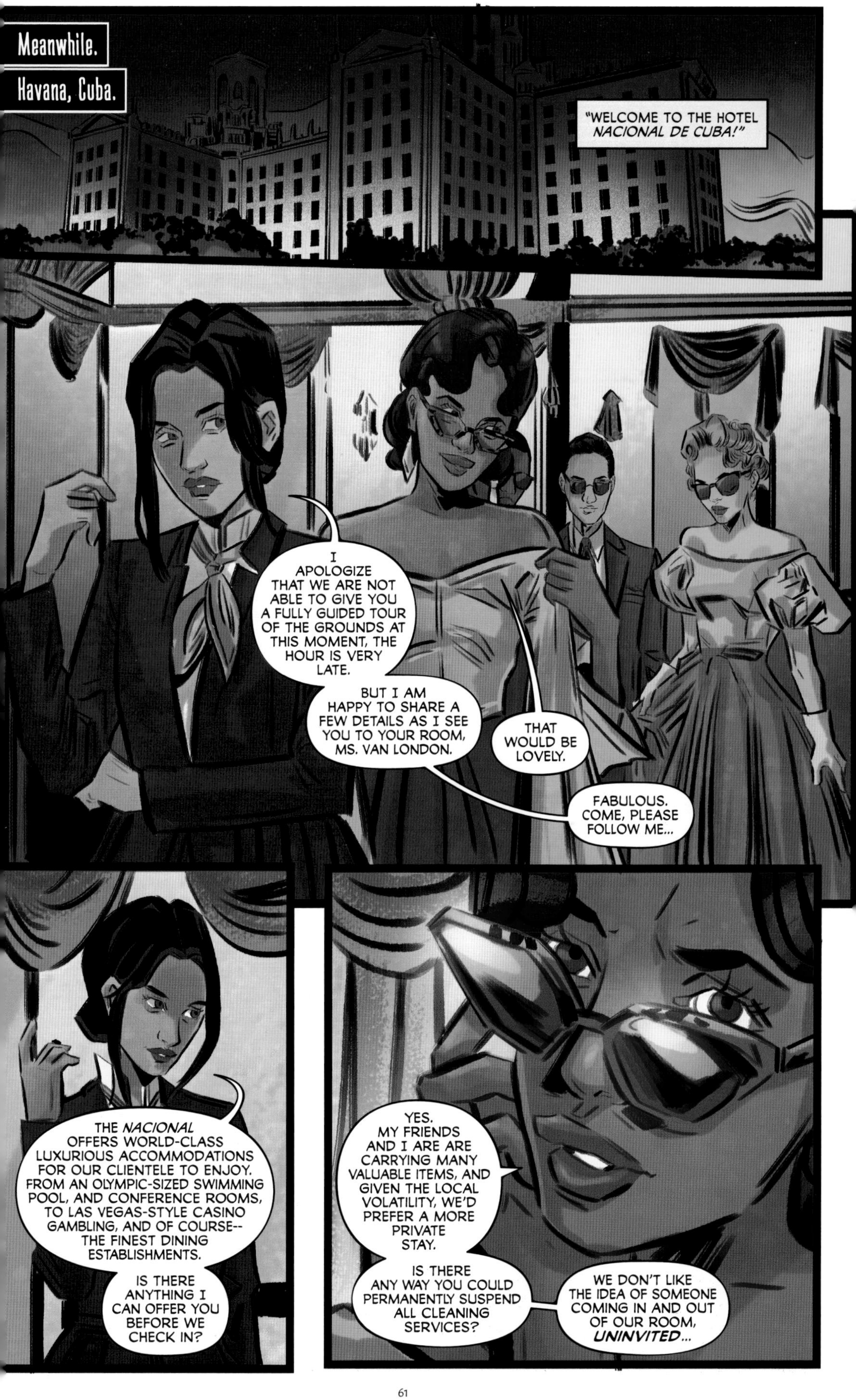

Meanwhile.
Havana, Cuba.
"WELCOME TO THE HOTEL *NACIONAL DE CUBA!*"
I APOLOGIZE THAT WE ARE NOT ABLE TO GIVE YOU A FULLY GUIDED TOUR OF THE GROUNDS AT THIS MOMENT, THE HOUR IS VERY LATE.
BUT I AM HAPPY TO SHARE A FEW DETAILS AS I SEE YOU TO YOUR ROOM, MS. VAN LONDON.
THAT WOULD BE LOVELY.
FABULOUS. COME, PLEASE FOLLOW ME...
THE *NACIONAL* OFFERS WORLD-CLASS LUXURIOUS ACCOMMODATIONS FOR OUR CLIENTELE TO ENJOY. FROM AN OLYMPIC-SIZED SWIMMING POOL, AND CONFERENCE ROOMS, TO LAS VEGAS-STYLE CASINO GAMBLING, AND OF COURSE-- THE FINEST DINING ESTABLISHMENTS.
IS THERE ANYTHING I CAN OFFER YOU BEFORE WE CHECK IN?
YES. MY FRIENDS AND I ARE ARE CARRYING MANY VALUABLE ITEMS, AND GIVEN THE LOCAL VOLATILITY, WE'D PREFER A MORE PRIVATE STAY.
IS THERE ANY WAY YOU COULD PERMANENTLY SUSPEND ALL CLEANING SERVICES?
WE DON'T LIKE THE IDEA OF SOMEONE COMING IN AND OUT OF OUR ROOM, ***UNINVITED***...

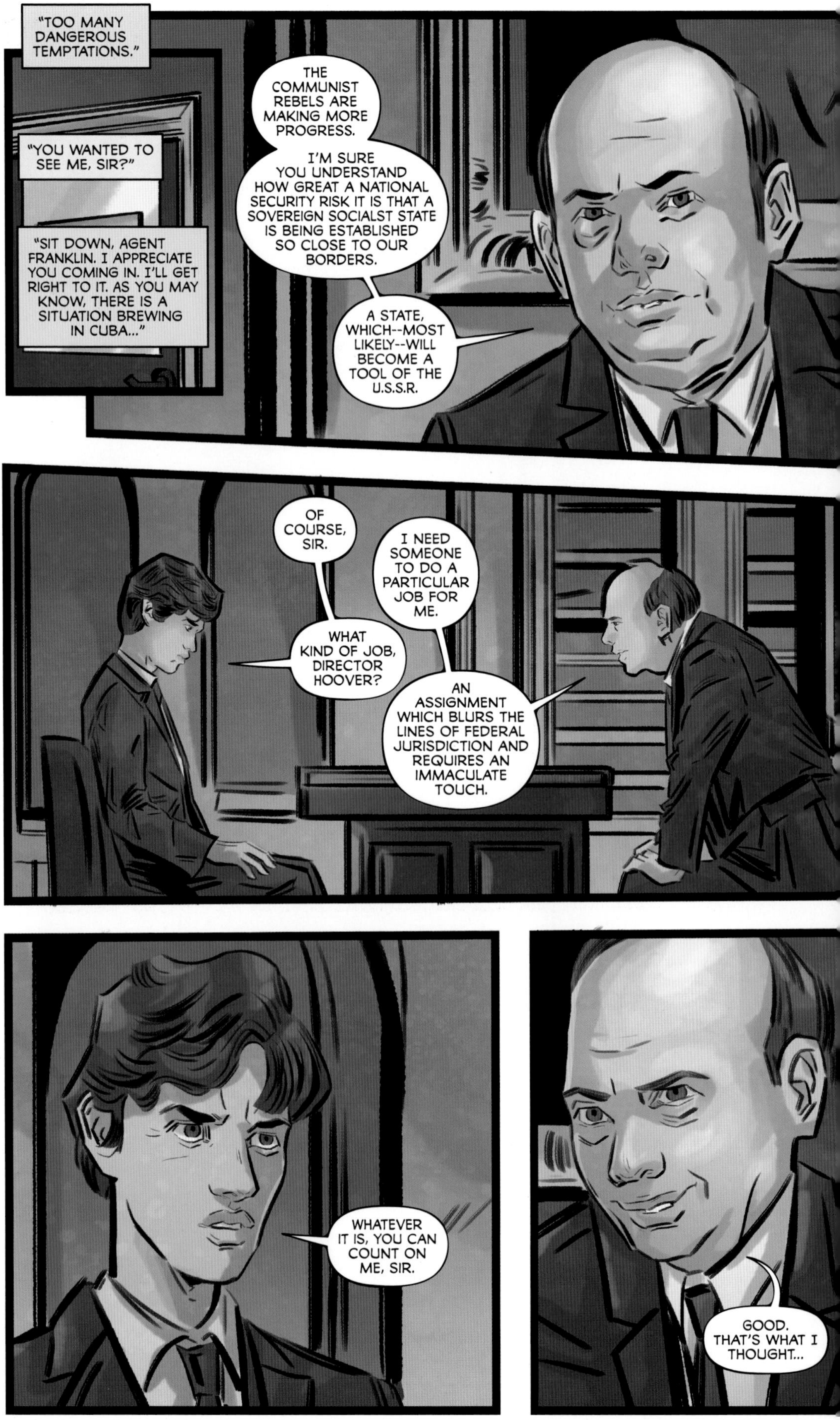
"TOO MANY DANGEROUS TEMPTATIONS."
"YOU WANTED TO SEE ME, SIR?"
"SIT DOWN, AGENT FRANKLIN. I APPRECIATE YOU COMING IN. I'LL GET RIGHT TO IT. AS YOU MAY KNOW, THERE IS A SITUATION BREWING IN CUBA..."
THE COMMUNIST REBELS ARE MAKING MORE PROGRESS.
I'M SURE YOU UNDERSTAND HOW GREAT A NATIONAL SECURITY RISK IT IS THAT A SOVEREIGN SOCIALST STATE IS BEING ESTABLISHED SO CLOSE TO OUR BORDERS.
A STATE, WHICH--MOST LIKELY--WILL BECOME A TOOL OF THE U.S.S.R.
OF COURSE, SIR.
I NEED SOMEONE TO DO A PARTICULAR JOB FOR ME.
WHAT KIND OF JOB, DIRECTOR HOOVER?
AN ASSIGNMENT WHICH BLURS THE LINES OF FEDERAL JURISDICTION AND REQUIRES AN IMMACULATE TOUCH.
WHATEVER IT IS, YOU CAN COUNT ON ME, SIR.
GOOD. THAT'S WHAT I THOUGHT...

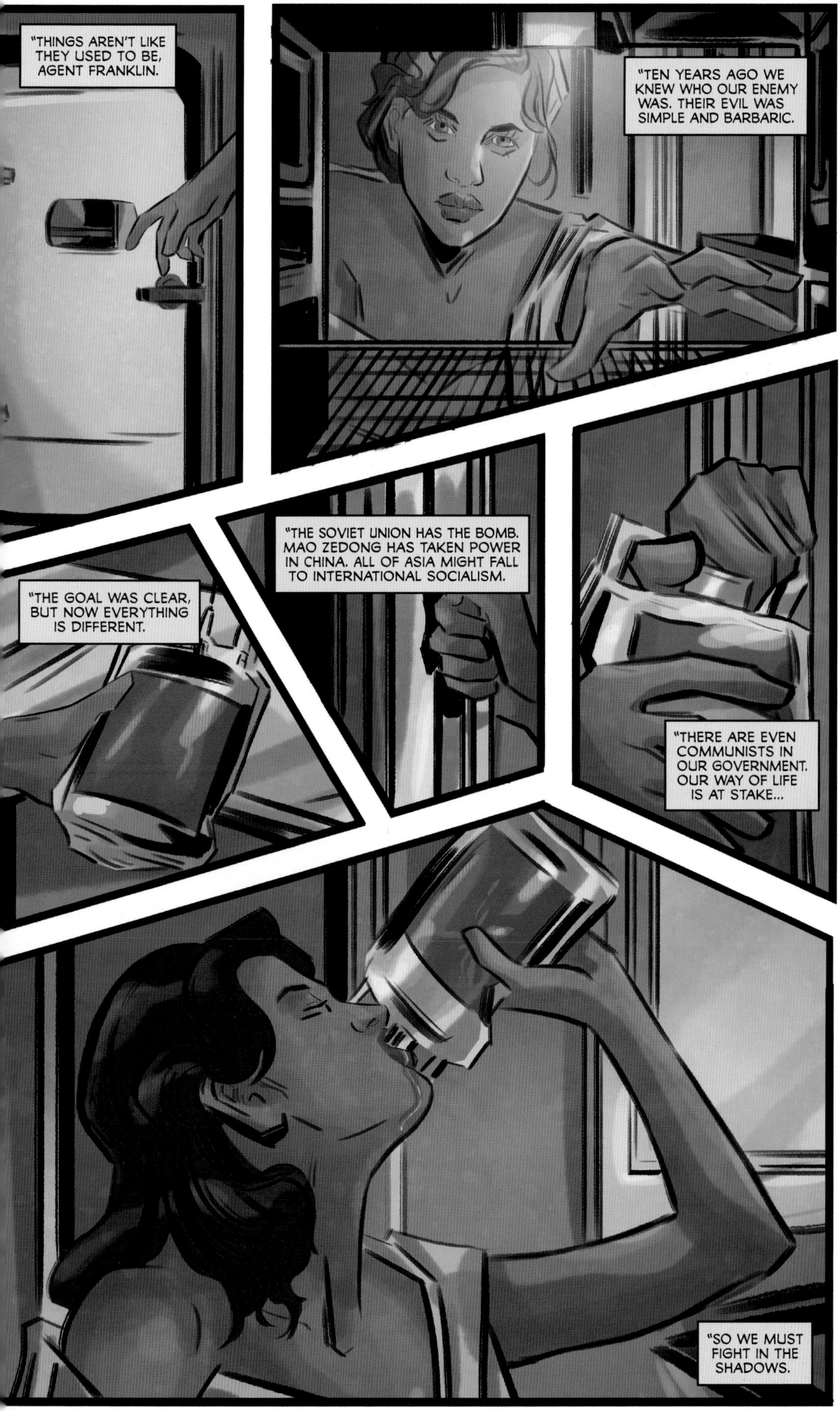
"THINGS AREN'T LIKE THEY USED TO BE, AGENT FRANKLIN.
"TEN YEARS AGO WE KNEW WHO OUR ENEMY WAS. THEIR EVIL WAS SIMPLE AND BARBARIC.
"THE GOAL WAS CLEAR, BUT NOW EVERYTHING IS DIFFERENT.
"THE SOVIET UNION HAS THE BOMB. MAO ZEDONG HAS TAKEN POWER IN CHINA. ALL OF ASIA MIGHT FALL TO INTERNATIONAL SOCIALISM.
"THERE ARE EVEN COMMUNISTS IN OUR GOVERNMENT. OUR WAY OF LIFE IS AT STAKE...
"SO WE MUST FIGHT IN THE SHADOWS.

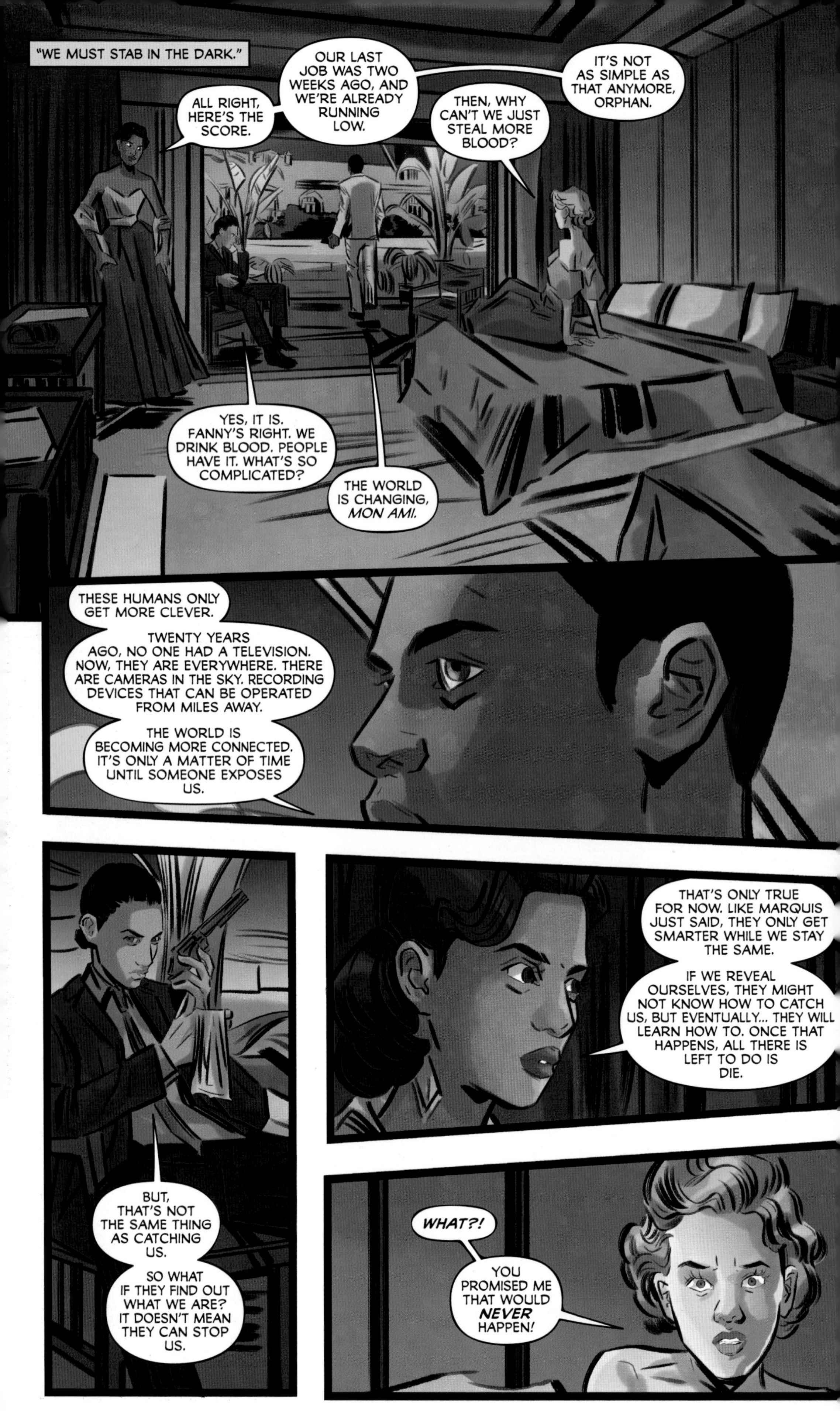
"WE MUST STAB IN THE DARK."
ALL RIGHT, HERE'S THE SCORE.
OUR LAST JOB WAS TWO WEEKS AGO, AND WE'RE ALREADY RUNNING LOW.
THEN, WHY CAN'T WE JUST STEAL MORE BLOOD?
IT'S NOT AS SIMPLE AS THAT ANYMORE, ORPHAN.
YES, IT IS. FANNY'S RIGHT. WE DRINK BLOOD. PEOPLE HAVE IT. WHAT'S SO COMPLICATED?
THE WORLD IS CHANGING, *MON AMI.*
THESE HUMANS ONLY GET MORE CLEVER.
TWENTY YEARS AGO, NO ONE HAD A TELEVISION. NOW, THEY ARE EVERYWHERE. THERE ARE CAMERAS IN THE SKY. RECORDING DEVICES THAT CAN BE OPERATED FROM MILES AWAY.
THE WORLD IS BECOMING MORE CONNECTED. IT'S ONLY A MATTER OF TIME UNTIL SOMEONE EXPOSES US.
BUT, THAT'S NOT THE SAME THING AS CATCHING US.
SO WHAT IF THEY FIND OUT WHAT WE ARE? IT DOESN'T MEAN THEY CAN STOP US.
THAT'S ONLY TRUE FOR NOW. LIKE MARQUIS JUST SAID, THEY ONLY GET SMARTER WHILE WE STAY THE SAME.
IF WE REVEAL OURSELVES, THEY MIGHT NOT KNOW HOW TO CATCH US, BUT EVENTUALLY... THEY WILL LEARN HOW TO. ONCE THAT HAPPENS, ALL THERE IS LEFT TO DO IS DIE.
WHAT?!
YOU PROMISED ME THAT WOULD ***NEVER*** HAPPEN!

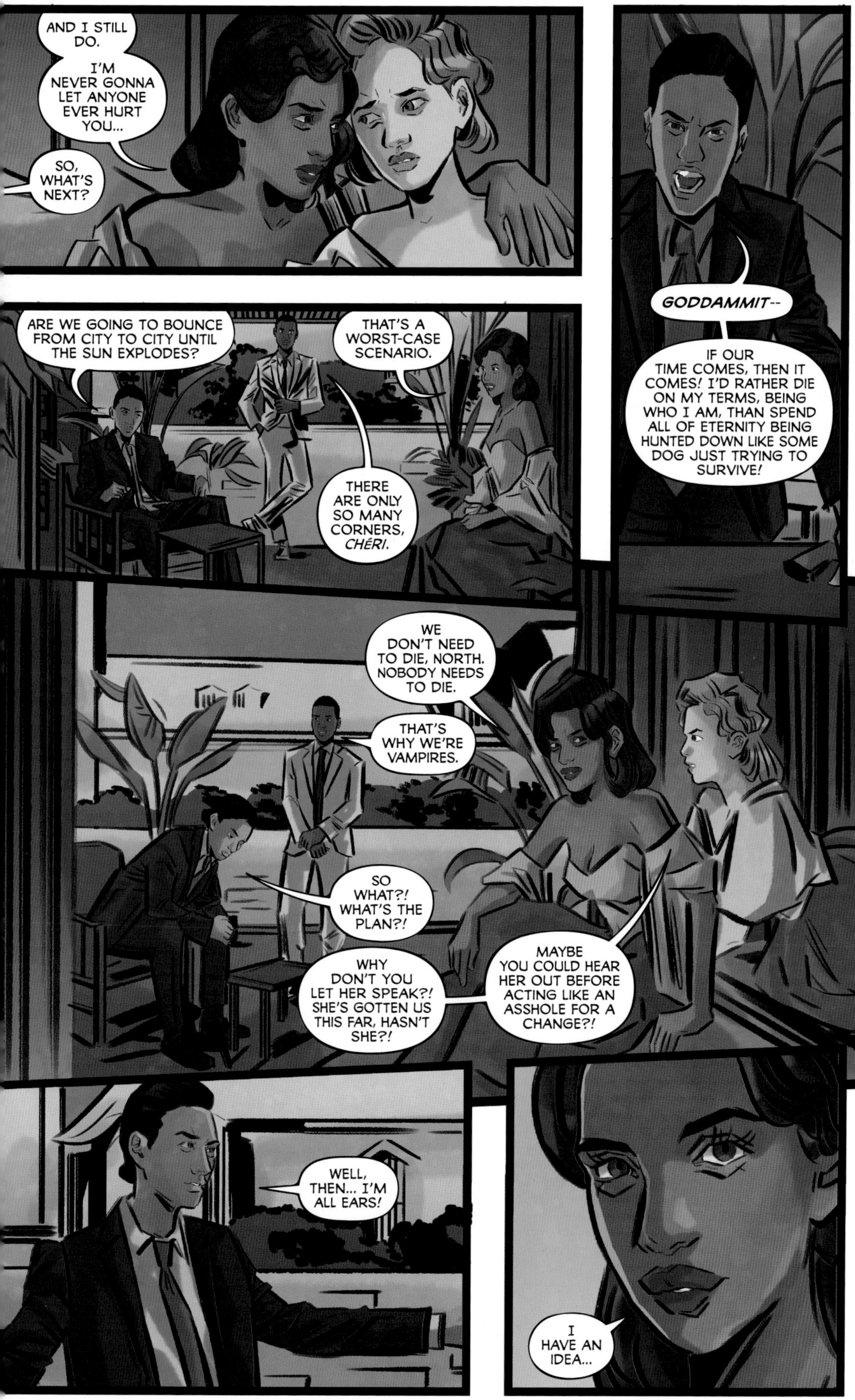
AND I STILL DO.
I'M NEVER GONNA LET ANYONE EVER HURT YOU...
SO, WHAT'S NEXT?
ARE WE GOING TO BOUNCE FROM CITY TO CITY UNTIL THE SUN EXPLODES?
THAT'S A WORST-CASE SCENARIO.
THERE ARE ONLY SO MANY CORNERS, *CHÉRI*.
GODDAMMIT--
IF OUR TIME COMES, THEN IT COMES! I'D RATHER DIE ON MY TERMS, BEING WHO I AM, THAN SPEND ALL OF ETERNITY BEING HUNTED DOWN LIKE SOME DOG JUST TRYING TO SURVIVE!
WE DON'T NEED TO DIE, NORTH. NOBODY NEEDS TO DIE.
THAT'S WHY WE'RE VAMPIRES.
SO WHAT?! WHAT'S THE PLAN?!
WHY DON'T YOU LET HER SPEAK?! SHE'S GOTTEN US THIS FAR, HASN'T SHE?!
MAYBE YOU COULD HEAR HER OUT BEFORE ACTING LIKE AN ASSHOLE FOR A CHANGE?!
WELL, THEN... I'M ALL EARS!
I HAVE AN IDEA...

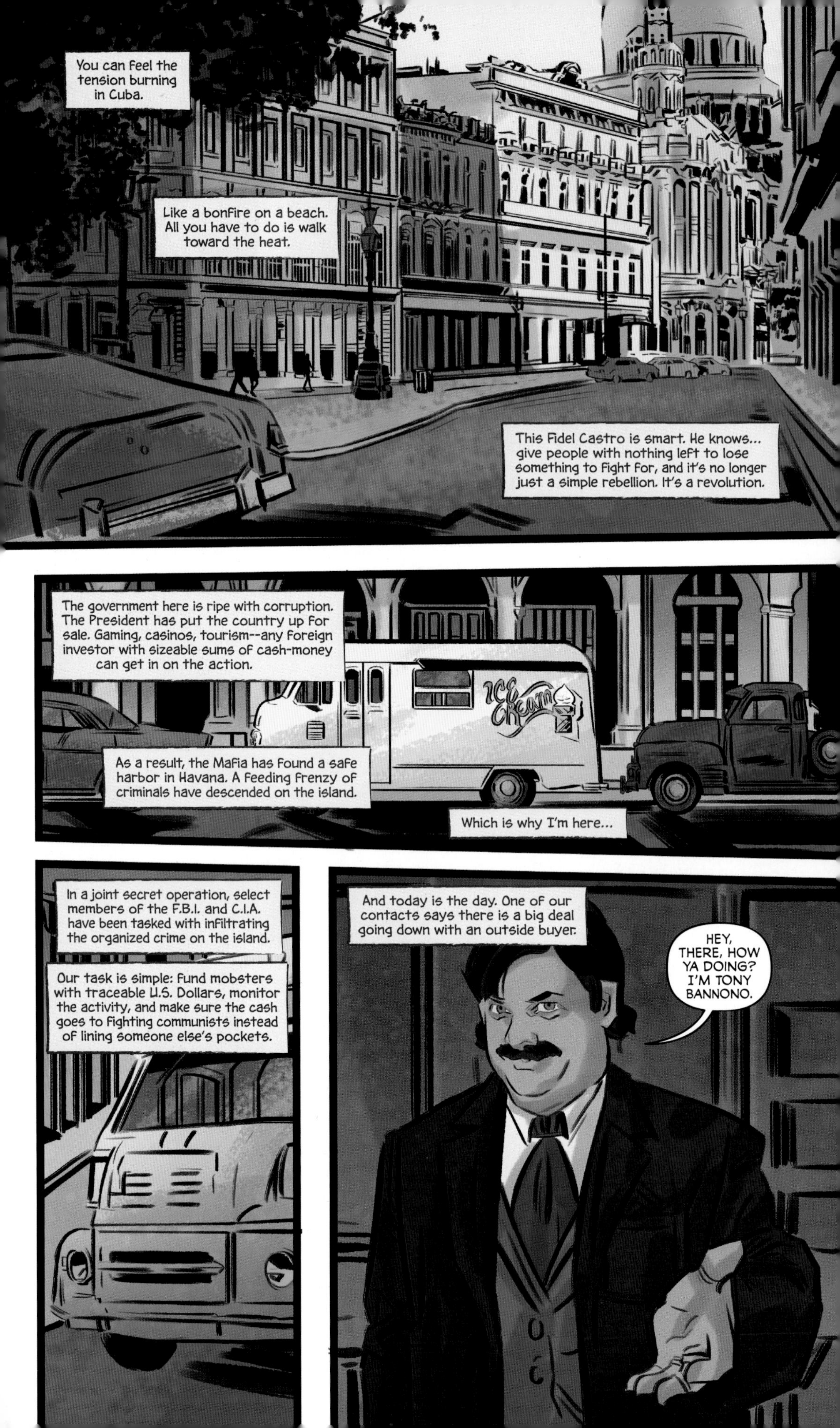

You can feel the tension burning in Cuba.
Like a bonfire on a beach. All you have to do is walk toward the heat.
This Fidel Castro is smart. He knows... give people with nothing left to lose something to fight for, and it's no longer just a simple rebellion. It's a revolution.
The government here is ripe with corruption. The President has put the country up for sale. Gaming, casinos, tourism--any foreign investor with sizeable sums of cash-money can get in on the action.
ICE CREAM
As a result, the Mafia has found a safe harbor in Havana. A feeding frenzy of criminals have descended on the island.
Which is why I'm here...
In a joint secret operation, select members of the F.B.I. and C.I.A. have been tasked with infiltrating the organized crime on the island.
Our task is simple: fund mobsters with traceable U.S. Dollars, monitor the activity, and make sure the cash goes to fighting communists instead of lining someone else's pockets.
And today is the day. One of our contacts says there is a big deal going down with an outside buyer.
HEY, THERE, HOW YA DOING? I'M TONY BANNONO.

Somebody with a lot of money who no one has ever heard of before.

MY FRIENDS CALL ME *TONY BANANAS*. SO *YOU* CAN CALL ME MR. BANNONO. *AYE!* I'M JUST KIDDING OVER HERE!

NICE TO MEET YOU, MR. BANNONO.

TONY, PLEASE.

NICE TO MEET YOU, TONY. I'M AGENT FRANKLIN. OVER ON THE CONTROLS IS MY COLLEAGUE, AGENT BIRCH. THANK YOU AGAIN FOR AGREEING TO WORK WITH US TODAY.

Since it's our job to survey the illegal activity of the entire country, we needed to put ears inside the room.

THIS RED CARNATION HAS A HIDDEN MICROPHONE ATTACHED TO A RECEIVER.

I'M GOING TO PIN THE MICROPHONE ON YOUR JACKET AND PLACE THE RECEIVER IN YOUR BREAST COAT POCKET. AGENT BIRCH AND I WILL BE LISTENING IN FROM HERE.

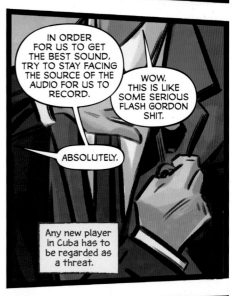

IN ORDER FOR US TO GET THE BEST SOUND, TRY TO STAY FACING THE SOURCE OF THE AUDIO FOR US TO RECORD.

WOW. THIS IS LIKE SOME SERIOUS FLASH GORDON SHIT.

ABSOLUTELY.

Any new player in Cuba has to be regarded as a threat.

NOW... TONY. IF THERE ARE ANY ISSUES, ANY PROBLEMS WHATSOEVER, JUST SAY, "WHO WANTS MORE COFFEE?" THAT WILL BE OUR CUE TO COME IN.

AYE, FUGGIT ABOUT IT. I'LL BE FINE!

They could be agents of the Cuban communist rebels.

AIN'T NO ONE KILLED OLD BANANAS, YET!

Perhaps even Soviet spies sent by the Kremlin directly. Or...

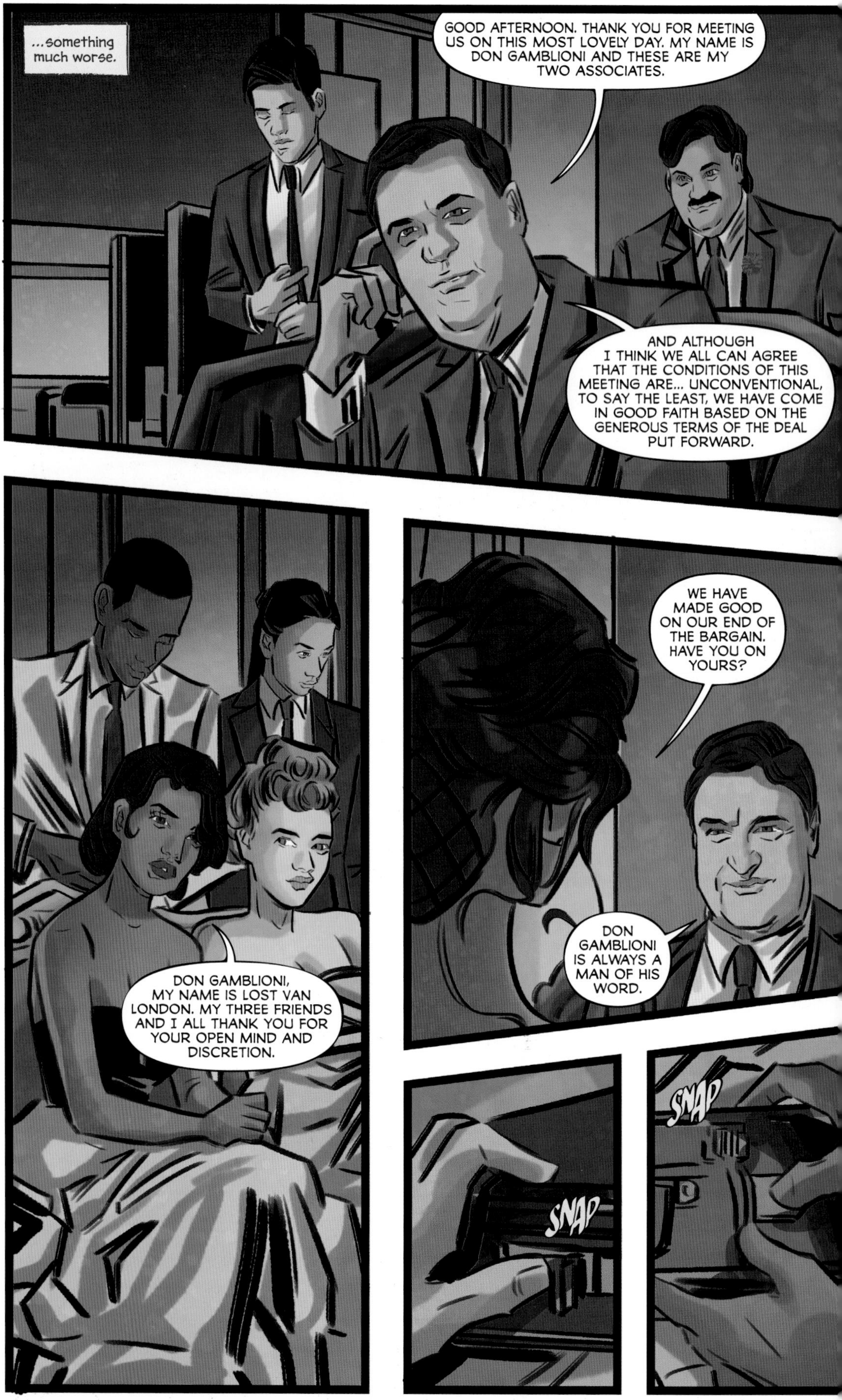
...something much worse.
GOOD AFTERNOON. THANK YOU FOR MEETING US ON THIS MOST LOVELY DAY. MY NAME IS DON GAMBLIONI AND THESE ARE MY TWO ASSOCIATES.
AND ALTHOUGH I THINK WE ALL CAN AGREE THAT THE CONDITIONS OF THIS MEETING ARE... UNCONVENTIONAL, TO SAY THE LEAST, WE HAVE COME IN GOOD FAITH BASED ON THE GENEROUS TERMS OF THE DEAL PUT FORWARD.
DON GAMBLIONI, MY NAME IS LOST VAN LONDON. MY THREE FRIENDS AND I ALL THANK YOU FOR YOUR OPEN MIND AND DISCRETION.
WE HAVE MADE GOOD ON OUR END OF THE BARGAIN. HAVE YOU ON YOURS?
DON GAMBLIONI IS ALWAYS A MAN OF HIS WORD.
SNAP
SNAP

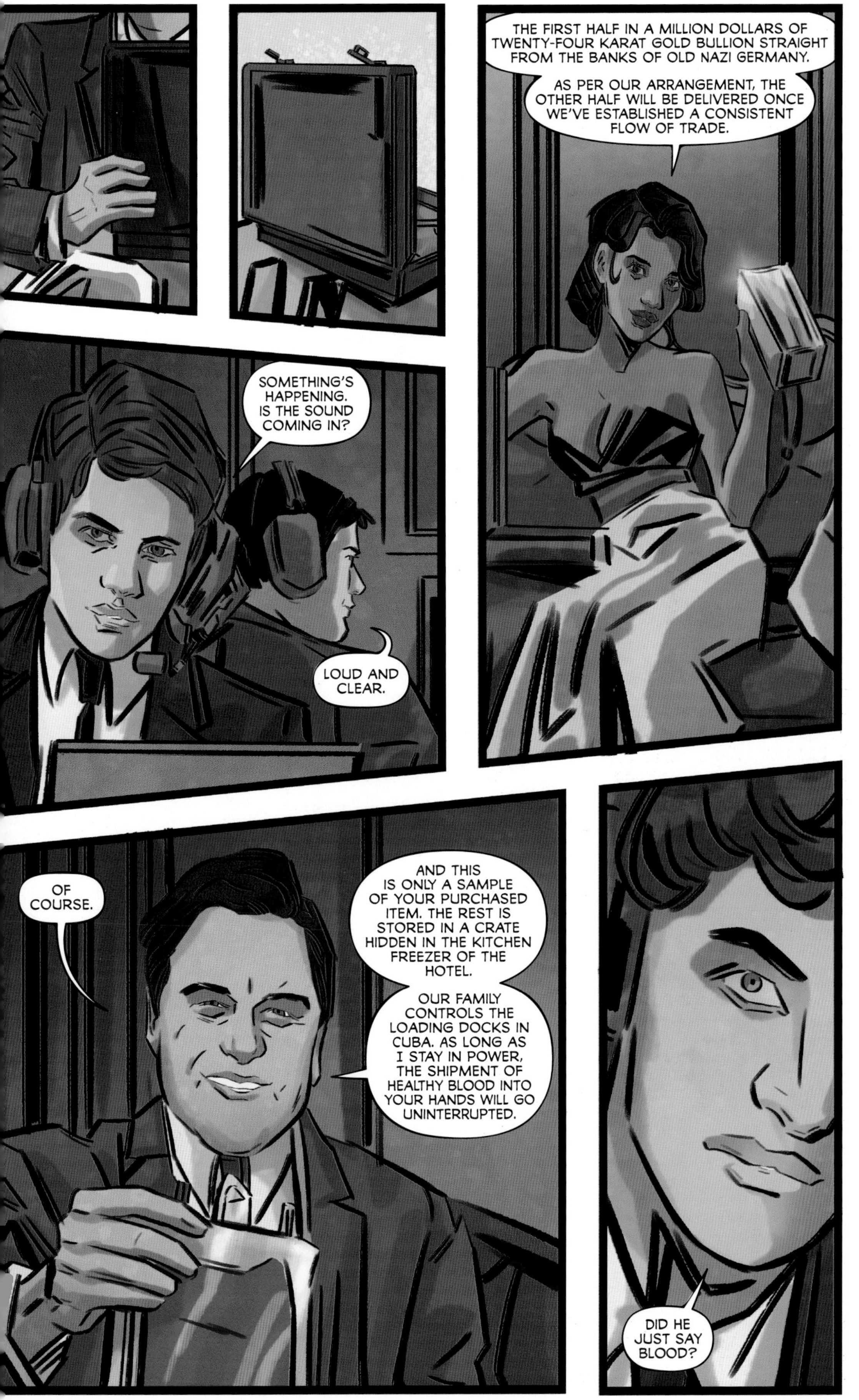
THE FIRST HALF IN A MILLION DOLLARS OF TWENTY-FOUR KARAT GOLD BULLION STRAIGHT FROM THE BANKS OF OLD NAZI GERMANY.
AS PER OUR ARRANGEMENT, THE OTHER HALF WILL BE DELIVERED ONCE WE'VE ESTABLISHED A CONSISTENT FLOW OF TRADE.
SOMETHING'S HAPPENING. IS THE SOUND COMING IN?
LOUD AND CLEAR.
OF COURSE.
AND THIS IS ONLY A SAMPLE OF YOUR PURCHASED ITEM. THE REST IS STORED IN A CRATE HIDDEN IN THE KITCHEN FREEZER OF THE HOTEL.
OUR FAMILY CONTROLS THE LOADING DOCKS IN CUBA. AS LONG AS I STAY IN POWER, THE SHIPMENT OF HEALTHY BLOOD INTO YOUR HANDS WILL GO UNINTERRUPTED.
DID HE JUST SAY BLOOD?

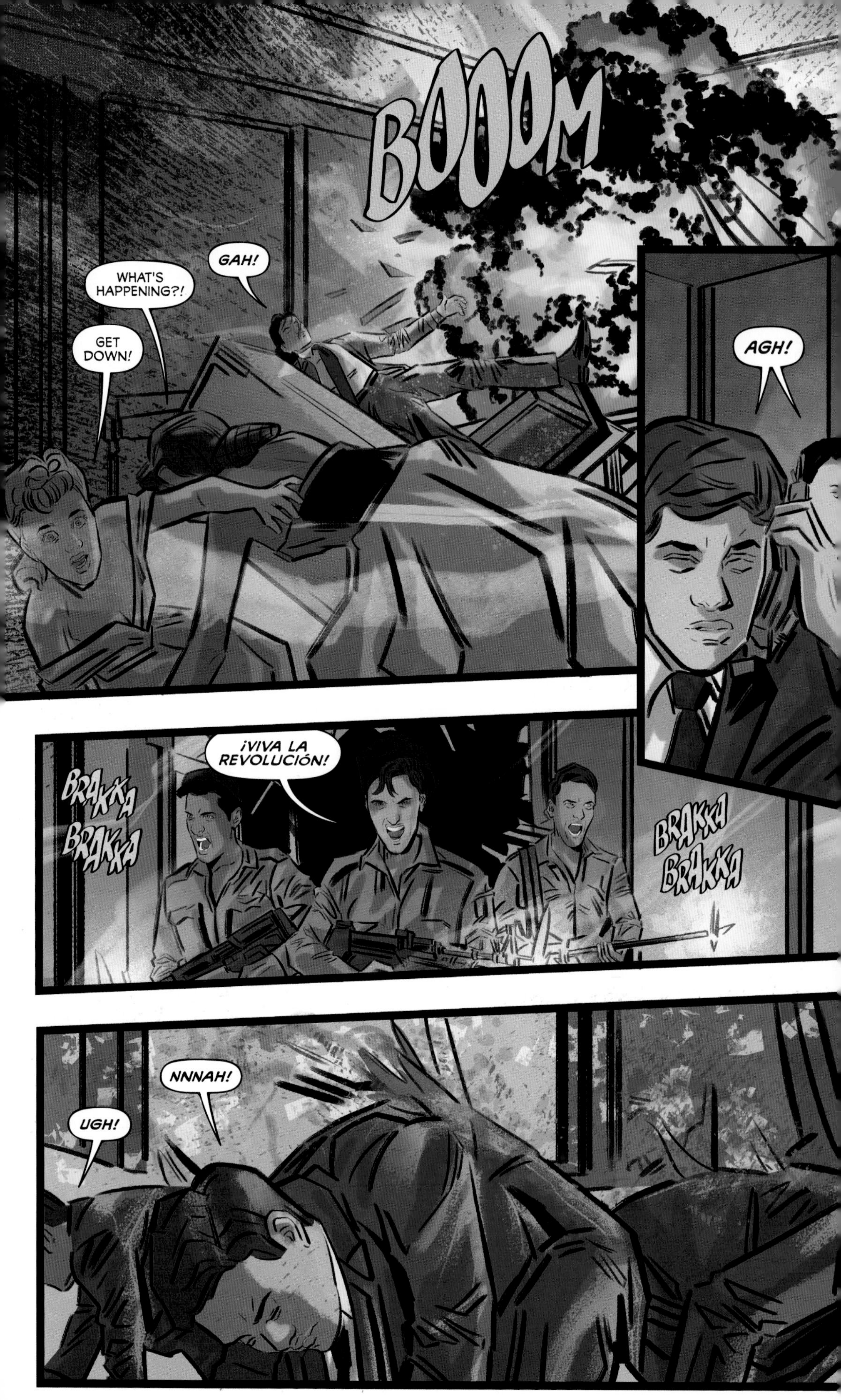
BOOOM
GAH!
WHAT'S HAPPENING?!
GET DOWN!
AGH!
¡VIVA LA REVOLUCIÓN!
BRAKKA BRAKKA
BRAKKA BRAKKA
NNNAH!
UGH!

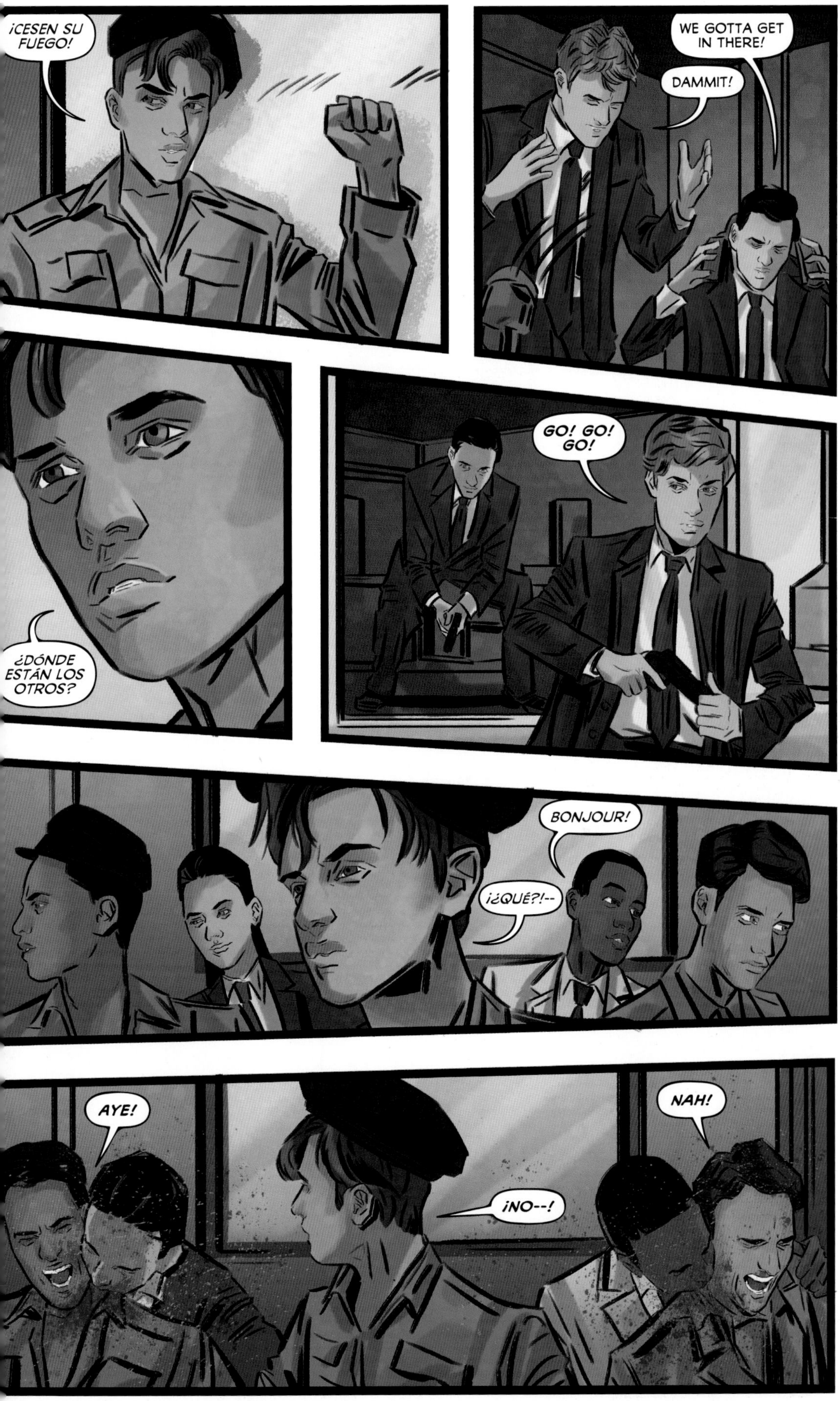
¡CESEN SU FUEGO!
WE GOTTA GET IN THERE!
DAMMIT!
¿DÓNDE ESTÁN LOS OTROS?
GO! GO! GO!
BONJOUR!
¡¿QUÉ?!--
AYE!
¡NO--!
NAH!

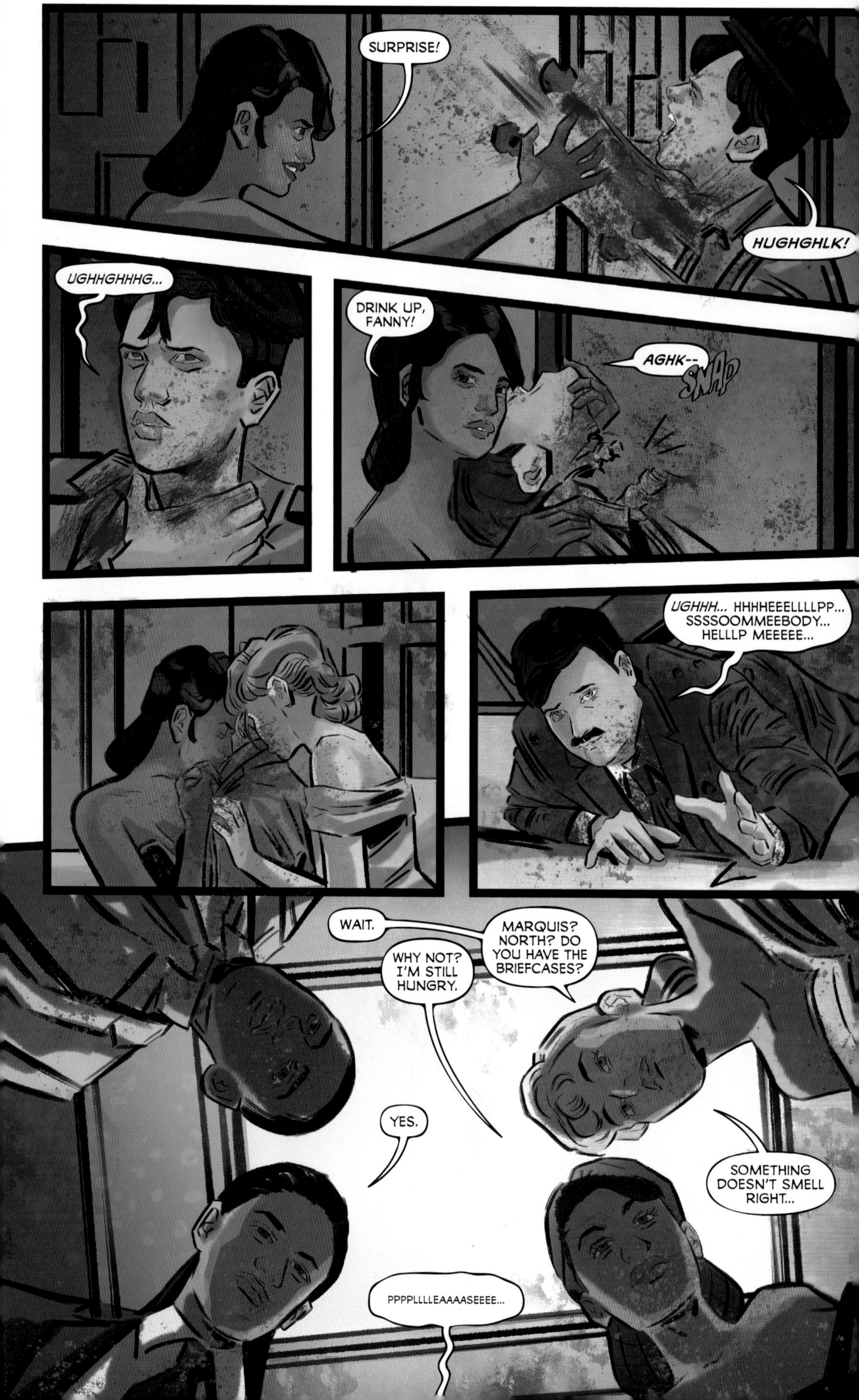
SURPRISE!
HUGHGHLK!
UGHHGHHHG...
DRINK UP, FANNY!
AGHK--
SNAP
UGHHH... HHHHEEELLLLPP... SSSSOOMMEEBODY... HELLLP MEEEEE...
WAIT.
MARQUIS? NORTH? DO YOU HAVE THE BRIEFCASES?
WHY NOT? I'M STILL HUNGRY.
YES.
SOMETHING DOESN'T SMELL RIGHT...
PPPPLLLLEAAAASEEEE...

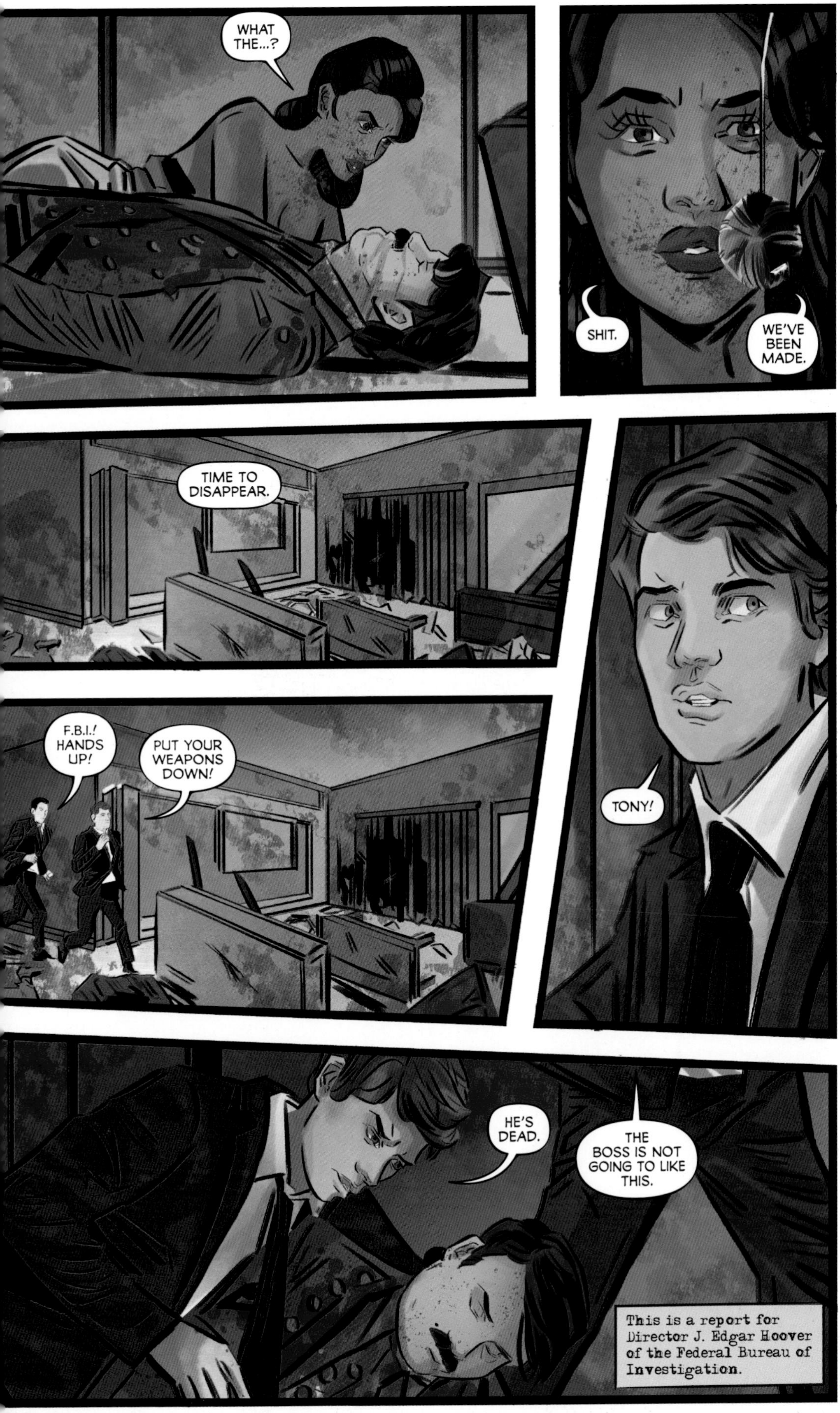
WHAT THE...?
SHIT.
WE'VE BEEN MADE.
TIME TO DISAPPEAR.
F.B.I.! HANDS UP!
PUT YOUR WEAPONS DOWN!
TONY!
HE'S DEAD.
THE BOSS IS NOT GOING TO LIKE THIS.
This is a report for Director J. Edgar Hoover of the Federal Bureau of Investigation.

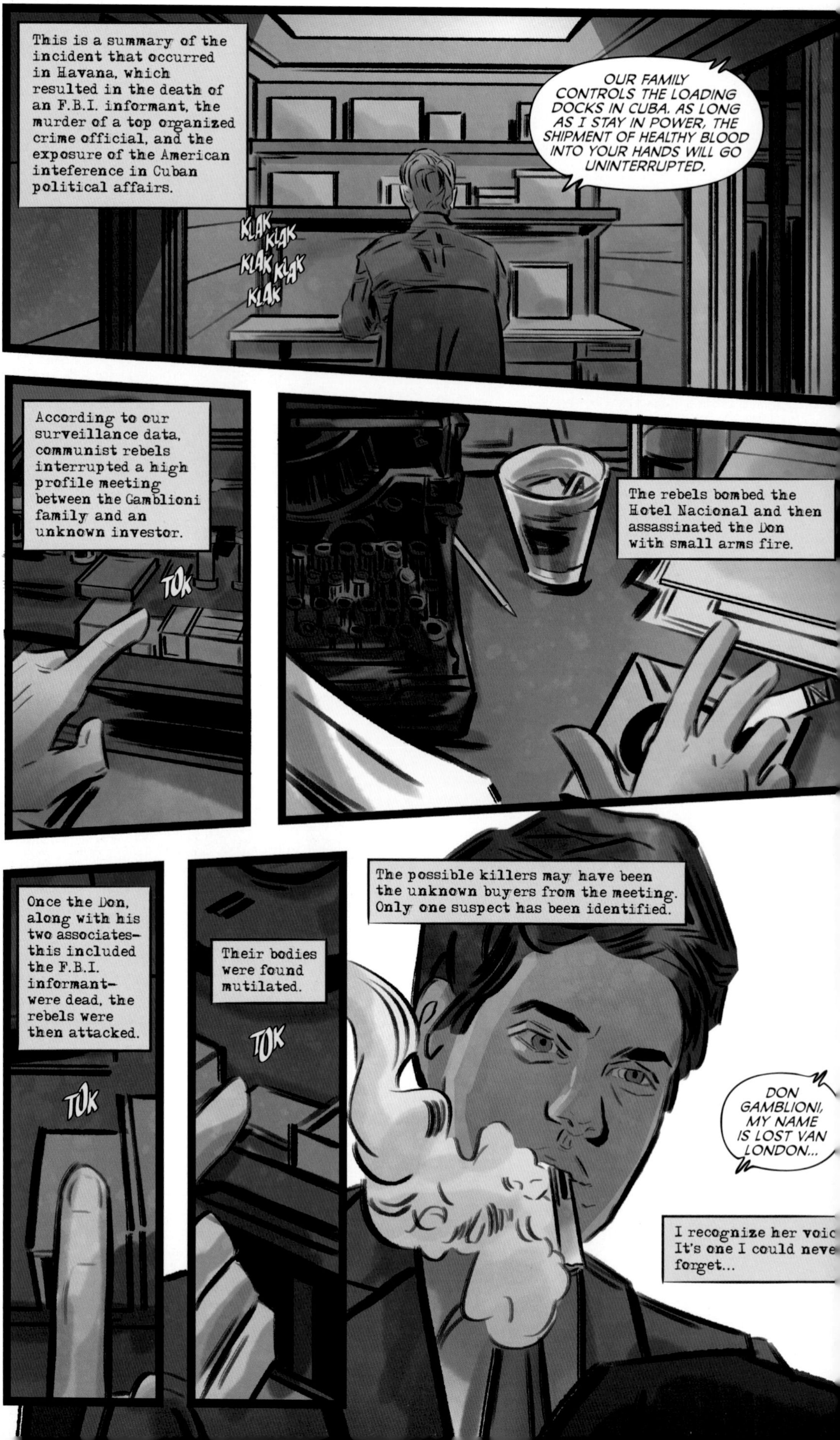

This is a summary of the incident that occurred in Havana, which resulted in the death of an F.B.I. informant, the murder of a top organized crime official, and the exposure of the American inteference in Cuban political affairs.
OUR FAMILY CONTROLS THE LOADING DOCKS IN CUBA. AS LONG AS I STAY IN POWER, THE SHIPMENT OF HEALTHY BLOOD INTO YOUR HANDS WILL GO UNINTERRUPTED.
KLAK KLAK KLAK KLAK KLAK
According to our surveillance data, communist rebels interrupted a high profile meeting between the Gamblioni family and an unknown investor.
TOK
The rebels bombed the Hotel Nacional and then assassinated the Don with small arms fire.
Once the Don, along with his two associates- this included the F.B.I. informant- were dead, the rebels were then attacked.
TOK
Their bodies were found mutilated.
TOK
The possible killers may have been the unknown buyers from the meeting. Only one suspect has been identified.
DON GAMBLIONI, MY NAME IS LOST VAN LONDON...
I recognize her voic It's one I could neve forget...

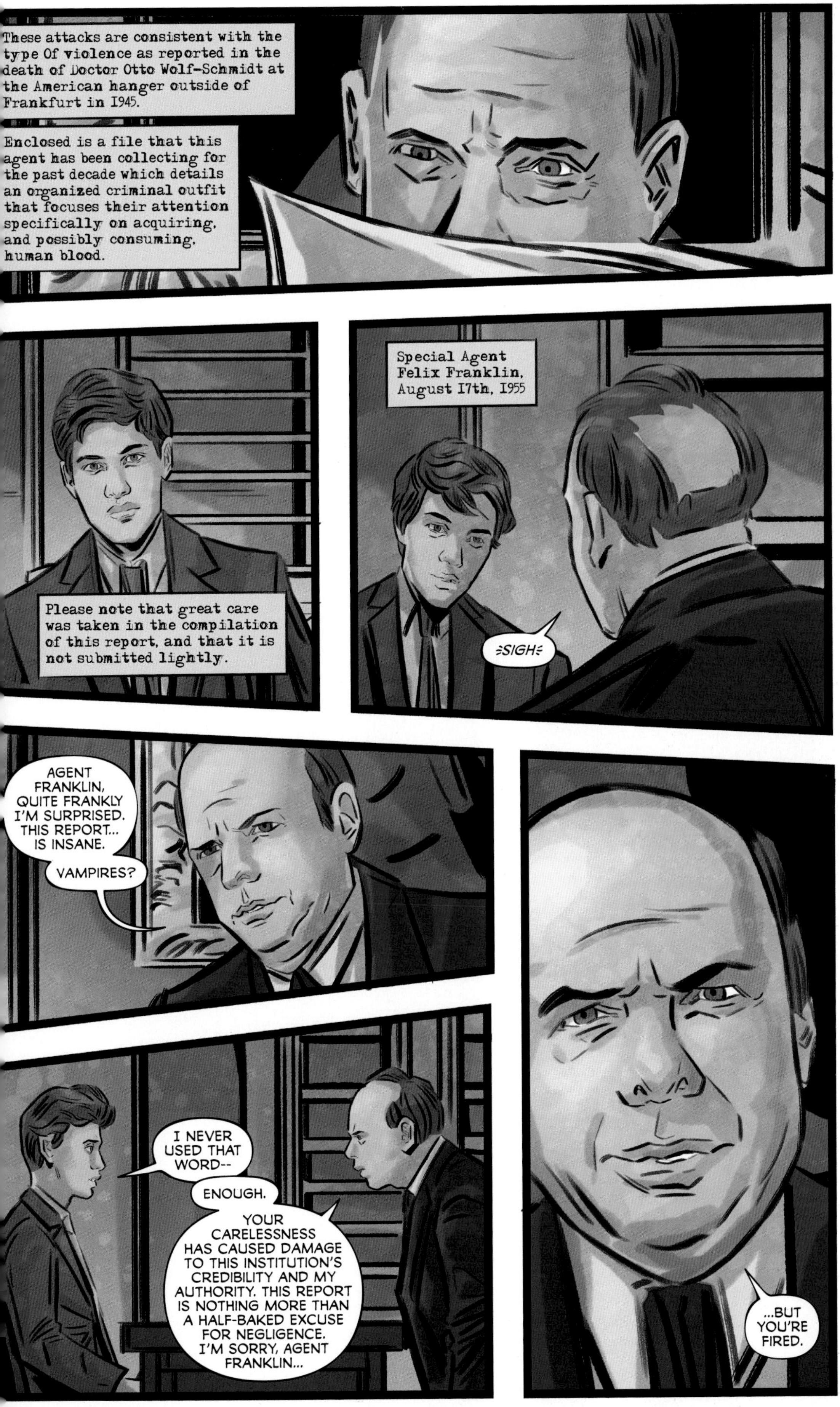
These attacks are consistent with the type Of violence as reported in the death of Doctor Otto Wolf-Schmidt at the American hanger outside of Frankfurt in 1945.
Enclosed is a file that this agent has been collecting for the past decade which details an organized criminal outfit that focuses their attention specifically on acquiring, and possibly consuming, human blood.
Please note that great care was taken in the compilation of this report, and that it is not submitted lightly.
Special Agent Felix Franklin, August 17th, 1955
SIGH
AGENT FRANKLIN, QUITE FRANKLY I'M SURPRISED. THIS REPORT... IS INSANE.
VAMPIRES?
I NEVER USED THAT WORD--
ENOUGH.
YOUR CARELESSNESS HAS CAUSED DAMAGE TO THIS INSTITUTION'S CREDIBILITY AND MY AUTHORITY. THIS REPORT IS NOTHING MORE THAN A HALF-BAKED EXCUSE FOR NEGLIGENCE. I'M SORRY, AGENT FRANKLIN...
...BUT YOU'RE FIRED.

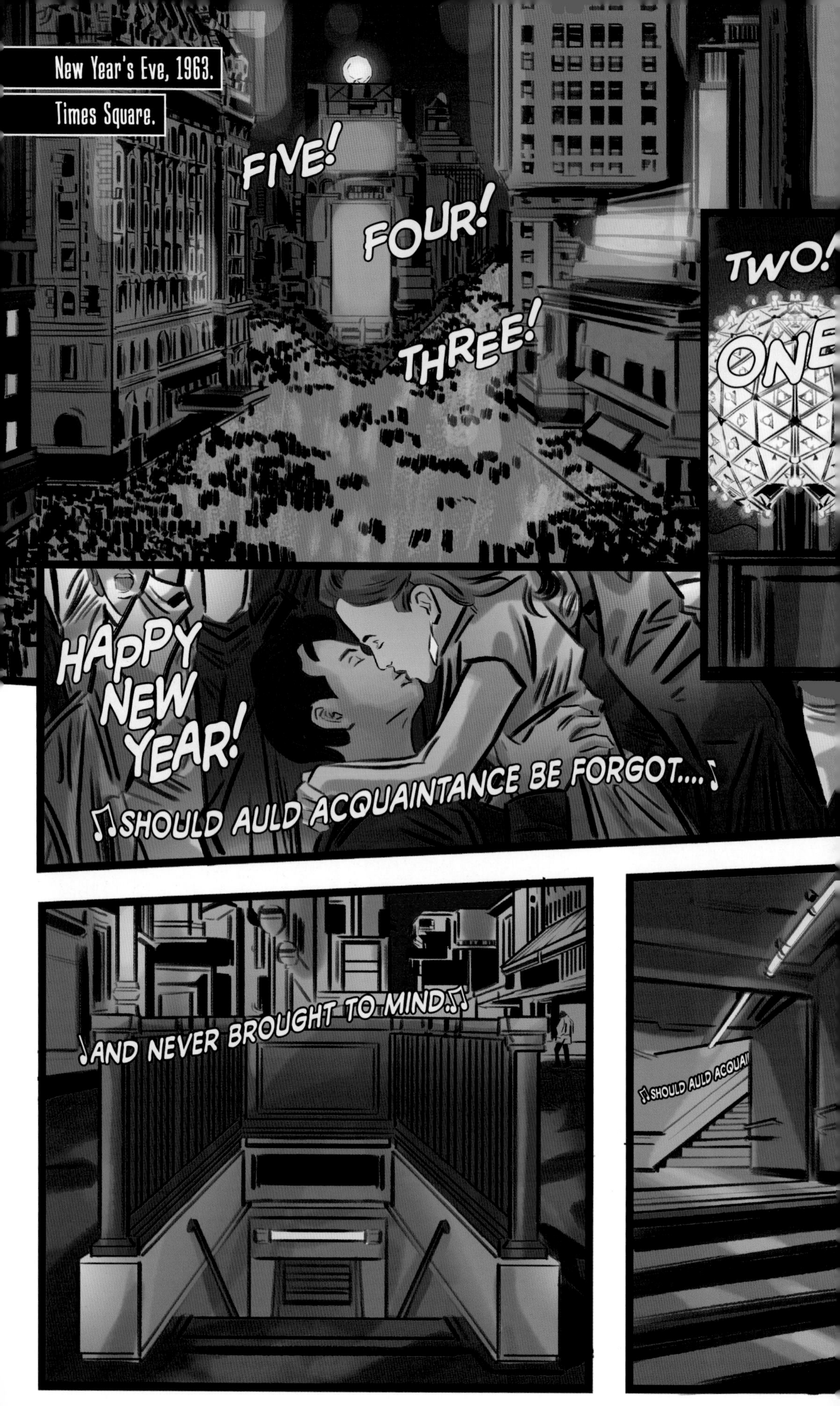
New Year's Eve, 1963.
Times Square.
FIVE!
FOUR!
THREE!
TWO!
ONE
HAPPY NEW YEAR!
♫SHOULD AULD ACQUAINTANCE BE FORGOT....♪
♪AND NEVER BROUGHT TO MIND♫
♫SHOULD AULD ACQUAI

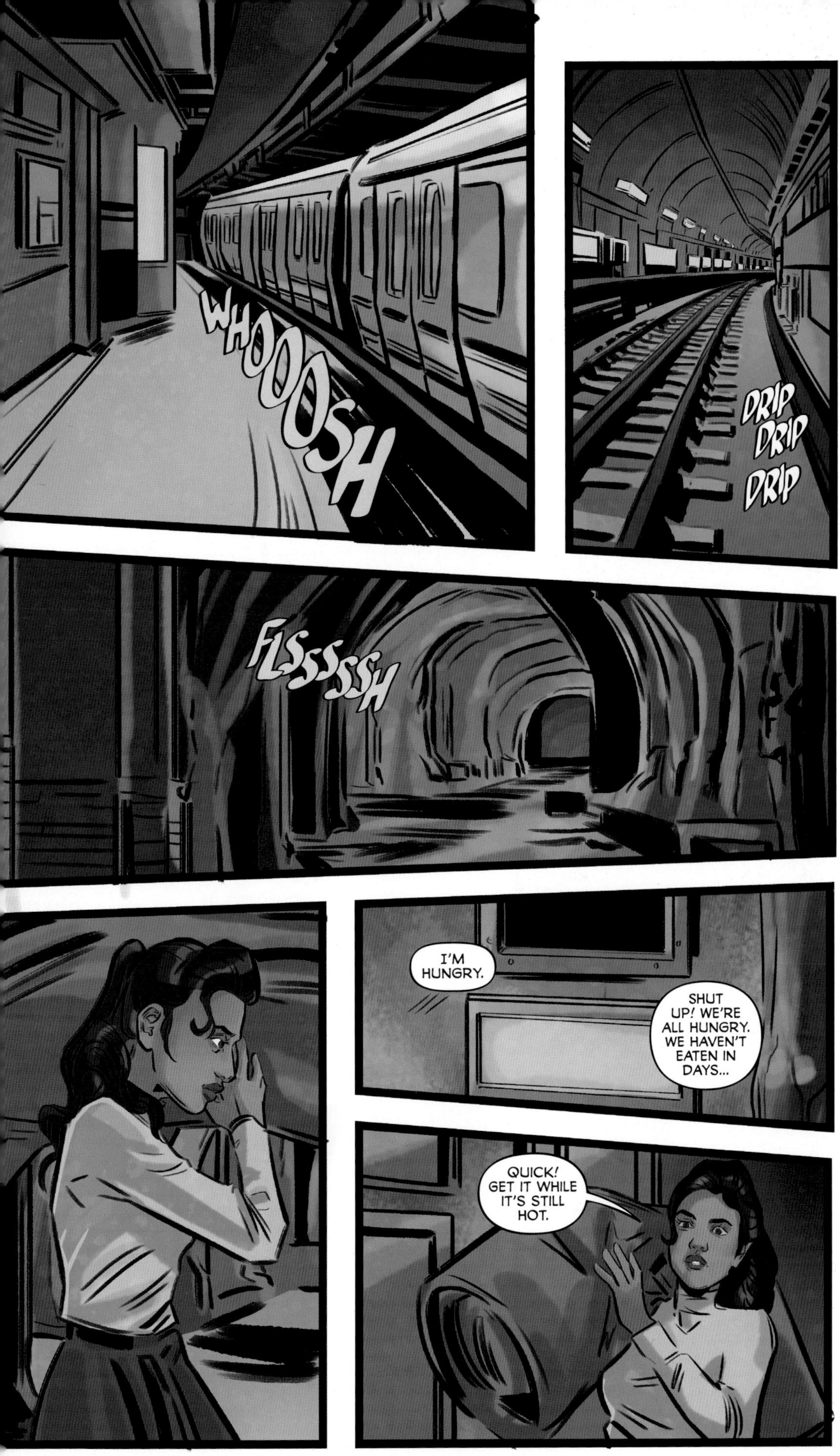
WHOOOOSH
DRIP
DRIP
DRIP
FLSSSSSH
I'M HUNGRY.
SHUT UP! WE'RE ALL HUNGRY. WE HAVEN'T EATEN IN DAYS...
QUICK! GET IT WHILE IT'S STILL HOT.

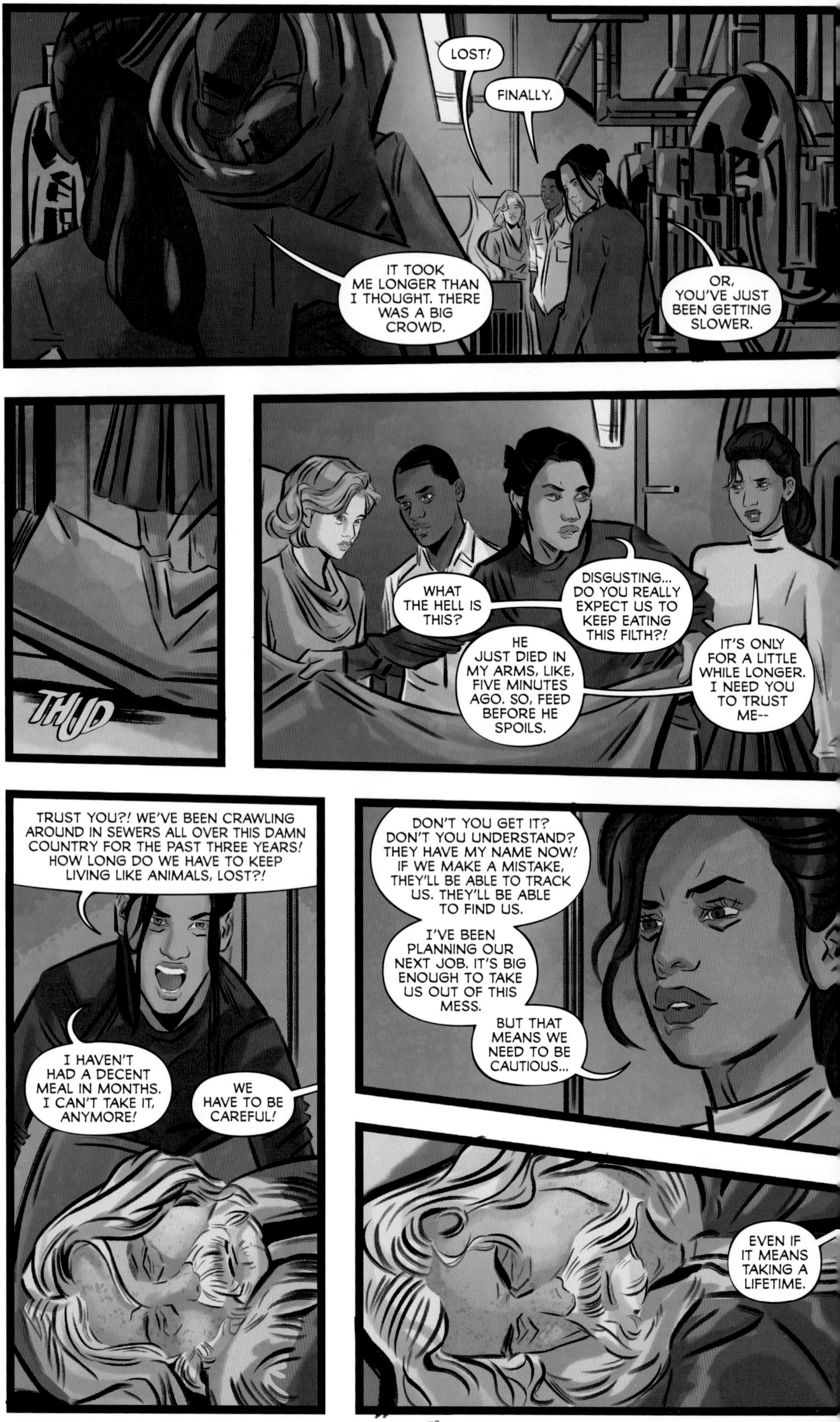
LOST!
FINALLY.
IT TOOK ME LONGER THAN I THOUGHT. THERE WAS A BIG CROWD.
OR, YOU'VE JUST BEEN GETTING SLOWER.
THUD
WHAT THE HELL IS THIS?
DISGUSTING... DO YOU REALLY EXPECT US TO KEEP EATING THIS FILTH?!
HE JUST DIED IN MY ARMS, LIKE, FIVE MINUTES AGO. SO, FEED BEFORE HE SPOILS.
IT'S ONLY FOR A LITTLE WHILE LONGER. I NEED YOU TO TRUST ME--
TRUST YOU?! WE'VE BEEN CRAWLING AROUND IN SEWERS ALL OVER THIS DAMN COUNTRY FOR THE PAST THREE YEARS! HOW LONG DO WE HAVE TO KEEP LIVING LIKE ANIMALS, LOST?!
I HAVEN'T HAD A DECENT MEAL IN MONTHS. I CAN'T TAKE IT, ANYMORE!
WE HAVE TO BE CAREFUL!
DON'T YOU GET IT? DON'T YOU UNDERSTAND? THEY HAVE MY NAME NOW! IF WE MAKE A MISTAKE, THEY'LL BE ABLE TO TRACK US. THEY'LL BE ABLE TO FIND US.
I'VE BEEN PLANNING OUR NEXT JOB. IT'S BIG ENOUGH TO TAKE US OUT OF THIS MESS.
BUT THAT MEANS WE NEED TO BE CAUTIOUS...
EVEN IF IT MEANS TAKING A LIFETIME.

CHAPTER

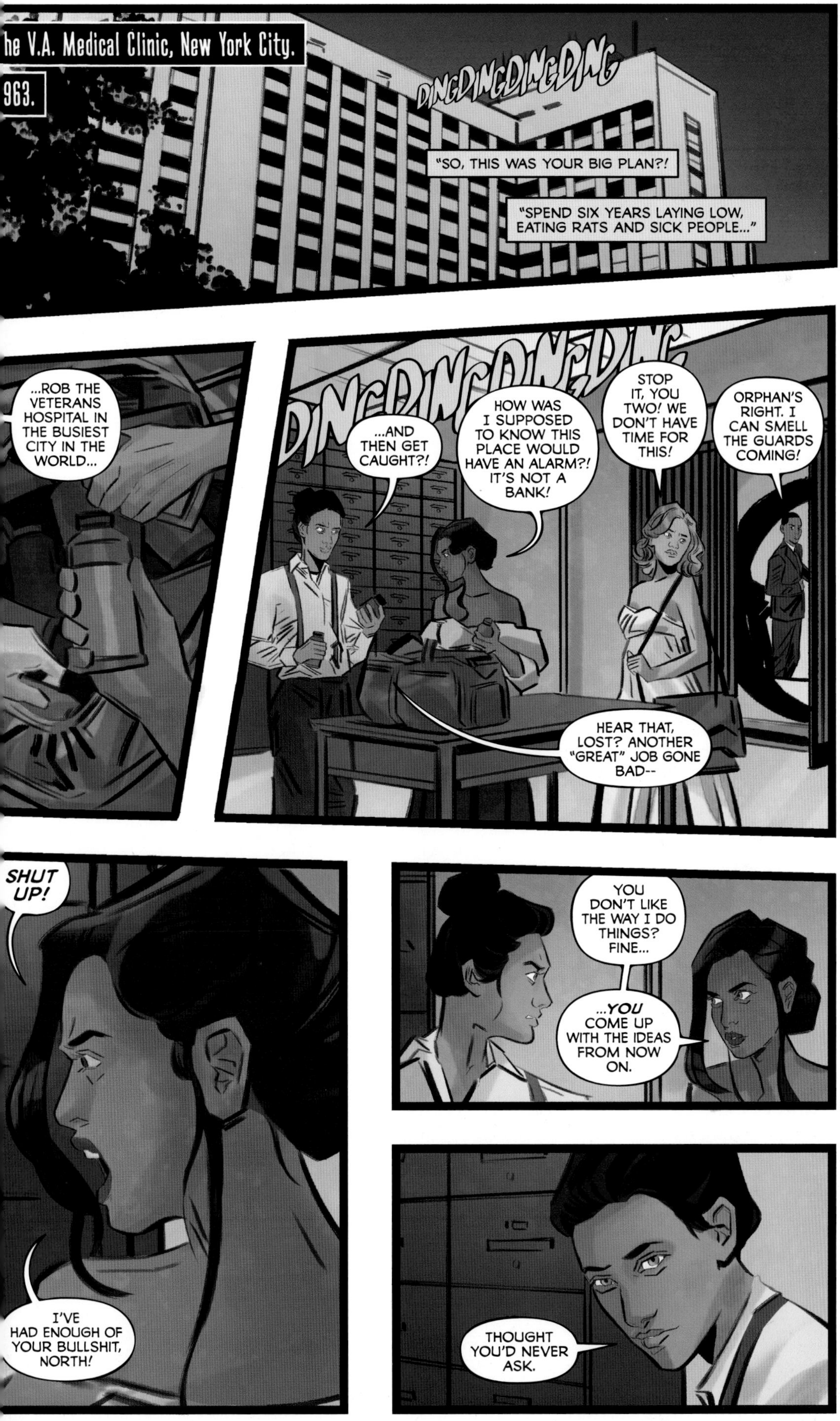
he V.A. Medical Clinic, New York City.
963.
DINGDINGDINGDING
"SO, THIS WAS YOUR BIG PLAN?!
"SPEND SIX YEARS LAYING LOW, EATING RATS AND SICK PEOPLE..."
...ROB THE VETERANS HOSPITAL IN THE BUSIEST CITY IN THE WORLD...
DINGDINGDINGDING
...AND THEN GET CAUGHT?!
HOW WAS I SUPPOSED TO KNOW THIS PLACE WOULD HAVE AN ALARM?! IT'S NOT A BANK!
STOP IT, YOU TWO! WE DON'T HAVE TIME FOR THIS!
ORPHAN'S RIGHT. I CAN SMELL THE GUARDS COMING!
HEAR THAT, LOST? ANOTHER "GREAT" JOB GONE BAD--
SHUT UP!
I'VE HAD ENOUGH OF YOUR BULLSHIT, NORTH!
YOU DON'T LIKE THE WAY I DO THINGS? FINE...
...YOU COME UP WITH THE IDEAS FROM NOW ON.
THOUGHT YOU'D NEVER ASK.

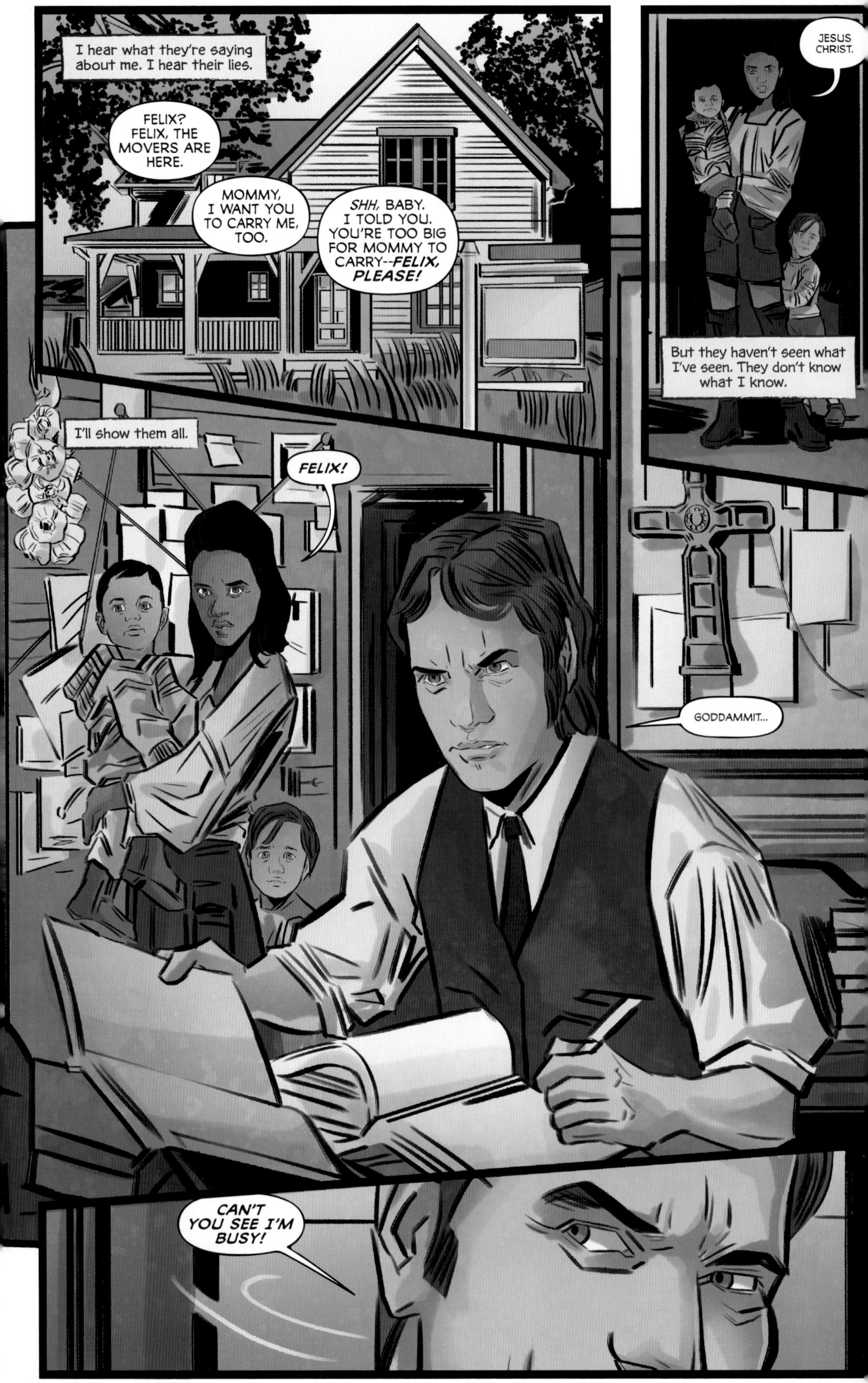
I hear what they're saying about me. I hear their lies.
FELIX? FELIX, THE MOVERS ARE HERE.
MOMMY, I WANT YOU TO CARRY ME, TOO.
SHH, BABY. I TOLD YOU. YOU'RE TOO BIG FOR MOMMY TO CARRY--FELIX, PLEASE!
JESUS CHRIST.
But they haven't seen what I've seen. They don't know what I know.
I'll show them all.
FELIX!
GODDAMMIT...
CAN'T YOU SEE I'M BUSY!

I DIDN'T REALIZE *THAT'S* WHAT YOU WERE CALLING IT, NOW.

IT'S RESEARCH. I'M WORKING.

HUNTING FOR VAMPIRES IS NOT A JOB.

GO AHEAD. MOCK ME. YOU'RE JUST LIKE ALL THE REST. YOU WOULDN'T UNDERSTAND.

FELIX, PLEASE... I WANT TO HELP YOU, BUT I'M SCARED. THE CHILDREN ARE SCARED. I TOLD YOU THAT WE WEREN'T GOING TO KEEP LIVING LIKE THIS, AND YOU DON'T EVEN CARE. IT'S LIKE WE DON'T EVEN *MATTER* ANYMORE.

I'M TAKING THE KIDS AND WE'RE GOING TO STAY WITH MY MOTHER FOR A COUPLE DAYS. I'M BEGGING YOU, FELIX. GET SOME HELP--

SHUT UP!

FELIX!

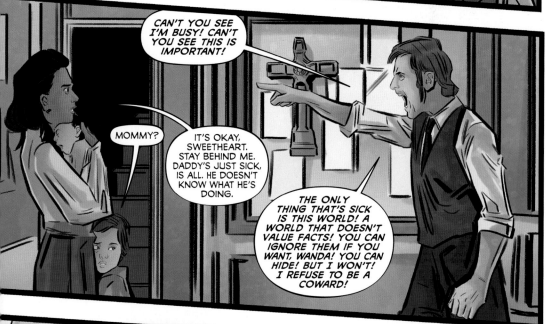

CAN'T YOU SEE I'M BUSY! CAN'T YOU SEE THIS IS IMPORTANT!

MOMMY?

IT'S OKAY, SWEETHEART. STAY BEHIND ME. DADDY'S JUST SICK, IS ALL. HE DOESN'T KNOW WHAT HE'S DOING.

THE ONLY THING THAT'S SICK IS THIS WORLD! A WORLD THAT DOESN'T VALUE FACTS! YOU CAN IGNORE THEM IF YOU WANT, WANDA! YOU CAN HIDE! BUT I WON'T! I REFUSE TO BE A COWARD!

I KNOW THEY'RE REAL. AND I'LL PROVE IT. I'LL PROVE IT TO ALL OF YOU.

"EVEN IF IT TAKES A LIFETIME."

FOLKS, WE HAVE AN EXCITING TREAT FOR YOU. OUR NEXT PERFORMER IS A VERY SPECIAL ONE. HE CLAIMS TO BE AN UNDEAD IMMORTAL POET FROM HELL, ITSELF. PLEASE GIVE IT UP FOR...

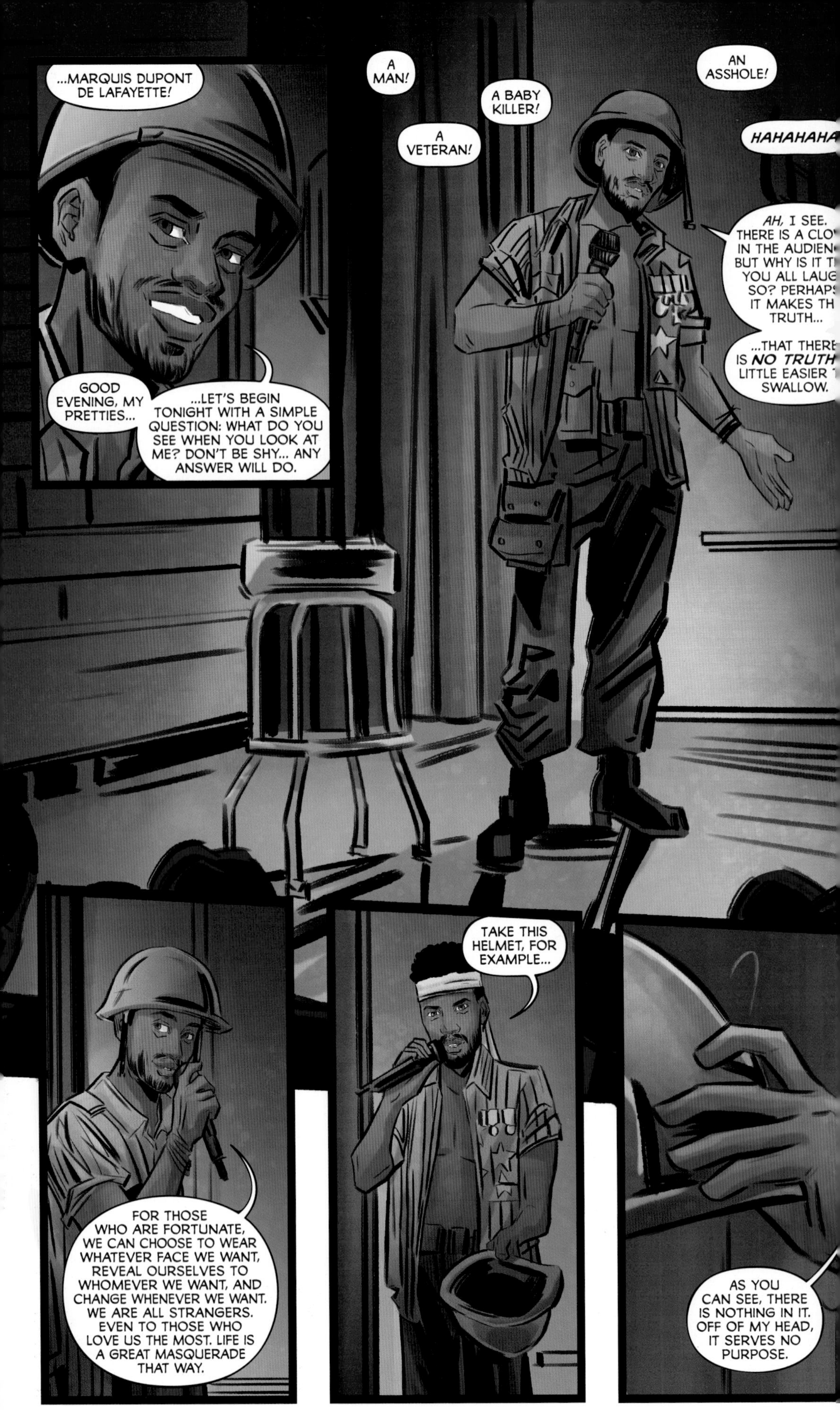
...MARQUIS DUPONT DE LAFAYETTE!
GOOD EVENING, MY PRETTIES...
...LET'S BEGIN TONIGHT WITH A SIMPLE QUESTION: WHAT DO YOU SEE WHEN YOU LOOK AT ME? DON'T BE SHY... ANY ANSWER WILL DO.
A MAN!
A VETERAN!
A BABY KILLER!
AN ASSHOLE!
HAHAHAHA
AH, I SEE. THERE IS A CLO IN THE AUDIEN BUT WHY IS IT T YOU ALL LAUG SO? PERHAP IT MAKES TH TRUTH...
...THAT THERE IS NO TRUTH LITTLE EASIER SWALLOW.
FOR THOSE WHO ARE FORTUNATE, WE CAN CHOOSE TO WEAR WHATEVER FACE WE WANT, REVEAL OURSELVES TO WHOMEVER WE WANT, AND CHANGE WHENEVER WE WANT. WE ARE ALL STRANGERS. EVEN TO THOSE WHO LOVE US THE MOST. LIFE IS A GREAT MASQUERADE THAT WAY.
TAKE THIS HELMET, FOR EXAMPLE...
AS YOU CAN SEE, THERE IS NOTHING IN IT. OFF OF MY HEAD, IT SERVES NO PURPOSE.

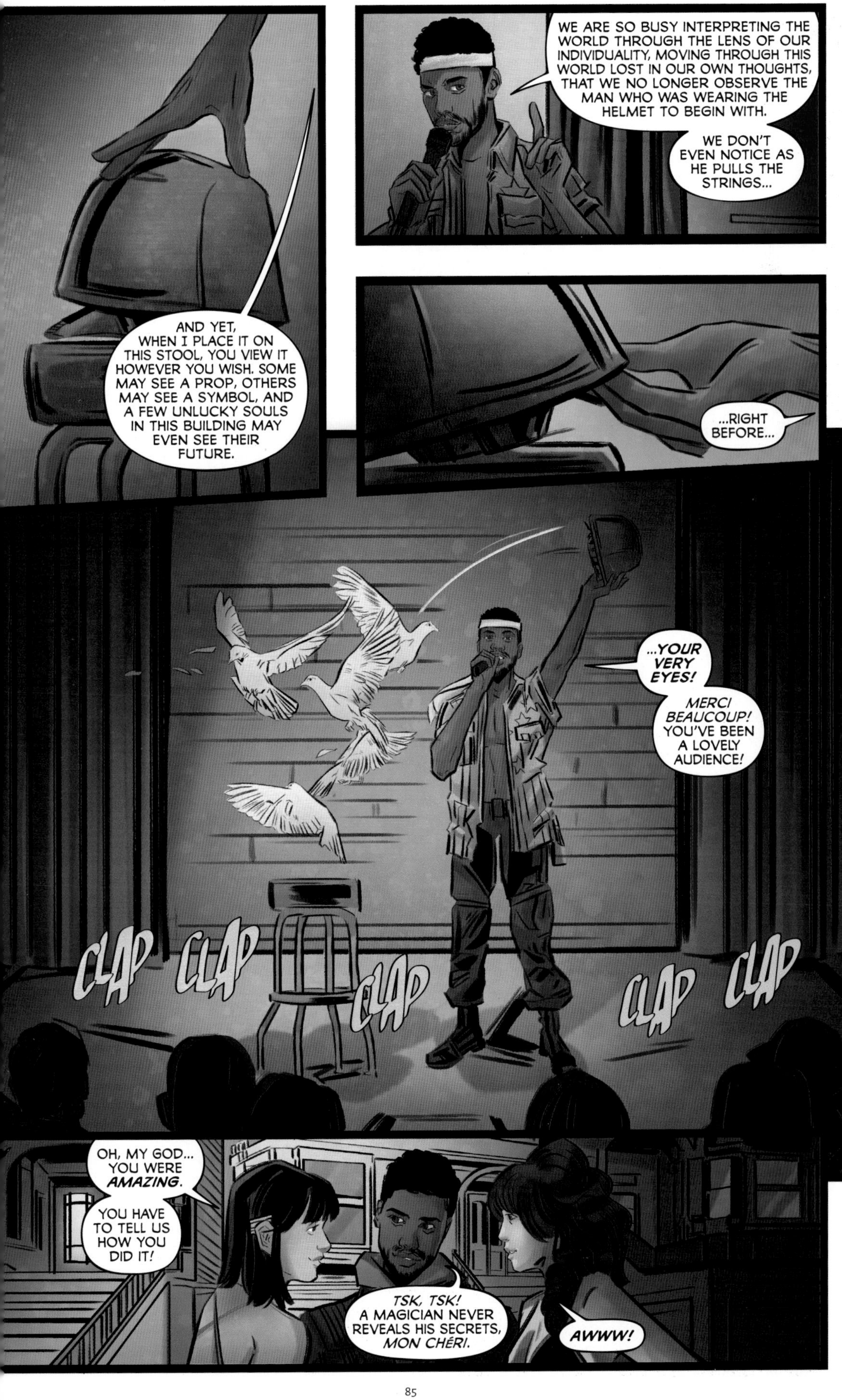
AND YET, WHEN I PLACE IT ON THIS STOOL, YOU VIEW IT HOWEVER YOU WISH. SOME MAY SEE A PROP, OTHERS MAY SEE A SYMBOL, AND A FEW UNLUCKY SOULS IN THIS BUILDING MAY EVEN SEE THEIR FUTURE.
WE ARE SO BUSY INTERPRETING THE WORLD THROUGH THE LENS OF OUR INDIVIDUALITY, MOVING THROUGH THIS WORLD LOST IN OUR OWN THOUGHTS, THAT WE NO LONGER OBSERVE THE MAN WHO WAS WEARING THE HELMET TO BEGIN WITH.
WE DON'T EVEN NOTICE AS HE PULLS THE STRINGS...
...RIGHT BEFORE...
...YOUR VERY EYES!
MERCI BEAUCOUP! YOU'VE BEEN A LOVELY AUDIENCE!
CLAP CLAP CLAP CLAP CLAP
OH, MY GOD... YOU WERE AMAZING.
YOU HAVE TO TELL US HOW YOU DID IT!
TSK, TSK! A MAGICIAN NEVER REVEALS HIS SECRETS, MON CHÉRI.
AWWW!

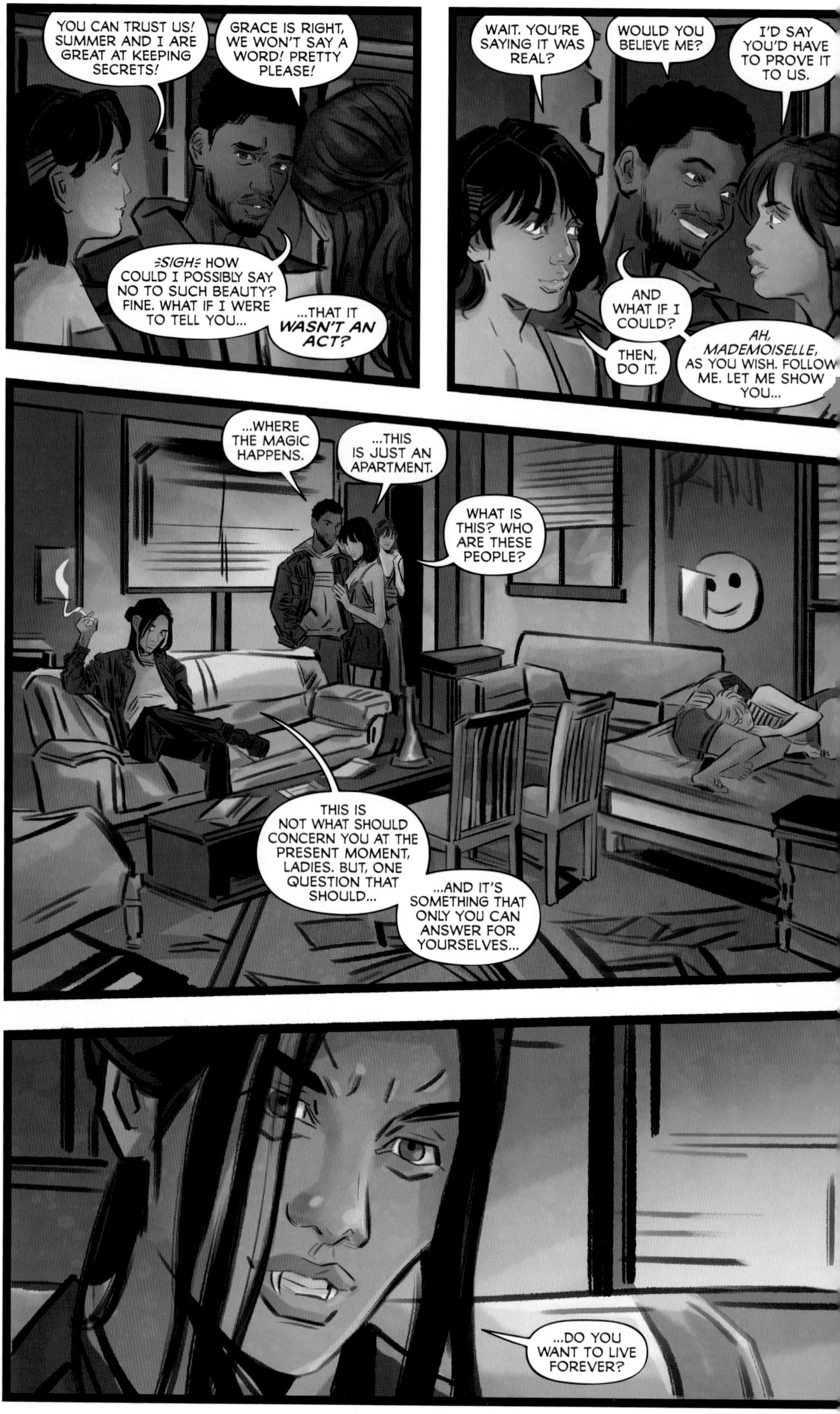
YOU CAN TRUST US! SUMMER AND I ARE GREAT AT KEEPING SECRETS!
GRACE IS RIGHT, WE WON'T SAY A WORD! PRETTY PLEASE!
≶SIGH≶ HOW COULD I POSSIBLY SAY NO TO SUCH BEAUTY? FINE. WHAT IF I WERE TO TELL YOU...
...THAT IT WASN'T AN ACT?
WAIT. YOU'RE SAYING IT WAS REAL?
WOULD YOU BELIEVE ME?
I'D SAY YOU'D HAVE TO PROVE IT TO US.
AND WHAT IF I COULD?
THEN, DO IT.
AH, MADEMOISELLE, AS YOU WISH. FOLLOW ME. LET ME SHOW YOU...
...WHERE THE MAGIC HAPPENS.
...THIS IS JUST AN APARTMENT.
WHAT IS THIS? WHO ARE THESE PEOPLE?
THIS IS NOT WHAT SHOULD CONCERN YOU AT THE PRESENT MOMENT, LADIES. BUT, ONE QUESTION THAT SHOULD...
...AND IT'S SOMETHING THAT ONLY YOU CAN ANSWER FOR YOURSELVES...
...DO YOU WANT TO LIVE FOREVER?

Central State Hospital. Petersburg, Virginia.

1967.

"I CAN'T IMAGINE HOW DIFFICULT THIS MUST BE FOR YOU, MRS. FRANKLIN, BUT LET ME ASSURE YOU..."

...YOUR HUSBAND WILL RECEIVE THE BEST CARE POSSIBLE, HERE. OUR PRACTICE IS FOCUSED ON IMPLEMENTING THE NEWEST AND MOST CUTTING-EDGE MEDICAL SCIENCE AVAILABLE TO US.

NOW, THAT BEING SAID, IT WOULD BE HELPFUL TO KNOW WHY YOUR HUSBAND ATTACKED A FEDERAL EMPLOYEE.

THANK YOU, DOCTOR.

MY HUSB-- FELIX... FELIX AND I...

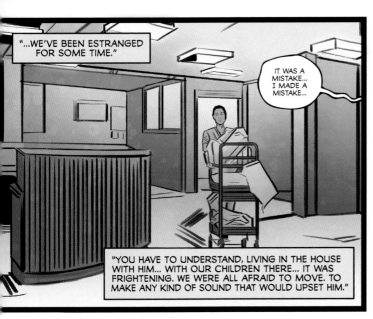

"...WE'VE BEEN ESTRANGED FOR SOME TIME."

IT WAS A MISTAKE... I MADE A MISTAKE...

"YOU HAVE TO UNDERSTAND, LIVING IN THE HOUSE WITH HIM... WITH OUR CHILDREN THERE... IT WAS FRIGHTENING. WE WERE ALL AFRAID TO MOVE. TO MAKE ANY KIND OF SOUND THAT WOULD UPSET HIM."

TIME FOR YOUR PILLS, MR. FRANKLIN.

HOW WAS I SUPPOSED TO KNOW? THE SUN WAS DOWN EARLY. IT WAS WINTER TIME.

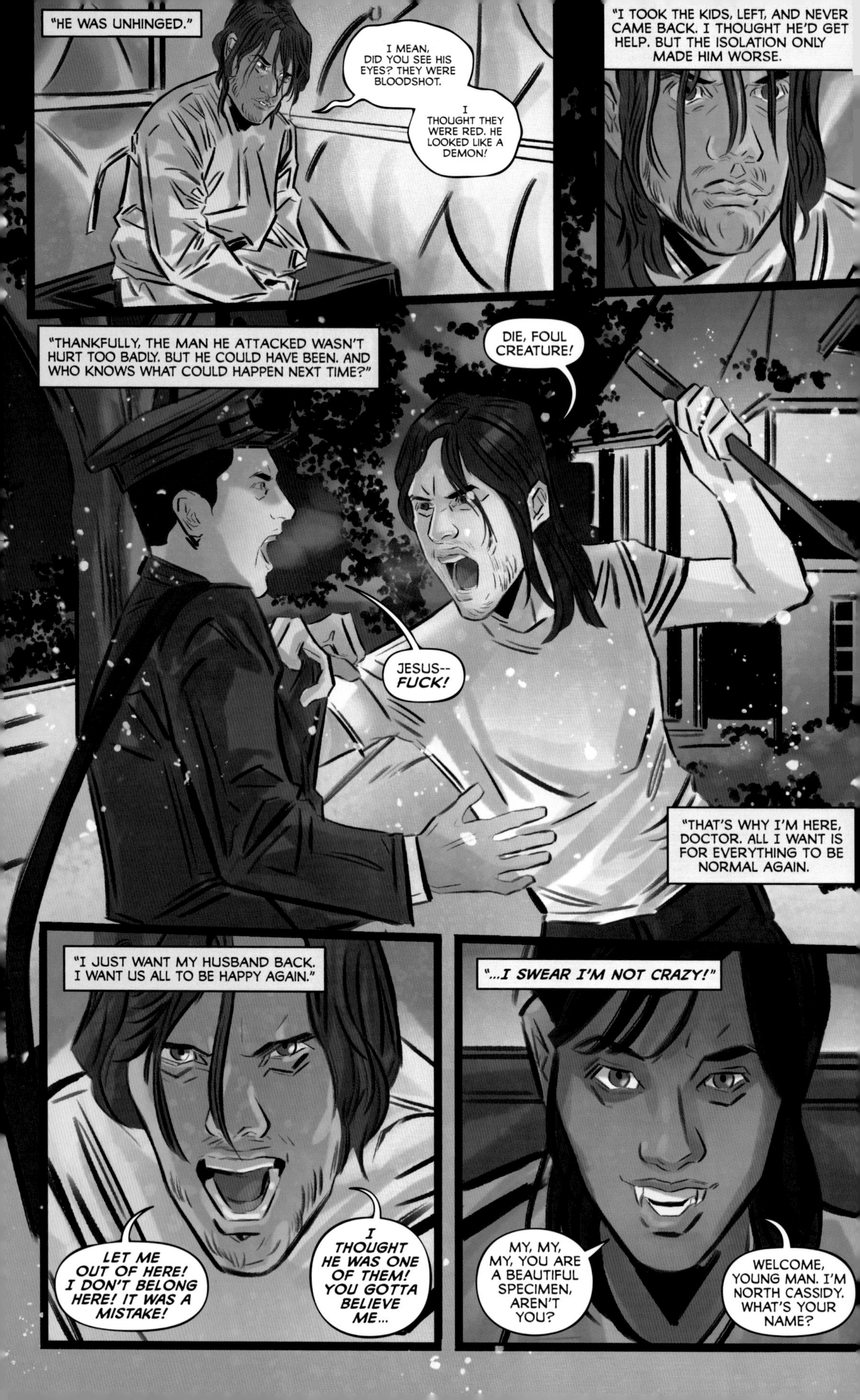
"HE WAS UNHINGED."
I MEAN, DID YOU SEE HIS EYES? THEY WERE BLOODSHOT.
I THOUGHT THEY WERE RED. HE LOOKED LIKE A DEMON!
"I TOOK THE KIDS, LEFT, AND NEVER CAME BACK. I THOUGHT HE'D GET HELP. BUT THE ISOLATION ONLY MADE HIM WORSE.
"THANKFULLY, THE MAN HE ATTACKED WASN'T HURT TOO BADLY. BUT HE COULD HAVE BEEN. AND WHO KNOWS WHAT COULD HAPPEN NEXT TIME?"
DIE, FOUL CREATURE!
JESUS--FUCK!
"THAT'S WHY I'M HERE, DOCTOR. ALL I WANT IS FOR EVERYTHING TO BE NORMAL AGAIN.
"I JUST WANT MY HUSBAND BACK. I WANT US ALL TO BE HAPPY AGAIN."
LET ME OUT OF HERE! I DON'T BELONG HERE! IT WAS A MISTAKE!
I THOUGHT HE WAS ONE OF THEM! YOU GOTTA BELIEVE ME...
"...I SWEAR I'M NOT CRAZY!"
MY, MY, MY, YOU ARE A BEAUTIFUL SPECIMEN, AREN'T YOU?
WELCOME, YOUNG MAN. I'M NORTH CASSIDY. WHAT'S YOUR NAME?

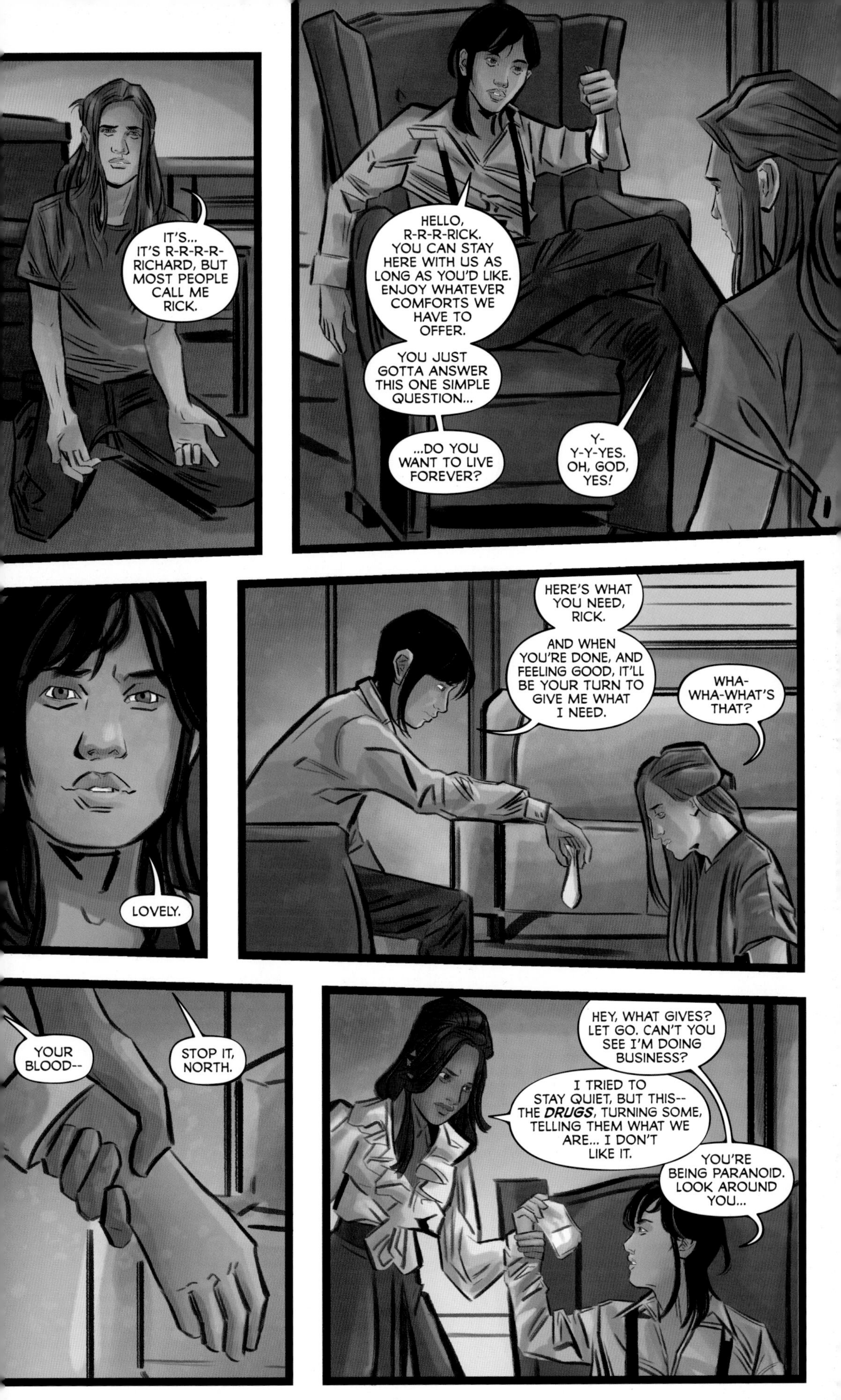
IT'S... IT'S R-R-R-R-RICHARD, BUT MOST PEOPLE CALL ME RICK.
HELLO, R-R-R-RICK. YOU CAN STAY HERE WITH US AS LONG AS YOU'D LIKE. ENJOY WHATEVER COMFORTS WE HAVE TO OFFER.
YOU JUST GOTTA ANSWER THIS ONE SIMPLE QUESTION...
...DO YOU WANT TO LIVE FOREVER?
Y-Y-Y-YES. OH, GOD, YES!
LOVELY.
HERE'S WHAT YOU NEED, RICK.
AND WHEN YOU'RE DONE, AND FEELING GOOD, IT'LL BE YOUR TURN TO GIVE ME WHAT I NEED.
WHA-WHA-WHAT'S THAT?
YOUR BLOOD--
STOP IT, NORTH.
HEY, WHAT GIVES? LET GO. CAN'T YOU SEE I'M DOING BUSINESS?
I TRIED TO STAY QUIET, BUT THIS-- THE DRUGS, TURNING SOME, TELLING THEM WHAT WE ARE... I DON'T LIKE IT.
YOU'RE BEING PARANOID. LOOK AROUND YOU...

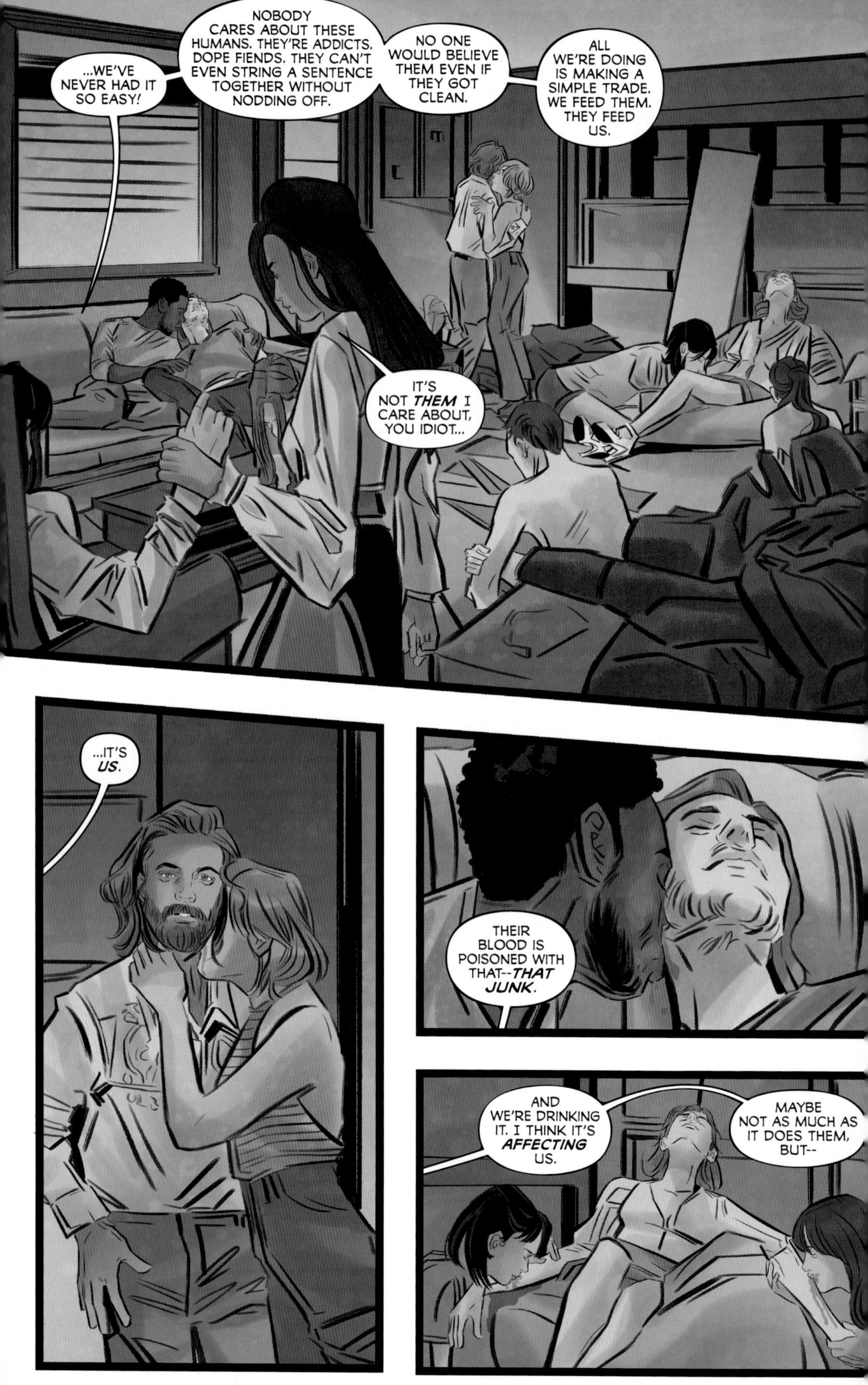
...WE'VE NEVER HAD IT SO EASY!
NOBODY CARES ABOUT THESE HUMANS. THEY'RE ADDICTS. DOPE FIENDS. THEY CAN'T EVEN STRING A SENTENCE TOGETHER WITHOUT NODDING OFF.
NO ONE WOULD BELIEVE THEM EVEN IF THEY GOT CLEAN.
ALL WE'RE DOING IS MAKING A SIMPLE TRADE. WE FEED THEM. THEY FEED US.
IT'S NOT *THEM* I CARE ABOUT, YOU IDIOT...
...IT'S *US*.
THEIR BLOOD IS POISONED WITH THAT--*THAT JUNK*.
AND WE'RE DRINKING IT. I THINK IT'S *AFFECTING* US.
MAYBE NOT AS MUCH AS IT DOES THEM, BUT--

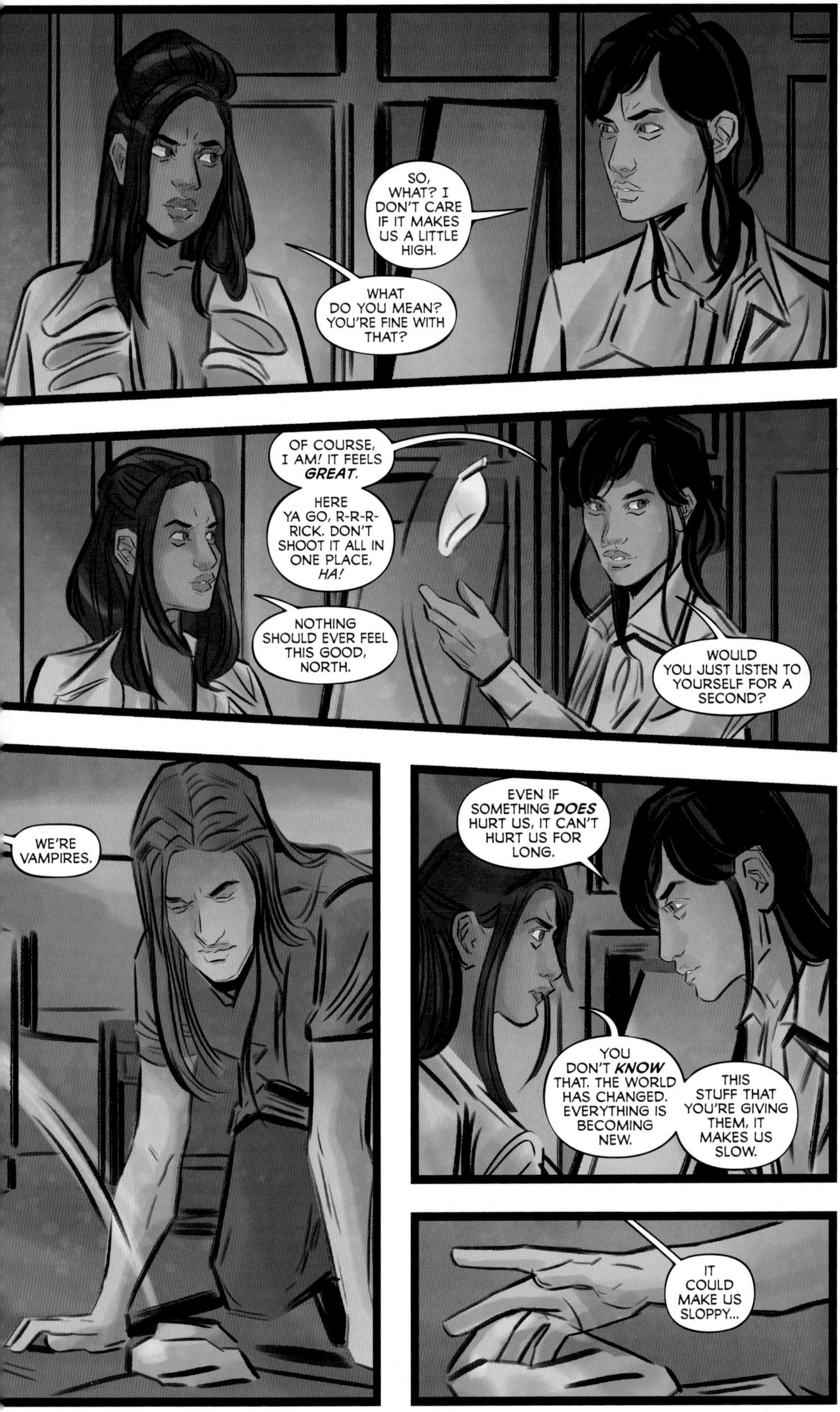
SO, WHAT? I DON'T CARE IF IT MAKES US A LITTLE HIGH.
WHAT DO YOU MEAN? YOU'RE FINE WITH THAT?
OF COURSE, I AM! IT FEELS GREAT.
HERE YA GO, R-R-R-RICK. DON'T SHOOT IT ALL IN ONE PLACE, HA!
NOTHING SHOULD EVER FEEL THIS GOOD, NORTH.
WOULD YOU JUST LISTEN TO YOURSELF FOR A SECOND?
WE'RE VAMPIRES.
EVEN IF SOMETHING DOES HURT US, IT CAN'T HURT US FOR LONG.
YOU DON'T KNOW THAT. THE WORLD HAS CHANGED. EVERYTHING IS BECOMING NEW.
THIS STUFF THAT YOU'RE GIVING THEM, IT MAKES US SLOW.
IT COULD MAKE US SLOPPY...

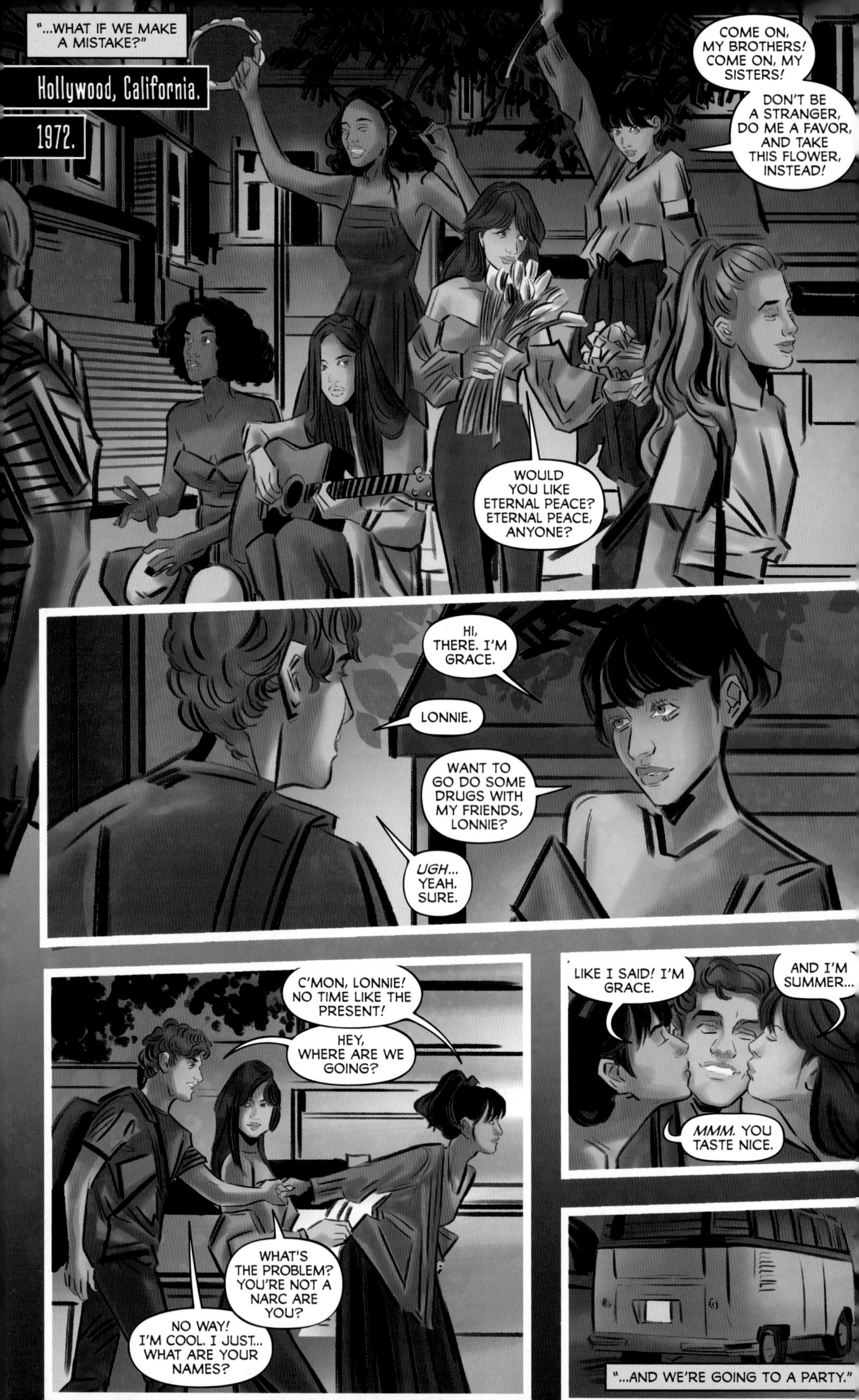
"...WHAT IF WE MAKE A MISTAKE?"
Hollywood, California.
1972.
COME ON, MY BROTHERS! COME ON, MY SISTERS!
DON'T BE A STRANGER, DO ME A FAVOR, AND TAKE THIS FLOWER, INSTEAD!
WOULD YOU LIKE ETERNAL PEACE? ETERNAL PEACE, ANYONE?
HI, THERE. I'M GRACE.
LONNIE.
WANT TO GO DO SOME DRUGS WITH MY FRIENDS, LONNIE?
UGH... YEAH. SURE.
C'MON, LONNIE! NO TIME LIKE THE PRESENT!
HEY, WHERE ARE WE GOING?
WHAT'S THE PROBLEM? YOU'RE NOT A NARC ARE YOU?
NO WAY! I'M COOL. I JUST... WHAT ARE YOUR NAMES?
LIKE I SAID! I'M GRACE.
AND I'M SUMMER...
MMM. YOU TASTE NICE.
"...AND WE'RE GOING TO A PARTY."

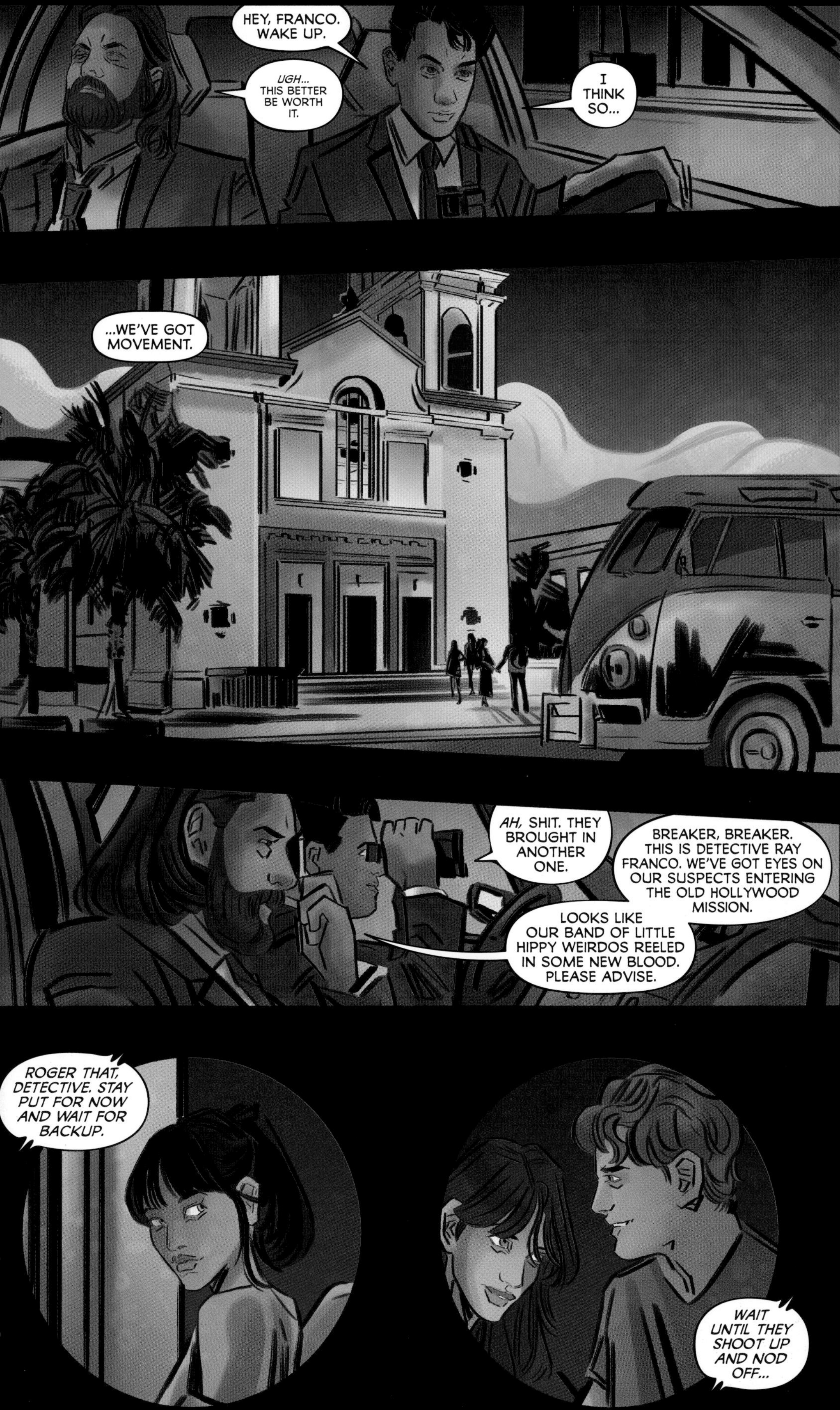
HEY, FRANCO. WAKE UP.
UGH... THIS BETTER BE WORTH IT.
I THINK SO...
...WE'VE GOT MOVEMENT.
AH, SHIT. THEY BROUGHT IN ANOTHER ONE.
BREAKER, BREAKER. THIS IS DETECTIVE RAY FRANCO. WE'VE GOT EYES ON OUR SUSPECTS ENTERING THE OLD HOLLYWOOD MISSION.
LOOKS LIKE OUR BAND OF LITTLE HIPPY WEIRDOS REELED IN SOME NEW BLOOD. PLEASE ADVISE.
ROGER THAT, DETECTIVE. STAY PUT FOR NOW AND WAIT FOR BACKUP.
WAIT UNTIL THEY SHOOT UP AND NOD OFF...

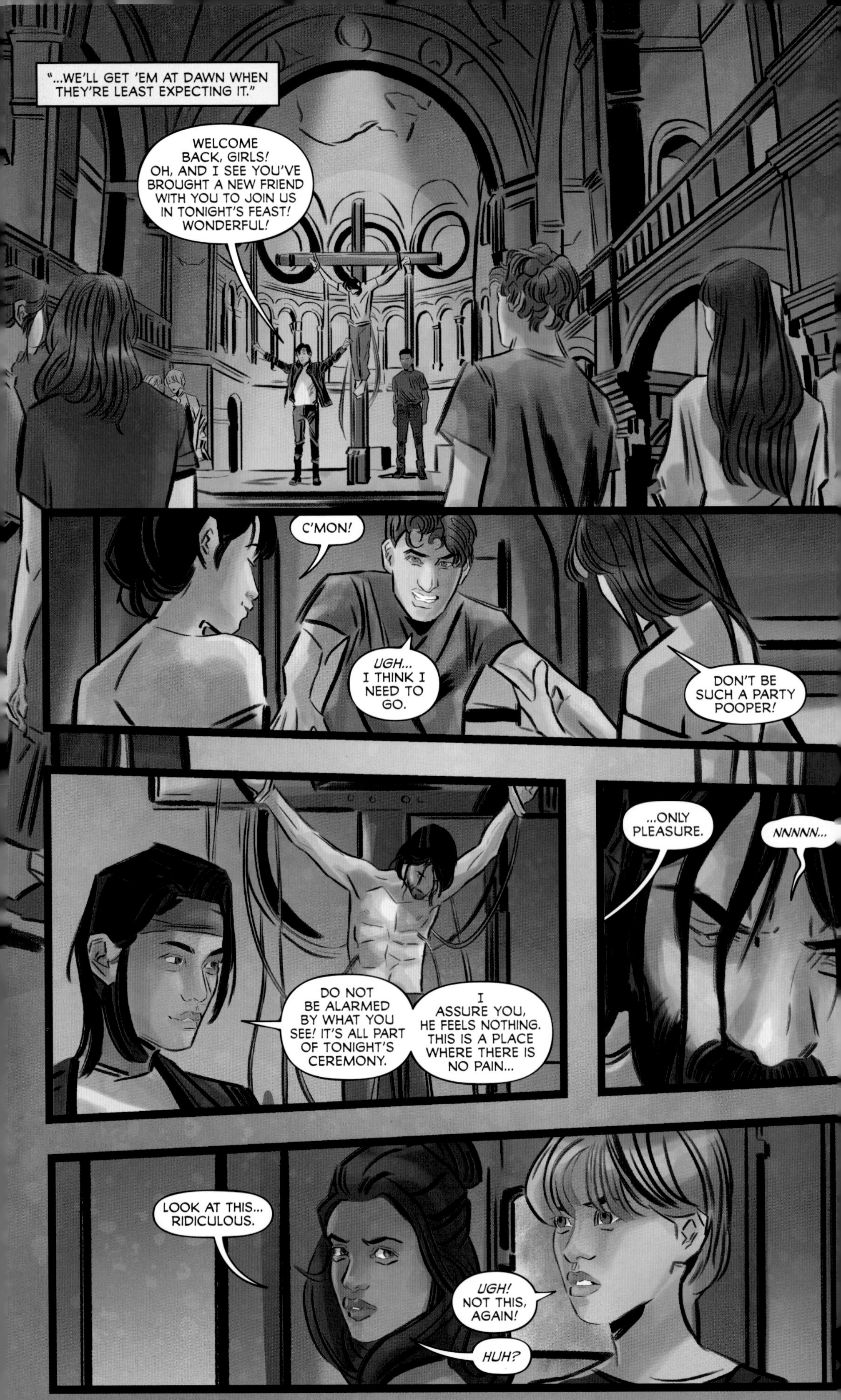
"...WE'LL GET 'EM AT DAWN WHEN THEY'RE LEAST EXPECTING IT."
WELCOME BACK, GIRLS! OH, AND I SEE YOU'VE BROUGHT A NEW FRIEND WITH YOU TO JOIN US IN TONIGHT'S FEAST! WONDERFUL!
C'MON!
UGH... I THINK I NEED TO GO.
DON'T BE SUCH A PARTY POOPER!
DO NOT BE ALARMED BY WHAT YOU SEE! IT'S ALL PART OF TONIGHT'S CEREMONY.
I ASSURE YOU, HE FEELS NOTHING. THIS IS A PLACE WHERE THERE IS NO PAIN...
...ONLY PLEASURE.
NNNNN...
LOOK AT THIS... RIDICULOUS.
UGH! NOT THIS, AGAIN!
HUH?

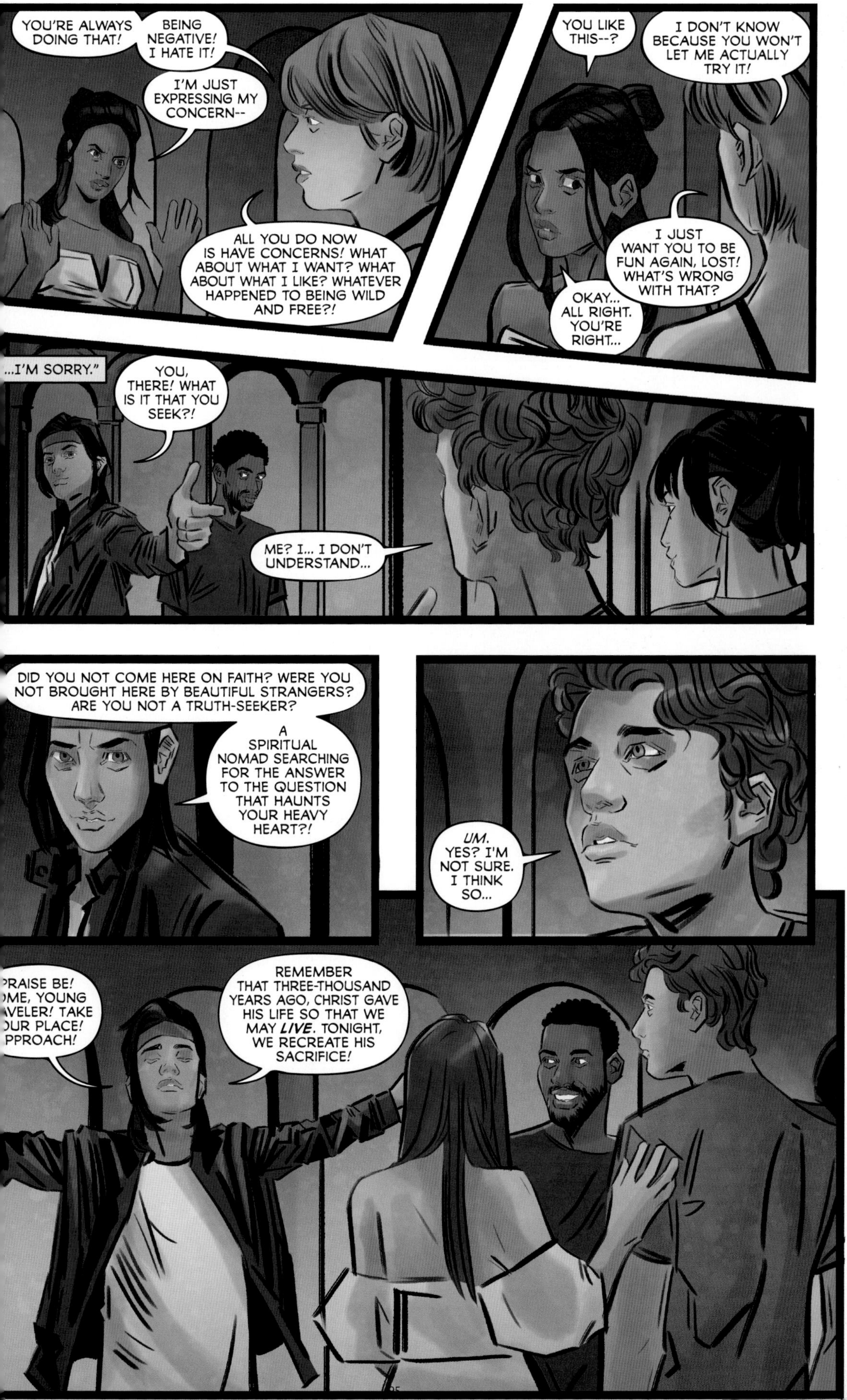
YOU'RE ALWAYS DOING THAT!
BEING NEGATIVE! I HATE IT!
I'M JUST EXPRESSING MY CONCERN--
ALL YOU DO NOW IS HAVE CONCERNS! WHAT ABOUT WHAT I WANT? WHAT ABOUT WHAT I LIKE? WHATEVER HAPPENED TO BEING WILD AND FREE?!
YOU LIKE THIS--?
I DON'T KNOW BECAUSE YOU WON'T LET ME ACTUALLY TRY IT!
I JUST WANT YOU TO BE FUN AGAIN, LOST! WHAT'S WRONG WITH THAT?
OKAY... ALL RIGHT. YOU'RE RIGHT...
...I'M SORRY."
YOU, THERE! WHAT IS IT THAT YOU SEEK?!
ME? I... I DON'T UNDERSTAND...
DID YOU NOT COME HERE ON FAITH? WERE YOU NOT BROUGHT HERE BY BEAUTIFUL STRANGERS? ARE YOU NOT A TRUTH-SEEKER?
A SPIRITUAL NOMAD SEARCHING FOR THE ANSWER TO THE QUESTION THAT HAUNTS YOUR HEAVY HEART?!
UM. YES? I'M NOT SURE. I THINK SO...
PRAISE BE! OME, YOUNG AVELER! TAKE OUR PLACE! PPROACH!
REMEMBER THAT THREE-THOUSAND YEARS AGO, CHRIST GAVE HIS LIFE SO THAT WE MAY LIVE. TONIGHT, WE RECREATE HIS SACRIFICE!

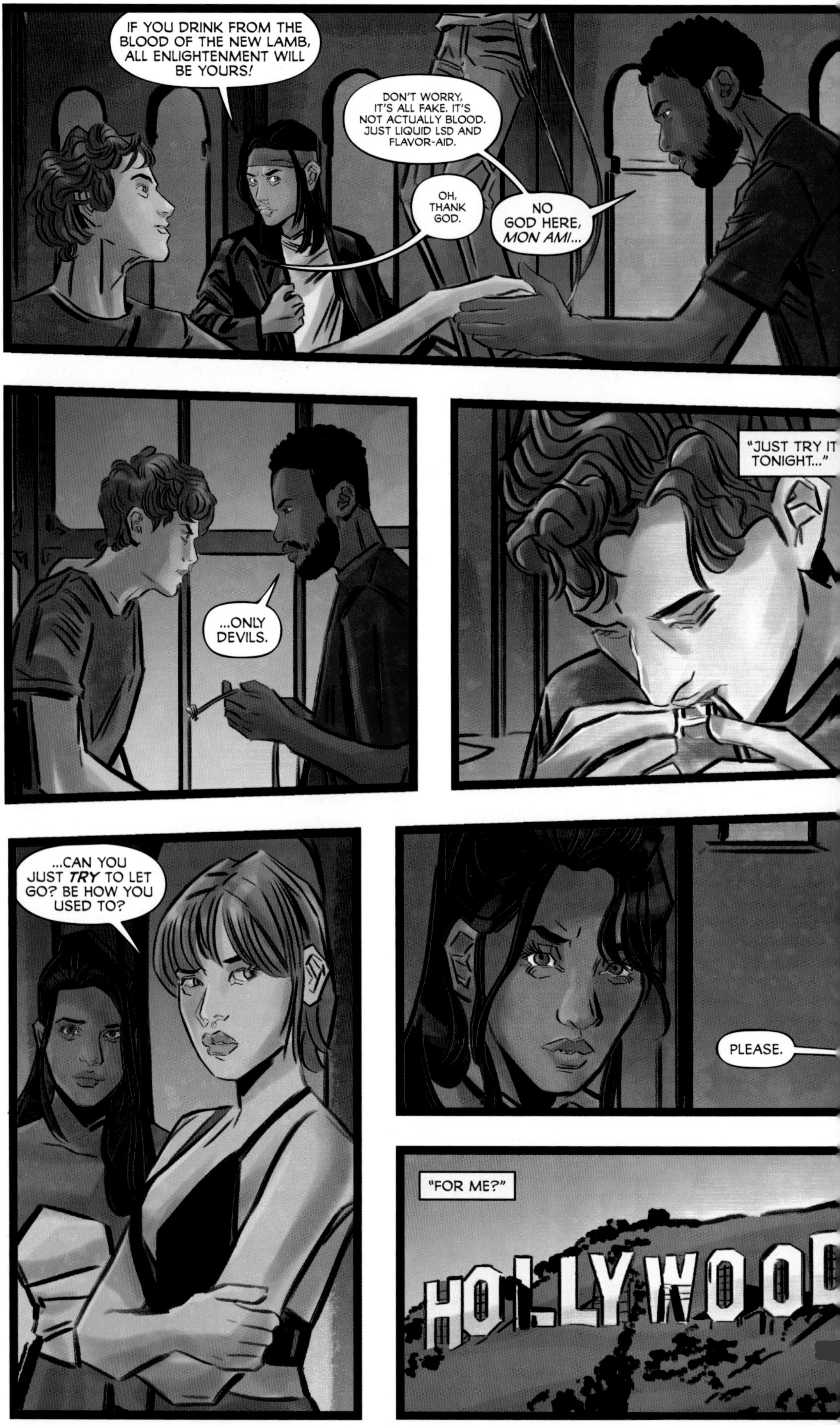
IF YOU DRINK FROM THE BLOOD OF THE NEW LAMB, ALL ENLIGHTENMENT WILL BE YOURS!
DON'T WORRY, IT'S ALL FAKE. IT'S NOT ACTUALLY BLOOD. JUST LIQUID LSD AND FLAVOR-AID.
OH, THANK GOD.
NO GOD HERE, *MON AMI*...
...ONLY DEVILS.
"JUST TRY IT TONIGHT..."
...CAN YOU JUST *TRY* TO LET GO? BE HOW YOU USED TO?
PLEASE.
"FOR ME?"
HOLLYWOOD

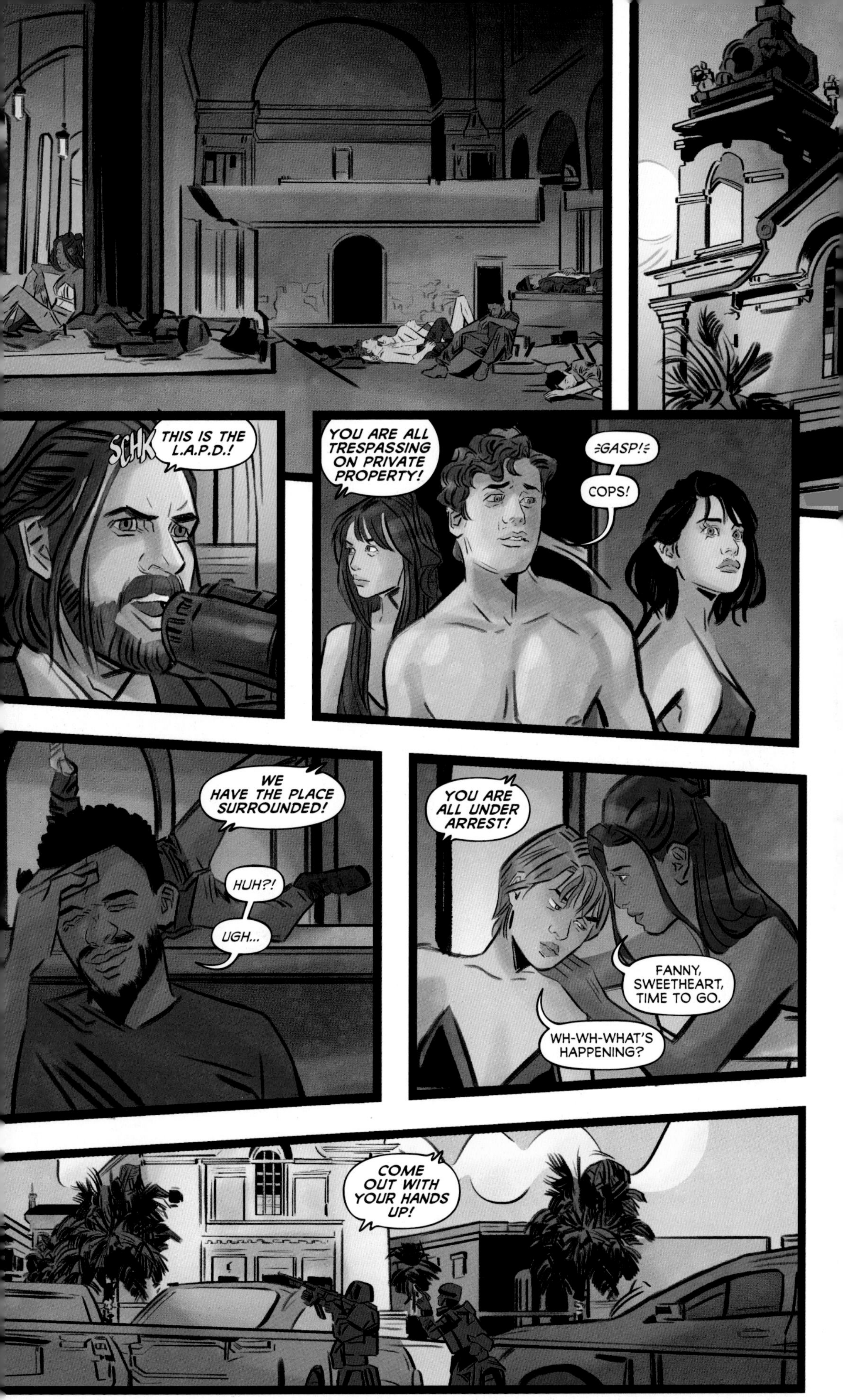
SCHK
THIS IS THE L.A.P.D.!
YOU ARE ALL TRESPASSING ON PRIVATE PROPERTY!
GASP!
COPS!
WE HAVE THE PLACE SURROUNDED!
HUH?!
UGH...
YOU ARE ALL UNDER ARREST!
FANNY, SWEETHEART, TIME TO GO.
WH-WH-WHAT'S HAPPENING?
COME OUT WITH YOUR HANDS UP!

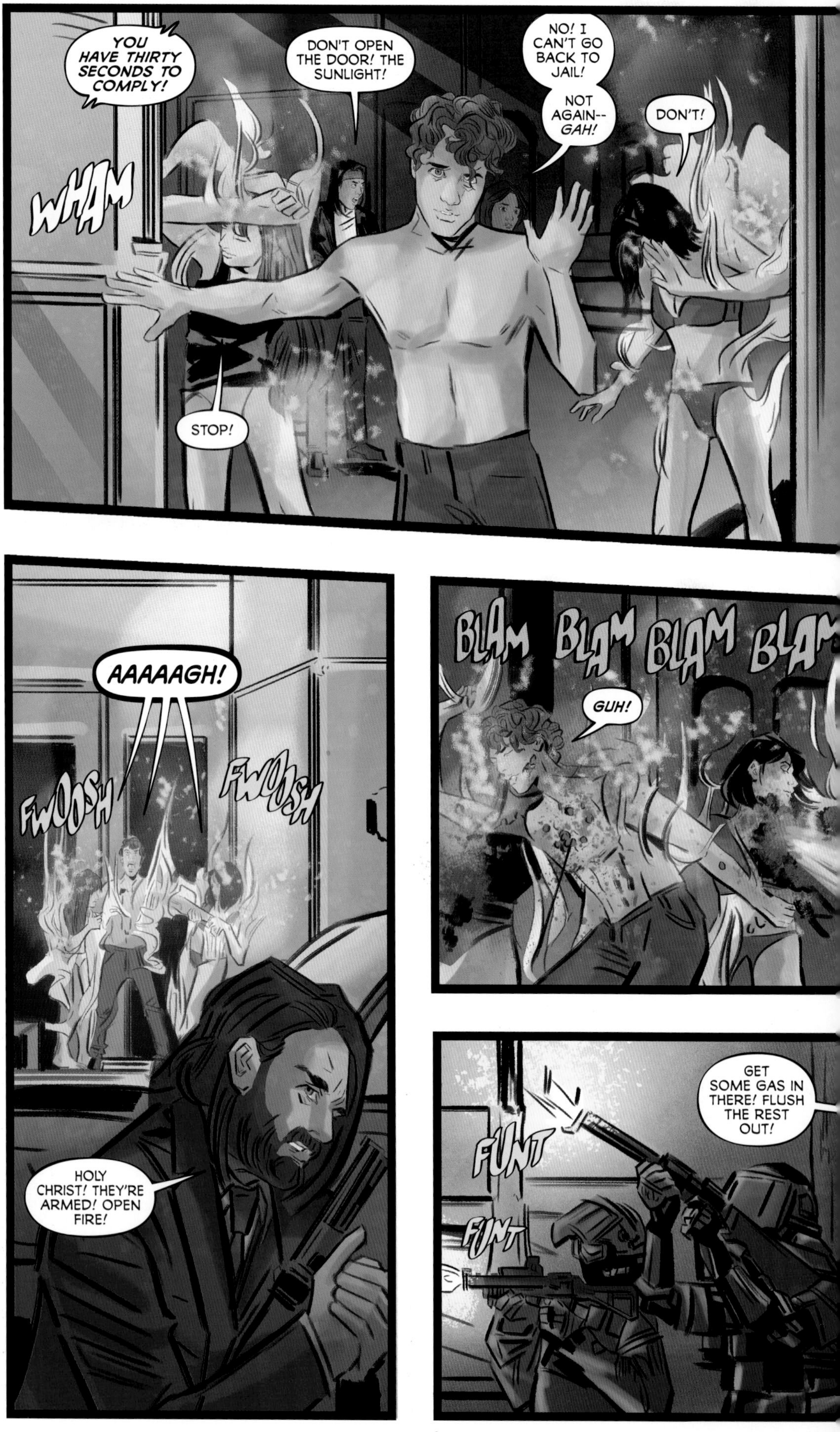
YOU HAVE THIRTY SECONDS TO COMPLY!
WHAM
DON'T OPEN THE DOOR! THE SUNLIGHT!
NO! I CAN'T GO BACK TO JAIL!
NOT AGAIN-- GAH!
DON'T!
STOP!
AAAAAGH!
FWOOSH
FWOOSH
HOLY CHRIST! THEY'RE ARMED! OPEN FIRE!
BLAM BLAM BLAM BLAM
GUH!
FUNT
FUNT
GET SOME GAS IN THERE! FLUSH THE REST OUT!

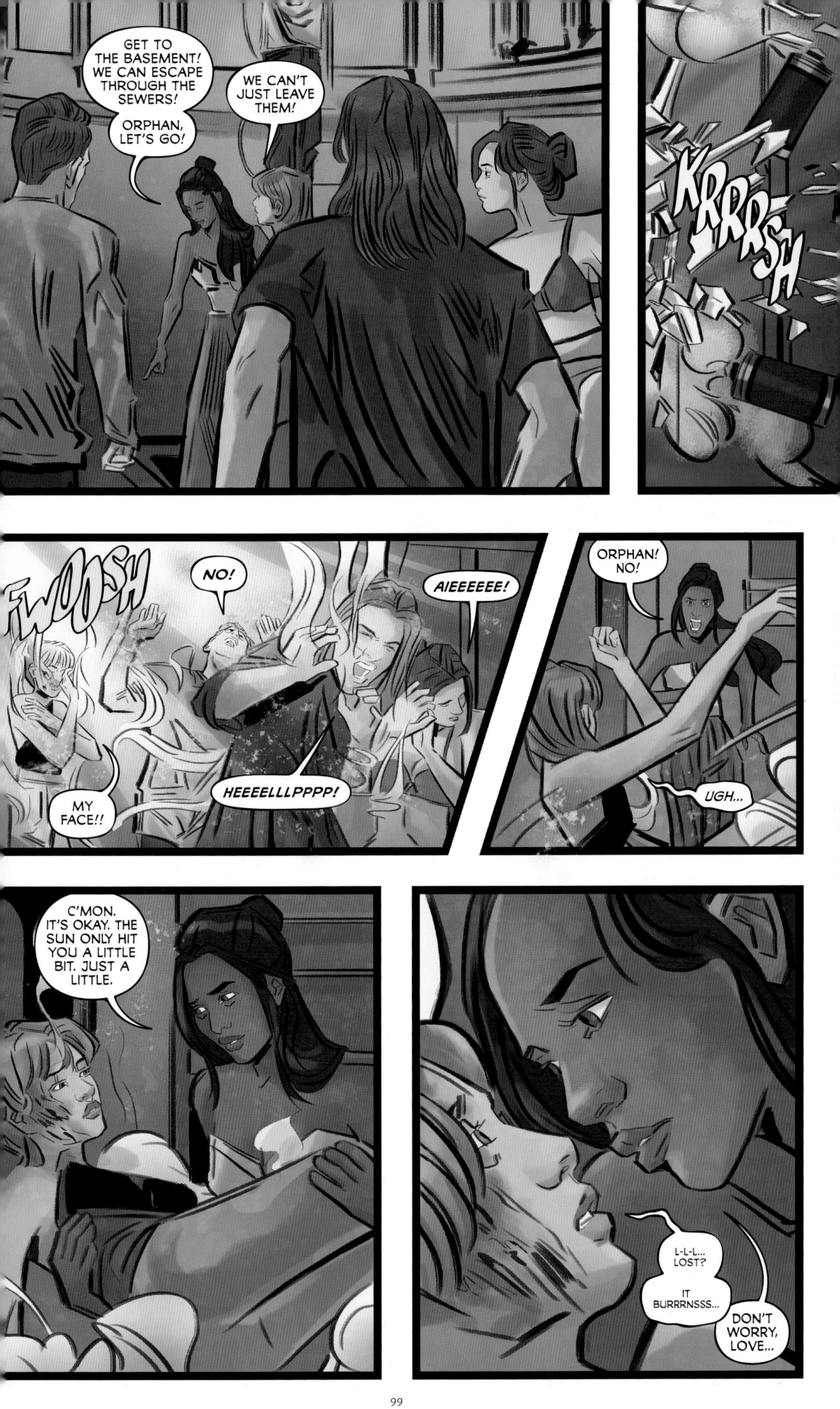
GET TO THE BASEMENT! WE CAN ESCAPE THROUGH THE SEWERS!
ORPHAN, LET'S GO!
WE CAN'T JUST LEAVE THEM!
KRRRSH
FWOOSH
NO!
AIEEEEEE!
MY FACE!!
HEEEELLLPPPP!
ORPHAN! NO!
UGH...
C'MON. IT'S OKAY. THE SUN ONLY HIT YOU A LITTLE BIT. JUST A LITTLE.
L-L-L... LOST?
IT BURRRNSSS...
DON'T WORRY, LOVE...

"...I'VE GOT YOU."
The Federal Bureau of Investigation.
"I'M AN OLD MAN, NOW. SO, I NEED YOU TO EXPLAIN THIS TO ME, SLOWLY. WHAT EXACTLY IS IT THAT YOU ARE TELLING ME?"
TO BE HONEST, DIRECTOR HOOVER, WE'RE NOT EXACTLY SURE, OURSELVES.
LOS ANGELES POLICE WERE WORKING A CASE ON SOME CULT ACTIVITY. DRUGS, KIDNAPPING, THE WORKS. THEY TRACKED THEM TO A SEEDY CHURCH IN OLD HOLLYWOOD.
IT WAS AN UGLY SCENE, SIR. MOST OF THE DEAD WERE BURNT TO A CRISP. WE WERE ONLY ABLE TO RECOVER ONE OF THE BODIES, STILL INTACT.
HE WAS CRUCIFIED, ALL THE BLOOD DRAINED FROM HIS BODY. ACCORDING TO THE OFFICIAL REPORT, THE RINGLEADERS MANAGED TO SLIP AWAY. THEY THINK THERE WERE AT LEAST FOUR OF THEM.
MOTHER OF MERCY, NOT AGAIN WITH THIS...
WHAT WAS THAT, SIR?
SHOULD WE OPEN UP A FORMAL INQUIRY INTO THE MATTER?
DID I SAY I WANTED YOU TO?! JUST BECAUSE I'M OLD DOESN'T MEAN YOU SHOULD PRESUME ANYTHING. JUST... OUT!
GET OUT! GODDAMMIT--

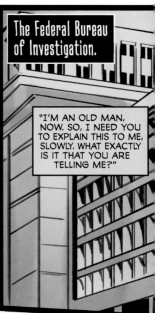

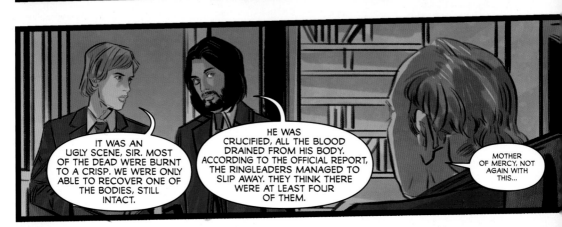

≠COUGH!≠
≠COUGH!≠
≠COUGH!≠

HHURMMM....

≠SIGH≠

SHNG

United States
Government
Memorandum.

March 3rd, 1972.

THIS IS MY
HOSPITAL, DAMMIT!
YOU CAN'T JUST
TAKE HIM!

NO CAN DO.
ORDERS ARE
ORDERS.

Subject: Felix Franklin.

TO: Petersburg, Virginia,
Police Department.

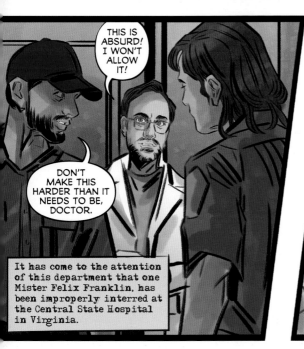

THIS IS
ABSURD!
I WON'T
ALLOW
IT!

DON'T
MAKE THIS
HARDER THAN IT
NEEDS TO BE,
DOCTOR.

It has come to the attention
of this department that one
Mister Felix Franklin, has
been improperly interred at
the Central State Hospital
in Virginia.

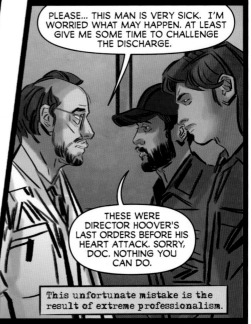

PLEASE... THIS MAN IS VERY SICK. I'M
WORRIED WHAT MAY HAPPEN. AT LEAST
GIVE ME SOME TIME TO CHALLENGE
THE DISCHARGE.

THESE WERE
DIRECTOR HOOVER'S
LAST ORDERS BEFORE HIS
HEART ATTACK. SORRY,
DOC. NOTHING YOU
CAN DO.

This unfortunate mistake is the
result of extreme professionalism.

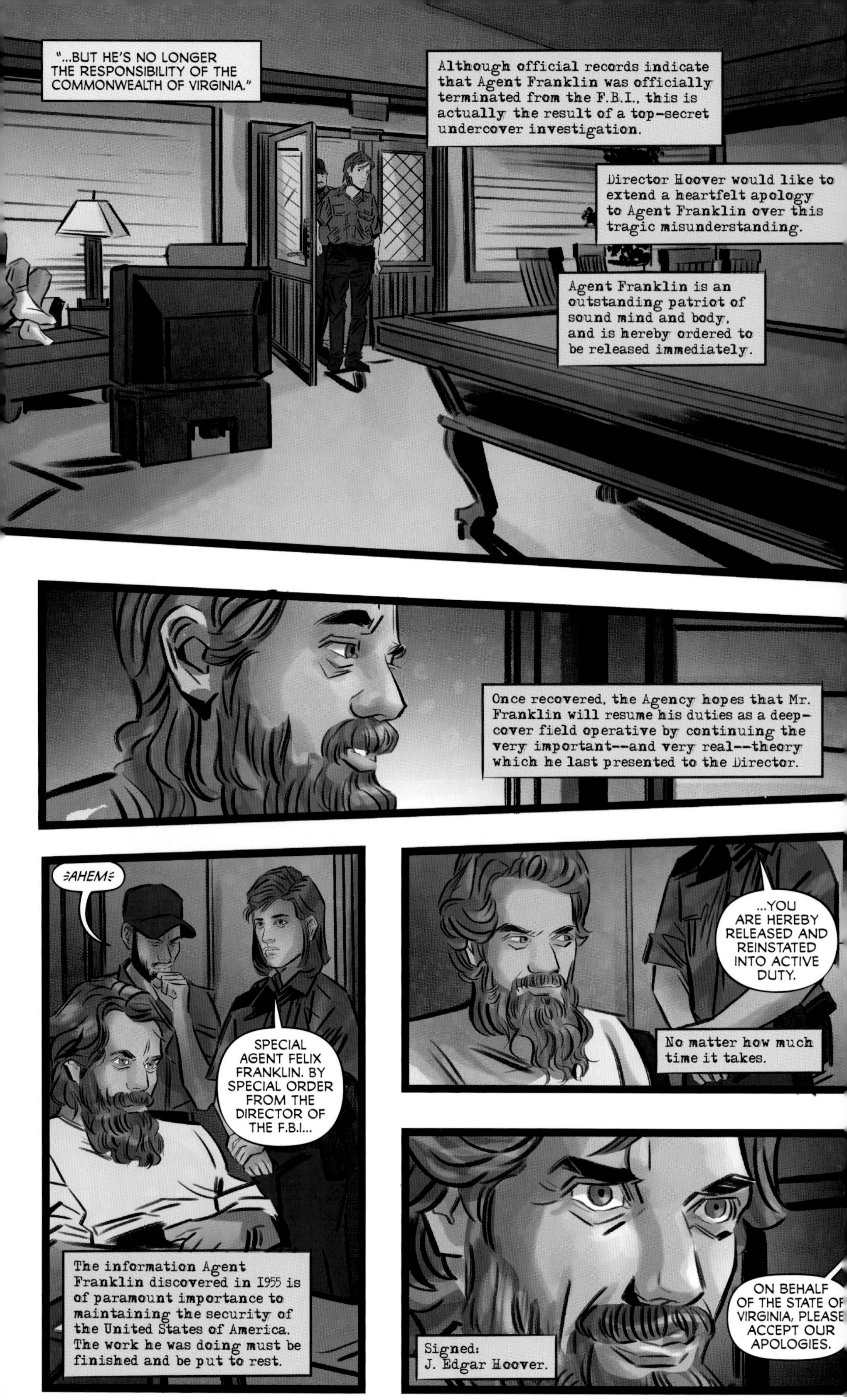
"...BUT HE'S NO LONGER THE RESPONSIBILITY OF THE COMMONWEALTH OF VIRGINIA."
Although official records indicate that Agent Franklin was officially terminated from the F.B.I., this is actually the result of a top-secret undercover investigation.
Director Hoover would like to extend a heartfelt apology to Agent Franklin over this tragic misunderstanding.
Agent Franklin is an outstanding patriot of sound mind and body, and is hereby ordered to be released immediately.
Once recovered, the Agency hopes that Mr. Franklin will resume his duties as a deep-cover field operative by continuing the very important--and very real--theory which he last presented to the Director.
AHEM
SPECIAL AGENT FELIX FRANKLIN. BY SPECIAL ORDER FROM THE DIRECTOR OF THE F.B.I...
The information Agent Franklin discovered in 1955 is of paramount importance to maintaining the security of the United States of America. The work he was doing must be finished and be put to rest.
...YOU ARE HEREBY RELEASED AND REINSTATED INTO ACTIVE DUTY.
No matter how much time it takes.
Signed: J. Edgar Hoover.
ON BEHALF OF THE STATE OF VIRGINIA, PLEASE ACCEPT OUR APOLOGIES.

CHAPTER

5

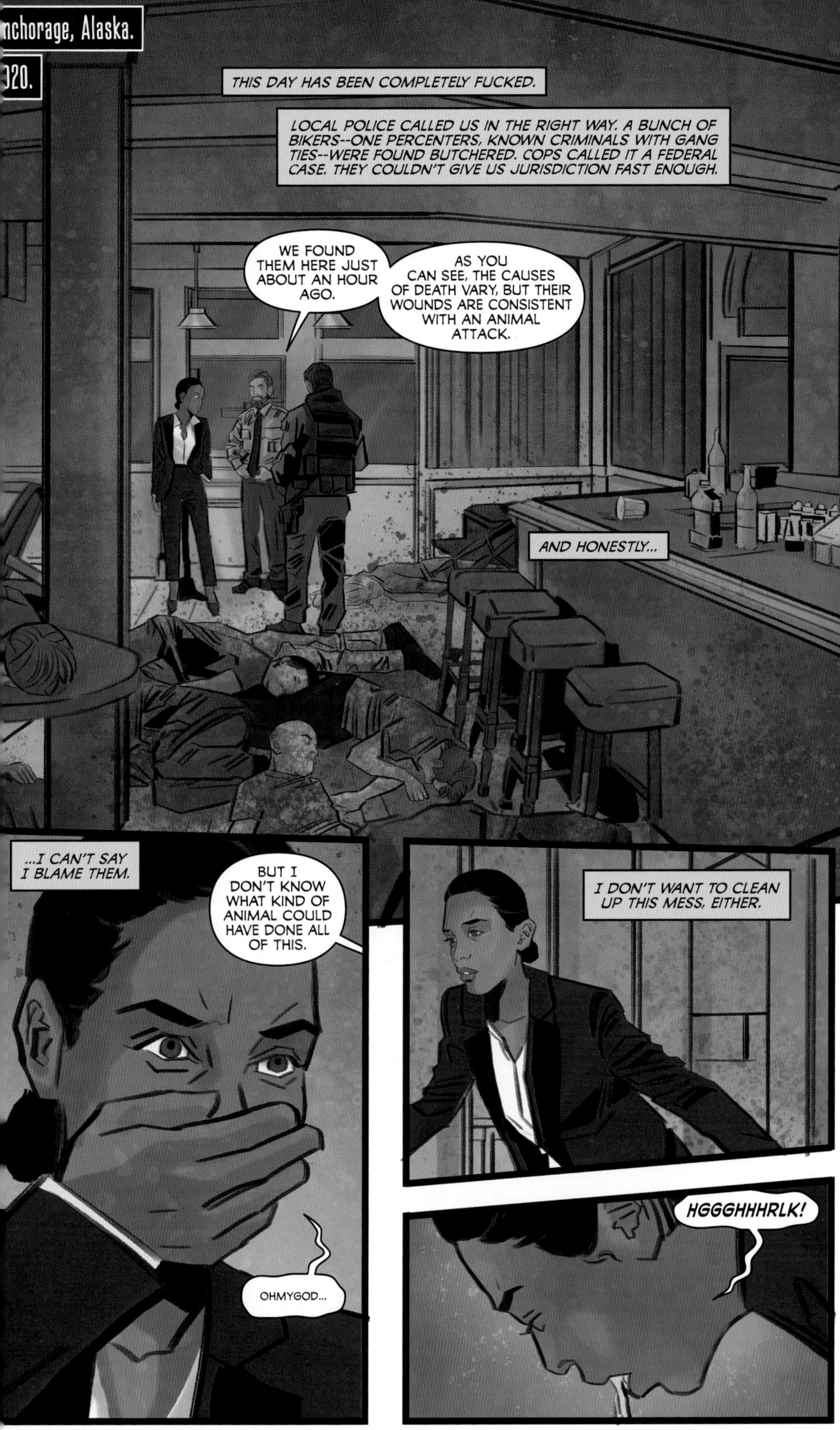

nchorage, Alaska.
020.
THIS DAY HAS BEEN COMPLETELY FUCKED.
LOCAL POLICE CALLED US IN THE RIGHT WAY. A BUNCH OF BIKERS--ONE PERCENTERS, KNOWN CRIMINALS WITH GANG TIES--WERE FOUND BUTCHERED. COPS CALLED IT A FEDERAL CASE. THEY COULDN'T GIVE US JURISDICTION FAST ENOUGH.
WE FOUND THEM HERE JUST ABOUT AN HOUR AGO.
AS YOU CAN SEE, THE CAUSES OF DEATH VARY, BUT THEIR WOUNDS ARE CONSISTENT WITH AN ANIMAL ATTACK.
AND HONESTLY...
...I CAN'T SAY I BLAME THEM.
BUT I DON'T KNOW WHAT KIND OF ANIMAL COULD HAVE DONE ALL OF THIS.
OHMYGOD...
I DON'T WANT TO CLEAN UP THIS MESS, EITHER.
HGGGHHHRLK!

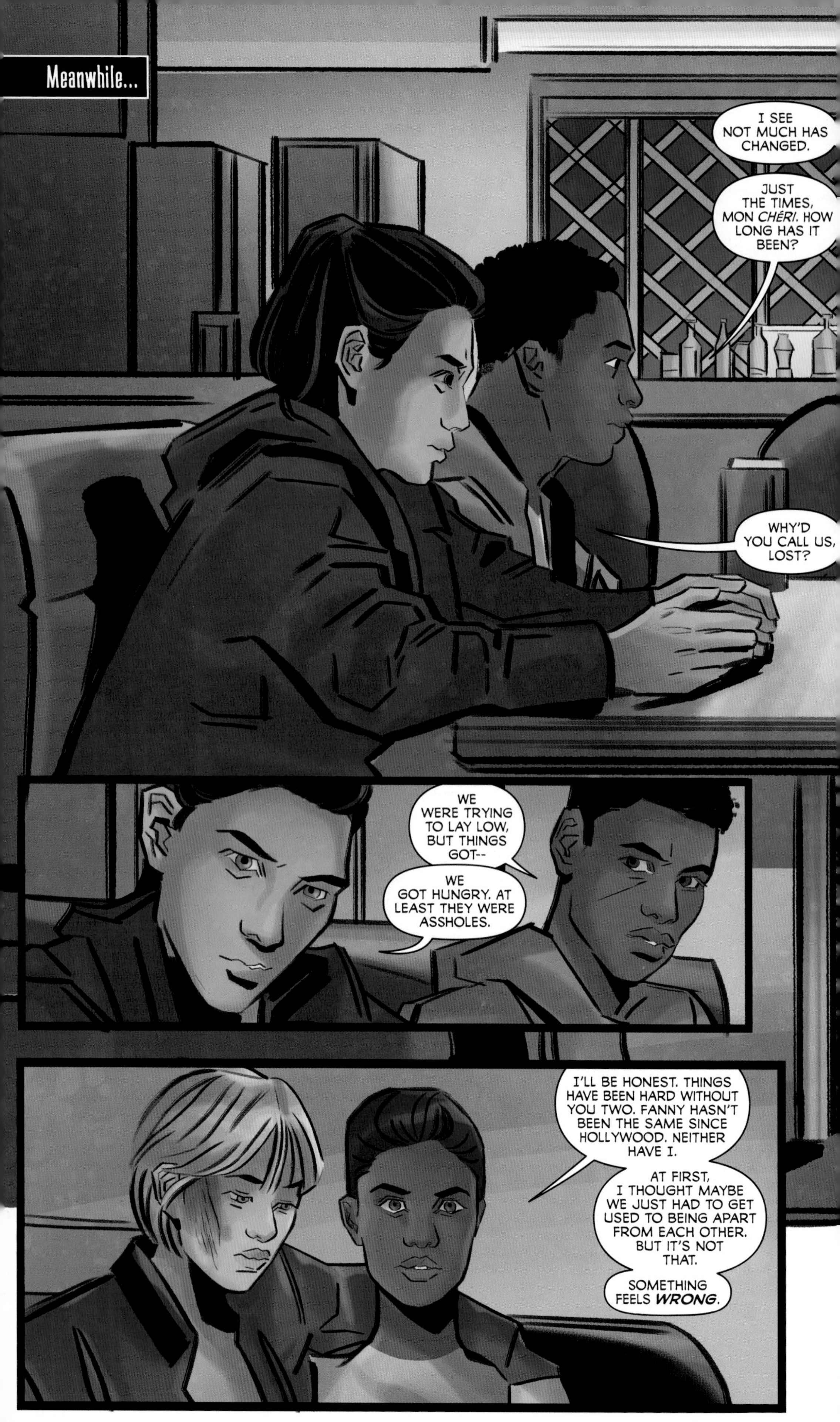
Meanwhile...
I SEE NOT MUCH HAS CHANGED.
JUST THE TIMES, MON *CHÉRI*. HOW LONG HAS IT BEEN?
WHY'D YOU CALL US, LOST?
WE WERE TRYING TO LAY LOW, BUT THINGS GOT--
WE GOT HUNGRY. AT LEAST THEY WERE ASSHOLES.
I'LL BE HONEST. THINGS HAVE BEEN HARD WITHOUT YOU TWO. FANNY HASN'T BEEN THE SAME SINCE HOLLYWOOD. NEITHER HAVE I.
AT FIRST, I THOUGHT MAYBE WE JUST HAD TO GET USED TO BEING APART FROM EACH OTHER. BUT IT'S NOT THAT.
SOMETHING FEELS ***WRONG***.

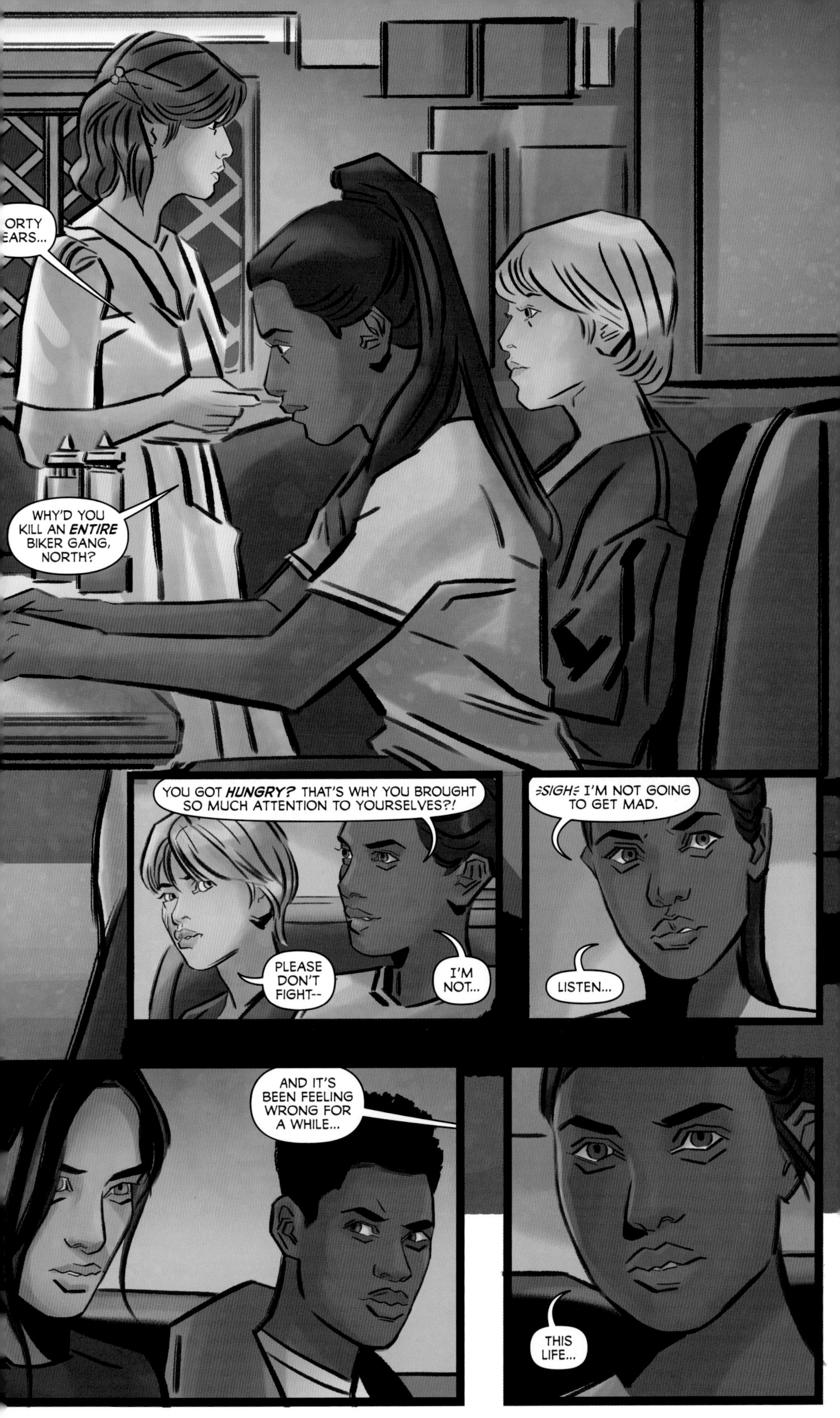
ORTY
EARS...
WHY'D YOU KILL AN *ENTIRE* BIKER GANG, NORTH?
YOU GOT *HUNGRY?* THAT'S WHY YOU BROUGHT SO MUCH ATTENTION TO YOURSELVES?!
PLEASE DON'T FIGHT--
I'M NOT...
SIGH I'M NOT GOING TO GET MAD.
LISTEN...
AND IT'S BEEN FEELING WRONG FOR A WHILE...
THIS LIFE...

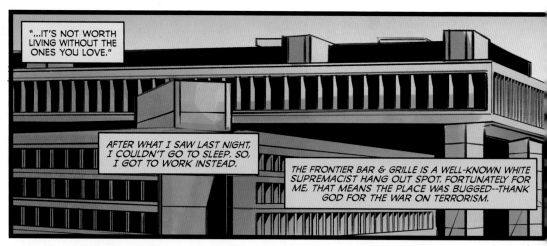

"...IT'S NOT WORTH LIVING WITHOUT THE ONES YOU LOVE."

AFTER WHAT I SAW LAST NIGHT, I COULDN'T GO TO SLEEP. SO, I GOT TO WORK INSTEAD.

THE FRONTIER BAR & GRILLE IS A WELL-KNOWN WHITE SUPREMACIST HANG OUT SPOT. FORTUNATELY FOR ME, THAT MEANS THE PLACE WAS BUGGED--THANK GOD FOR THE WAR ON TERRORISM.

THE MUSIC WAS LOUD AND I WASN'T ABLE TO HEAR MUCH...

I LISTENED TO THE TAPE SEVERAL TIMES AND I WAS ABLE TO IDENTIFY THE SOUND OF TWO MALE VOICES ESCALATING AN ARGUMENT WITH THE LOCALS.

KLIK KLAK TAKA-LAK

TAK

"I WANT TO DRINK YOUR BLOOD."

THEN THE SCREAMING BEGINS.

ACCORDING TO THE OFFICIAL REPORT, FORENSICS WAS SUGGESTING THAT BLOOD WAS CONSUMED FROM THE VICTIMS.

LIKE THEY WERE FUCKING VAMPIRES.

SO, I CROSS-CHECKED ANY OPEN CASE WITH "BLOOD RELATED CRIMES AND FELONIES" ON THE F.B.I. DIGITAL LIBRARY...

WHAT THE HELL IS THIS?

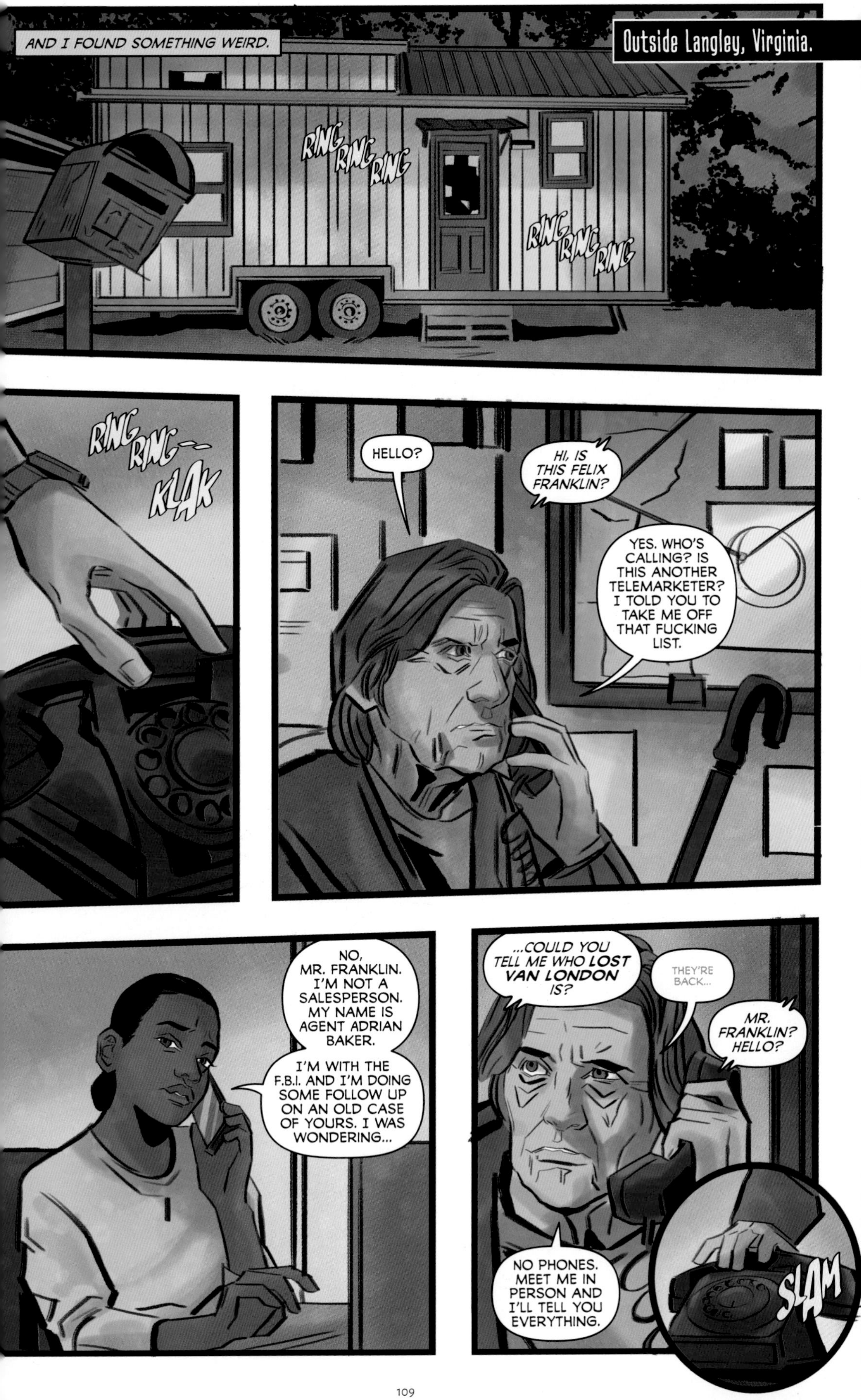
AND I FOUND SOMETHING WEIRD.
Outside Langley, Virginia.
RING RING RING
RING RING RING
RING RING--
KLAK
HELLO?
HI, IS THIS FELIX FRANKLIN?
YES. WHO'S CALLING? IS THIS ANOTHER TELEMARKETER? I TOLD YOU TO TAKE ME OFF THAT FUCKING LIST.
NO, MR. FRANKLIN. I'M NOT A SALESPERSON. MY NAME IS AGENT ADRIAN BAKER.
I'M WITH THE F.B.I. AND I'M DOING SOME FOLLOW UP ON AN OLD CASE OF YOURS. I WAS WONDERING...
...COULD YOU TELL ME WHO LOST VAN LONDON IS?
THEY'RE BACK...
MR. FRANKLIN? HELLO?
NO PHONES. MEET ME IN PERSON AND I'LL TELL YOU EVERYTHING.
SLAM

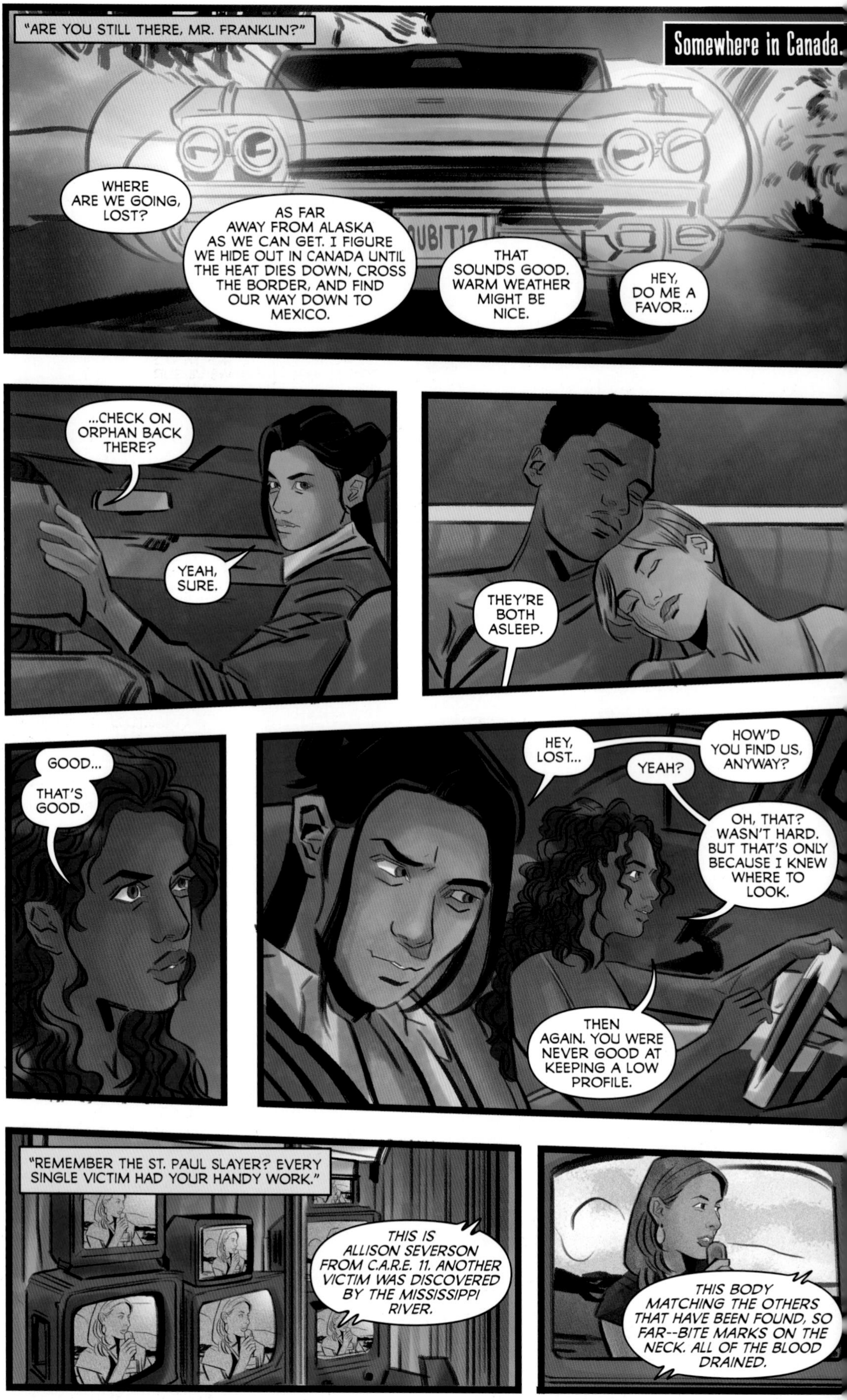
"ARE YOU STILL THERE, MR. FRANKLIN?"
Somewhere in Canada.
WHERE ARE WE GOING, LOST?
AS FAR AWAY FROM ALASKA AS WE CAN GET. I FIGURE WE HIDE OUT IN CANADA UNTIL THE HEAT DIES DOWN, CROSS THE BORDER, AND FIND OUR WAY DOWN TO MEXICO.
THAT SOUNDS GOOD. WARM WEATHER MIGHT BE NICE.
HEY, DO ME A FAVOR...
...CHECK ON ORPHAN BACK THERE?
YEAH, SURE.
THEY'RE BOTH ASLEEP.
GOOD...
THAT'S GOOD.
HEY, LOST...
YEAH?
HOW'D YOU FIND US, ANYWAY?
OH, THAT? WASN'T HARD. BUT THAT'S ONLY BECAUSE I KNEW WHERE TO LOOK.
THEN AGAIN. YOU WERE NEVER GOOD AT KEEPING A LOW PROFILE.
"REMEMBER THE ST. PAUL SLAYER? EVERY SINGLE VICTIM HAD YOUR HANDY WORK."
THIS IS ALLISON SEVERSON FROM C.A.R.E. 11. ANOTHER VICTIM WAS DISCOVERED BY THE MISSISSIPPI RIVER.
THIS BODY MATCHING THE OTHERS THAT HAVE BEEN FOUND, SO FAR--BITE MARKS ON THE NECK. ALL OF THE BLOOD DRAINED.

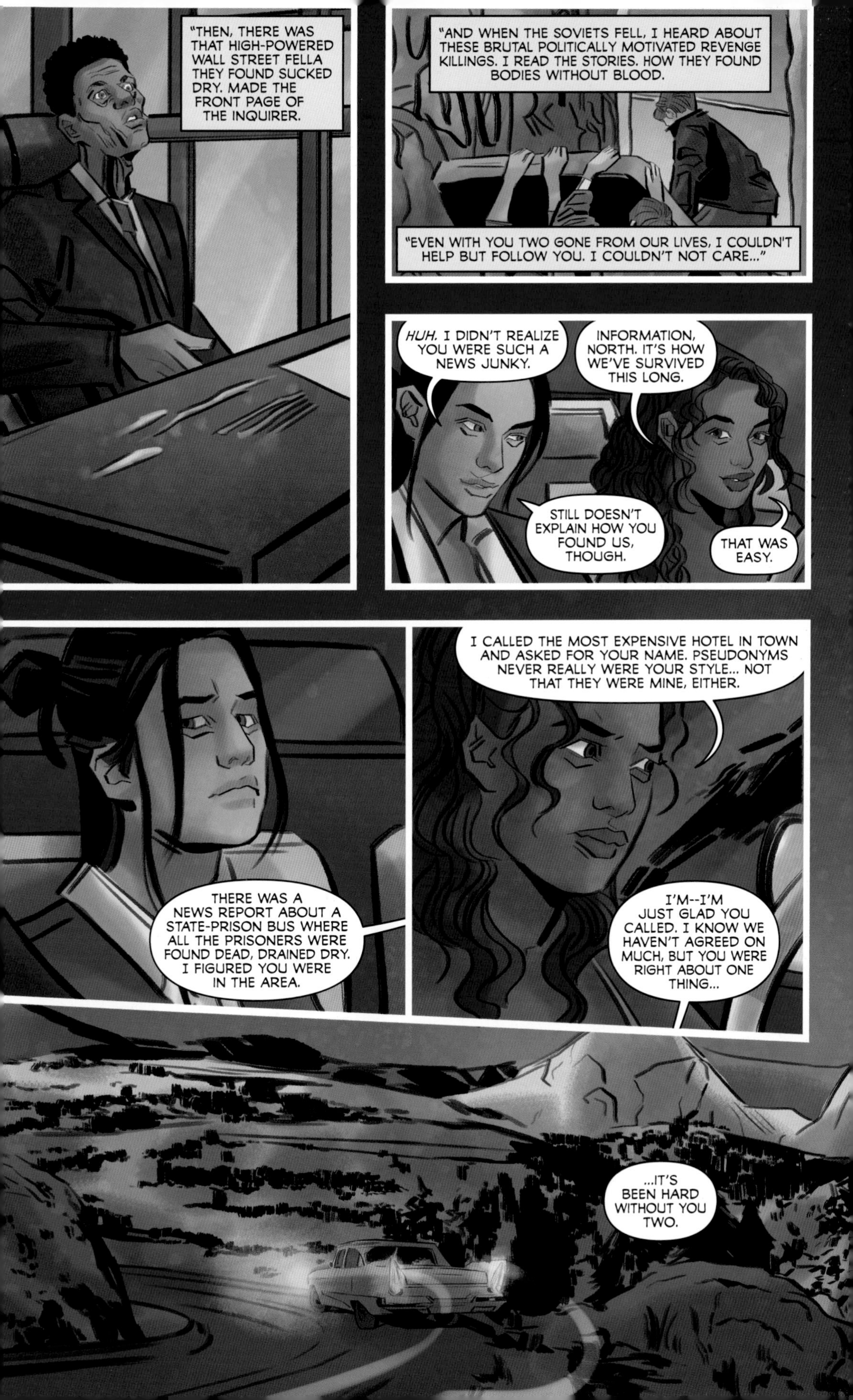
"THEN, THERE WAS THAT HIGH-POWERED WALL STREET FELLA THEY FOUND SUCKED DRY. MADE THE FRONT PAGE OF THE INQUIRER.
"AND WHEN THE SOVIETS FELL, I HEARD ABOUT THESE BRUTAL POLITICALLY MOTIVATED REVENGE KILLINGS. I READ THE STORIES. HOW THEY FOUND BODIES WITHOUT BLOOD.
"EVEN WITH YOU TWO GONE FROM OUR LIVES, I COULDN'T HELP BUT FOLLOW YOU. I COULDN'T NOT CARE..."
HUH. I DIDN'T REALIZE YOU WERE SUCH A NEWS JUNKY.
INFORMATION, NORTH. IT'S HOW WE'VE SURVIVED THIS LONG.
STILL DOESN'T EXPLAIN HOW YOU FOUND US, THOUGH.
THAT WAS EASY.
I CALLED THE MOST EXPENSIVE HOTEL IN TOWN AND ASKED FOR YOUR NAME. PSEUDONYMS NEVER REALLY WERE YOUR STYLE... NOT THAT THEY WERE MINE, EITHER.
THERE WAS A NEWS REPORT ABOUT A STATE-PRISON BUS WHERE ALL THE PRISONERS WERE FOUND DEAD, DRAINED DRY. I FIGURED YOU WERE IN THE AREA.
I'M--I'M JUST GLAD YOU CALLED. I KNOW WE HAVEN'T AGREED ON MUCH, BUT YOU WERE RIGHT ABOUT ONE THING...
...IT'S BEEN HARD WITHOUT YOU TWO.

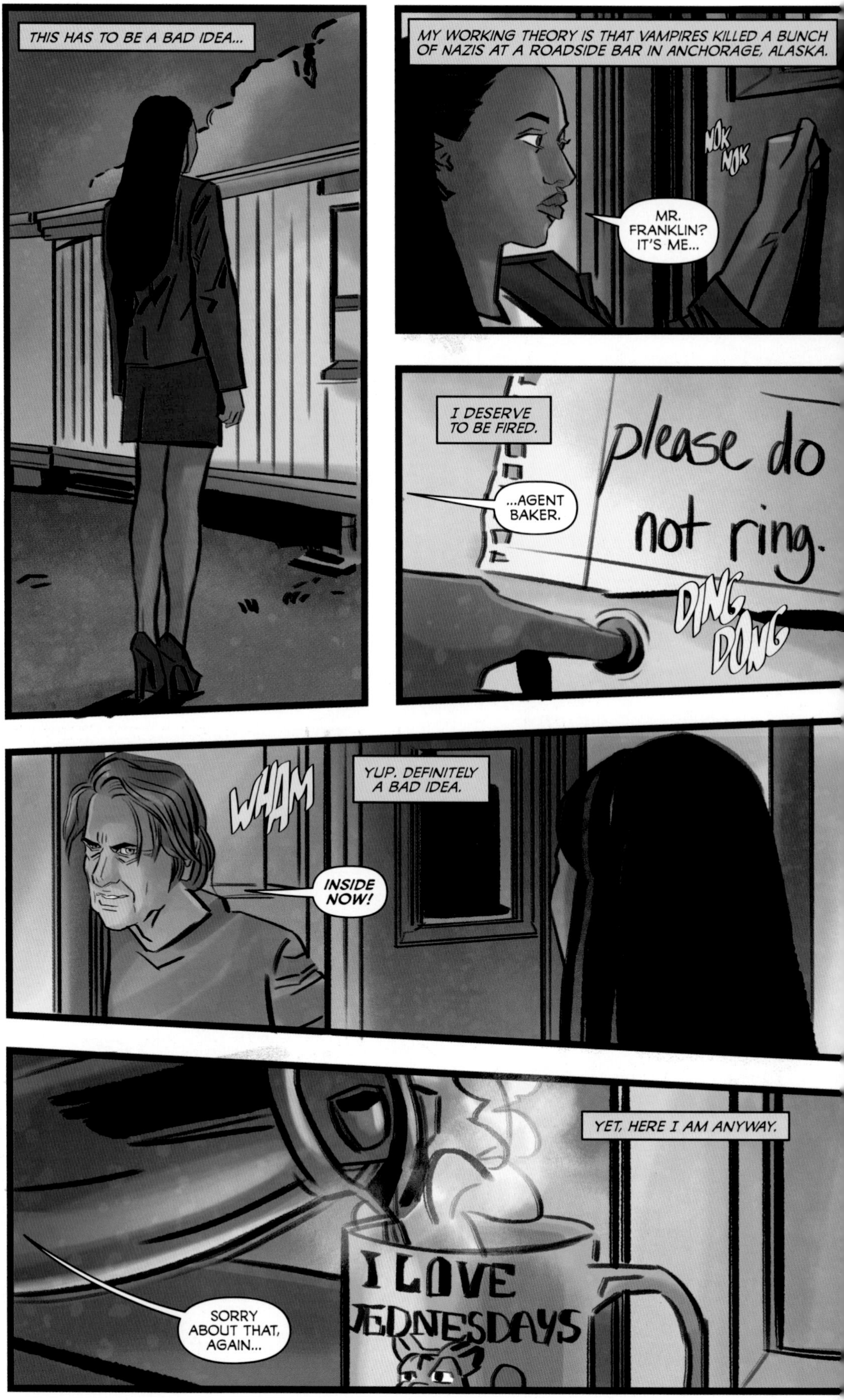
THIS HAS TO BE A BAD IDEA...
MY WORKING THEORY IS THAT VAMPIRES KILLED A BUNCH OF NAZIS AT A ROADSIDE BAR IN ANCHORAGE, ALASKA.
NOK NOK
MR. FRANKLIN? IT'S ME...
I DESERVE TO BE FIRED.
please do not ring.
...AGENT BAKER.
DING DONG
WHAM
YUP. DEFINITELY A BAD IDEA.
INSIDE NOW!
YET, HERE I AM ANYWAY.
I LOVE
SORRY ABOUT THAT, AGAIN...

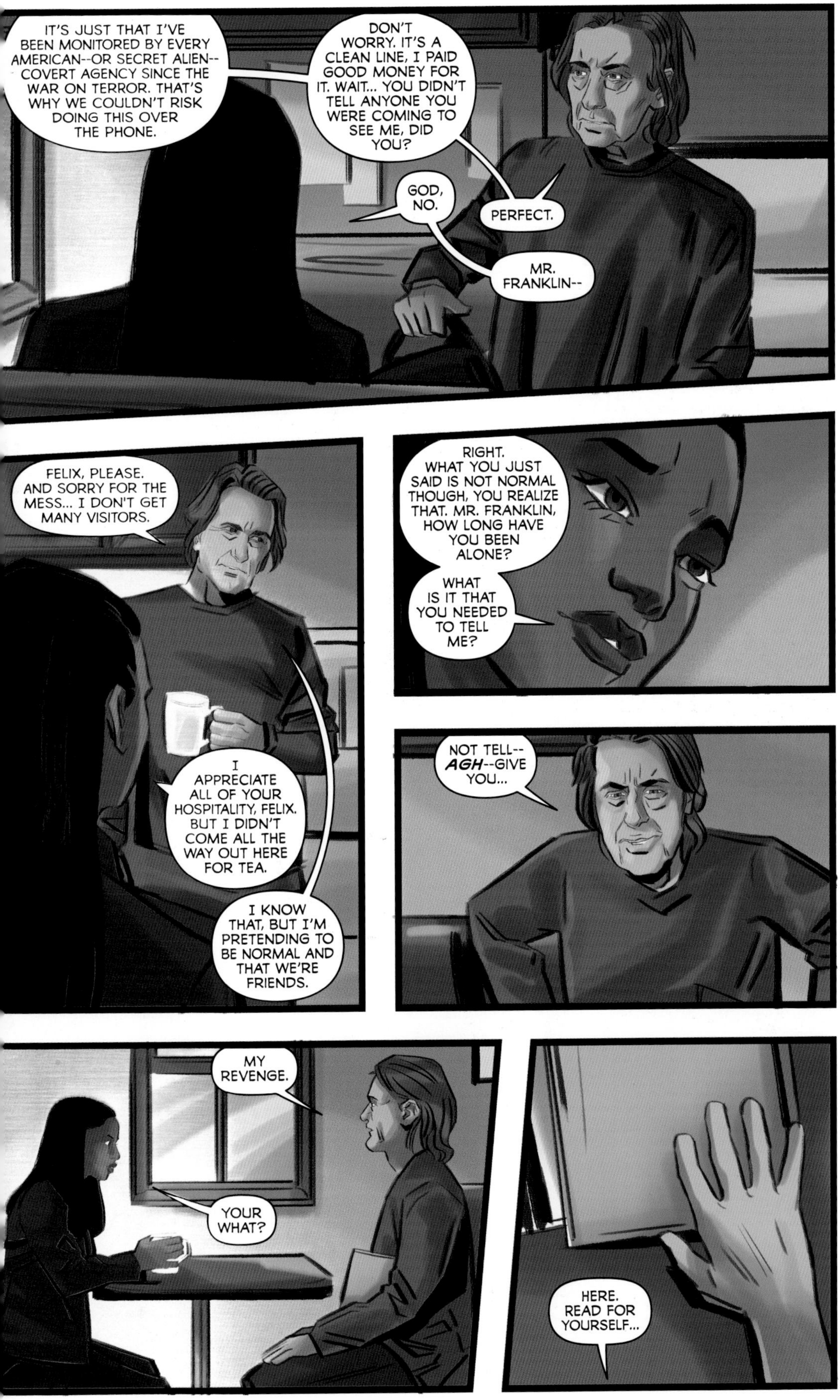
IT'S JUST THAT I'VE BEEN MONITORED BY EVERY AMERICAN--OR SECRET ALIEN--COVERT AGENCY SINCE THE WAR ON TERROR. THAT'S WHY WE COULDN'T RISK DOING THIS OVER THE PHONE.
DON'T WORRY. IT'S A CLEAN LINE, I PAID GOOD MONEY FOR IT. WAIT... YOU DIDN'T TELL ANYONE YOU WERE COMING TO SEE ME, DID YOU?
GOD, NO.
PERFECT.
MR. FRANKLIN--
FELIX, PLEASE. AND SORRY FOR THE MESS... I DON'T GET MANY VISITORS.
I APPRECIATE ALL OF YOUR HOSPITALITY, FELIX. BUT I DIDN'T COME ALL THE WAY OUT HERE FOR TEA.
I KNOW THAT, BUT I'M PRETENDING TO BE NORMAL AND THAT WE'RE FRIENDS.
RIGHT. WHAT YOU JUST SAID IS NOT NORMAL THOUGH, YOU REALIZE THAT. MR. FRANKLIN, HOW LONG HAVE YOU BEEN ALONE?
WHAT IS IT THAT YOU NEEDED TO TELL ME?
NOT TELL--AGH--GIVE YOU...
MY REVENGE.
YOUR WHAT?
HERE. READ FOR YOURSELF...

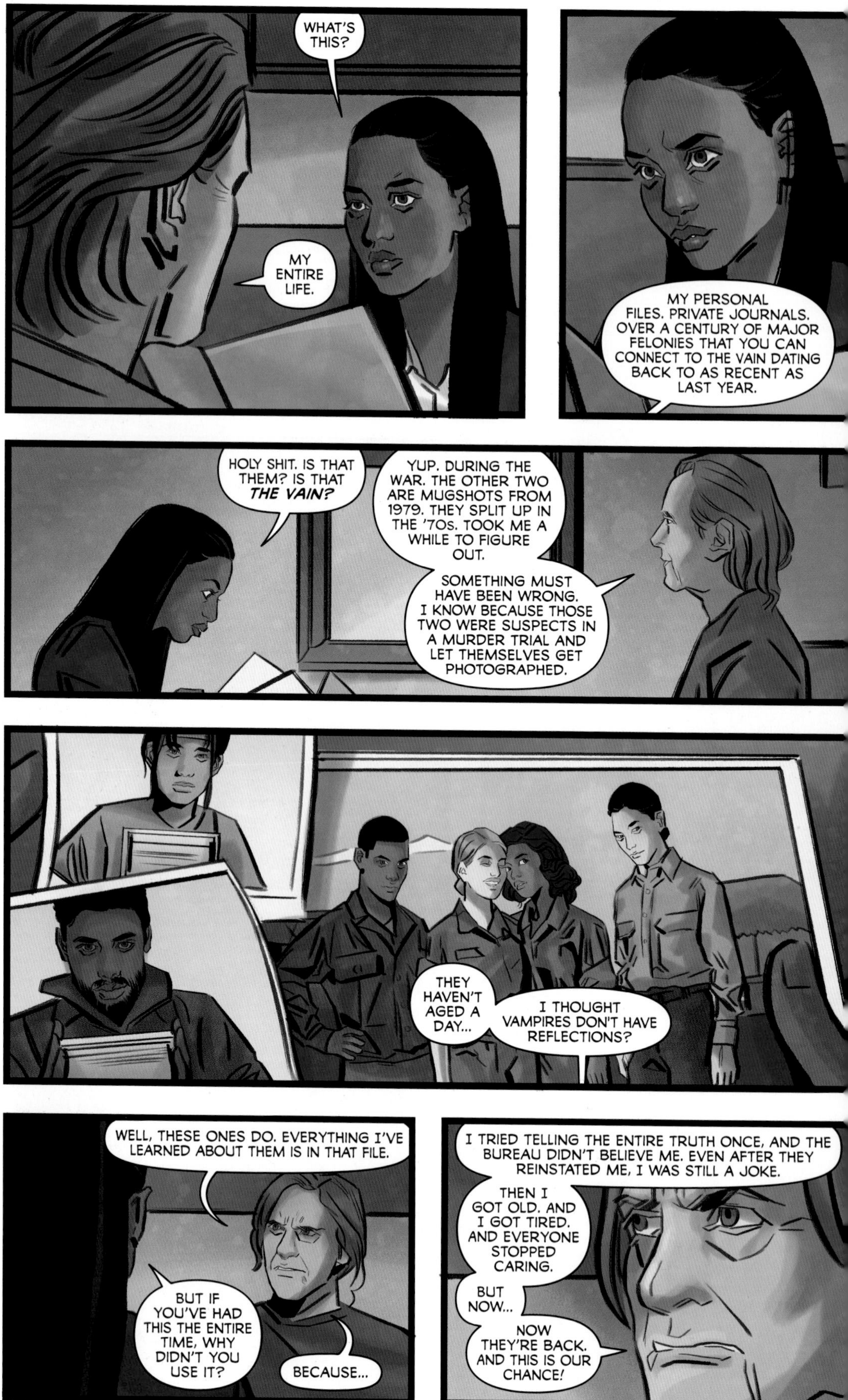
WHAT'S THIS?
MY ENTIRE LIFE.
MY PERSONAL FILES. PRIVATE JOURNALS. OVER A CENTURY OF MAJOR FELONIES THAT YOU CAN CONNECT TO THE VAIN DATING BACK TO AS RECENT AS LAST YEAR.
HOLY SHIT. IS THAT THEM? IS THAT *THE VAIN?*
YUP. DURING THE WAR. THE OTHER TWO ARE MUGSHOTS FROM 1979. THEY SPLIT UP IN THE '70s. TOOK ME A WHILE TO FIGURE OUT.
SOMETHING MUST HAVE BEEN WRONG. I KNOW BECAUSE THOSE TWO WERE SUSPECTS IN A MURDER TRIAL AND LET THEMSELVES GET PHOTOGRAPHED.
THEY HAVEN'T AGED A DAY...
I THOUGHT VAMPIRES DON'T HAVE REFLECTIONS?
WELL, THESE ONES DO. EVERYTHING I'VE LEARNED ABOUT THEM IS IN THAT FILE.
BUT IF YOU'VE HAD THIS THE ENTIRE TIME, WHY DIDN'T YOU USE IT?
BECAUSE...
I TRIED TELLING THE ENTIRE TRUTH ONCE, AND THE BUREAU DIDN'T BELIEVE ME. EVEN AFTER THEY REINSTATED ME, I WAS STILL A JOKE.
THEN I GOT OLD. AND I GOT TIRED. AND EVERYONE STOPPED CARING.
BUT NOW...
NOW THEY'RE BACK. AND THIS IS OUR CHANCE!

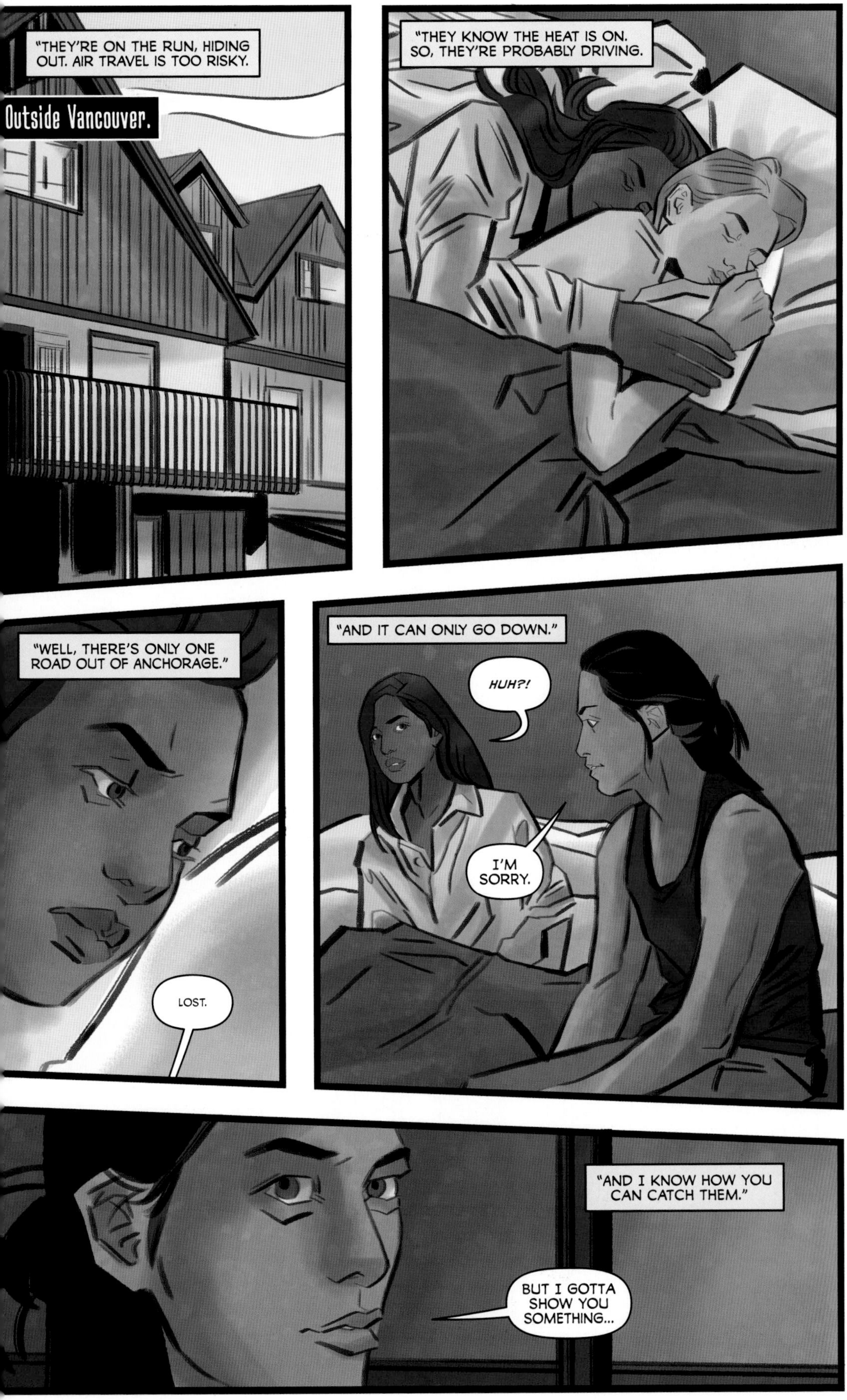
"THEY'RE ON THE RUN, HIDING OUT. AIR TRAVEL IS TOO RISKY.
Outside Vancouver.
"THEY KNOW THE HEAT IS ON. SO, THEY'RE PROBABLY DRIVING.
"WELL, THERE'S ONLY ONE ROAD OUT OF ANCHORAGE."
LOST.
"AND IT CAN ONLY GO DOWN."
HUH?!
I'M SORRY.
"AND I KNOW HOW YOU CAN CATCH THEM."
BUT I GOTTA SHOW YOU SOMETHING...

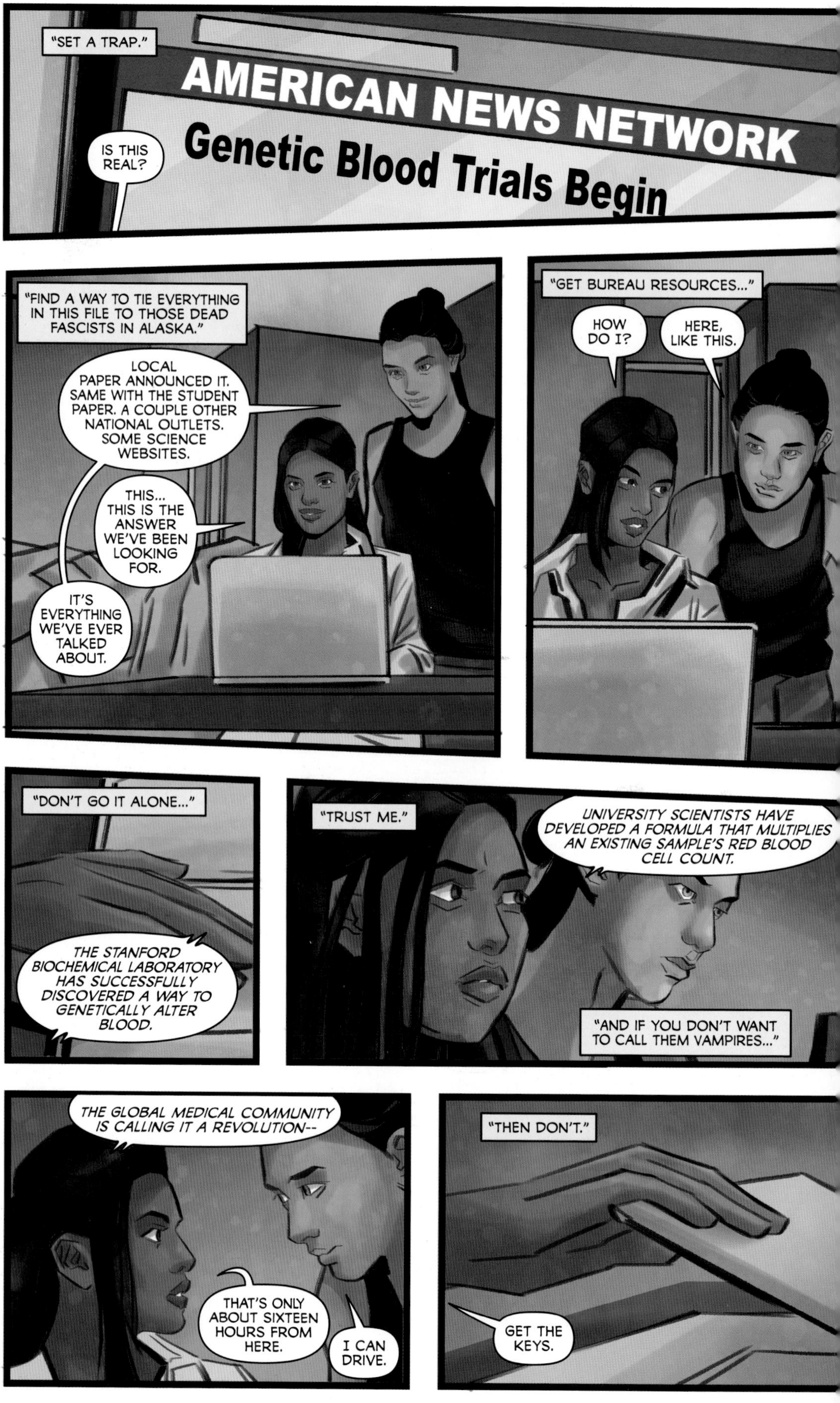
"SET A TRAP."
AMERICAN NEWS NETWORK
Genetic Blood Trials Begin
IS THIS REAL?
"FIND A WAY TO TIE EVERYTHING IN THIS FILE TO THOSE DEAD FASCISTS IN ALASKA."
LOCAL PAPER ANNOUNCED IT. SAME WITH THE STUDENT PAPER. A COUPLE OTHER NATIONAL OUTLETS. SOME SCIENCE WEBSITES.
THIS... THIS IS THE ANSWER WE'VE BEEN LOOKING FOR.
IT'S EVERYTHING WE'VE EVER TALKED ABOUT.
"GET BUREAU RESOURCES..."
HOW DO I?
HERE, LIKE THIS.
"DON'T GO IT ALONE..."
THE STANFORD BIOCHEMICAL LABORATORY HAS SUCCESSFULLY DISCOVERED A WAY TO GENETICALLY ALTER BLOOD.
"TRUST ME."
UNIVERSITY SCIENTISTS HAVE DEVELOPED A FORMULA THAT MULTIPLIES AN EXISTING SAMPLE'S RED BLOOD CELL COUNT.
"AND IF YOU DON'T WANT TO CALL THEM VAMPIRES..."
THE GLOBAL MEDICAL COMMUNITY IS CALLING IT A REVOLUTION--
THAT'S ONLY ABOUT SIXTEEN HOURS FROM HERE.
I CAN DRIVE.
"THEN DON'T."
GET THE KEYS.

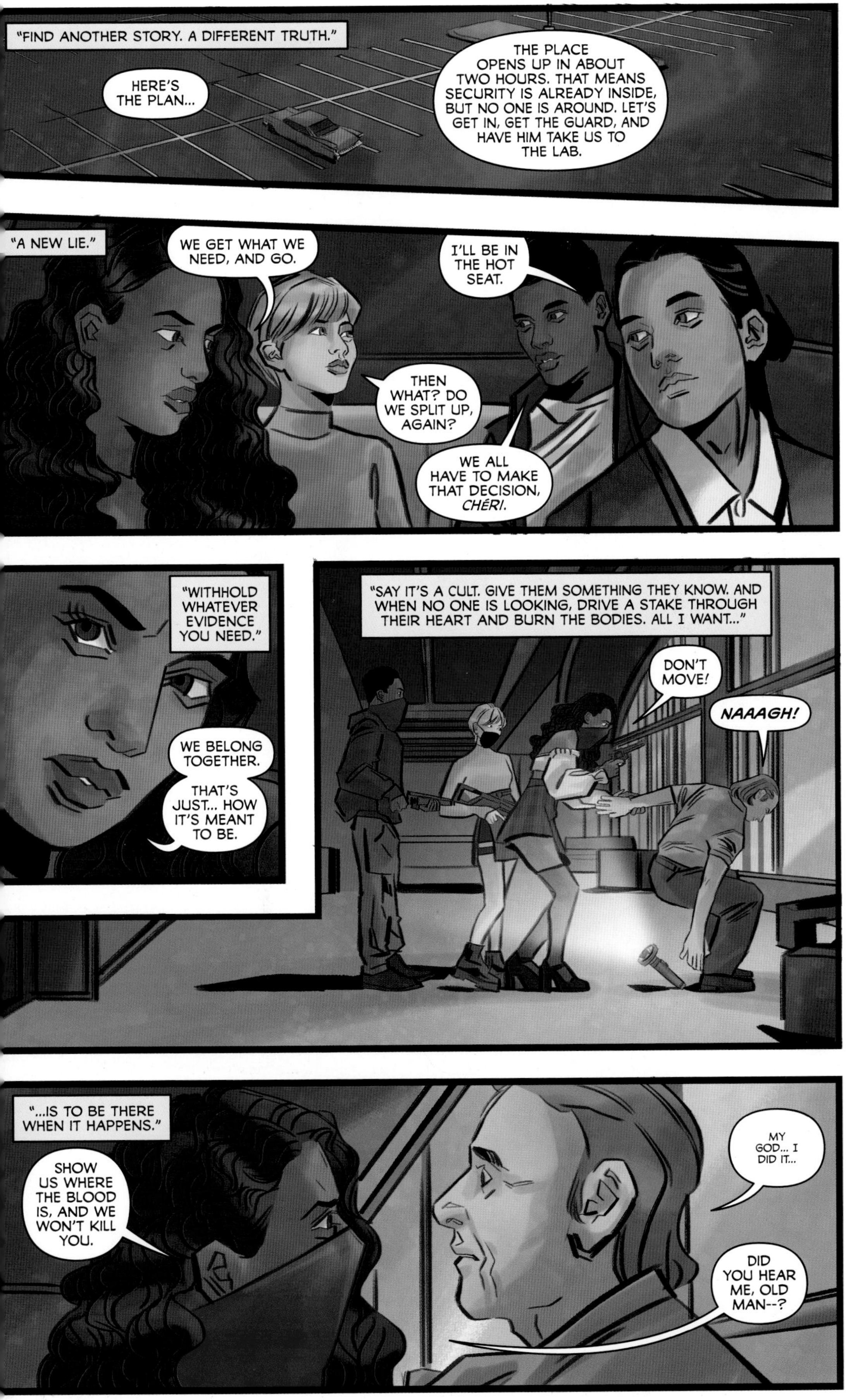
"FIND ANOTHER STORY. A DIFFERENT TRUTH."
HERE'S THE PLAN...
THE PLACE OPENS UP IN ABOUT TWO HOURS. THAT MEANS SECURITY IS ALREADY INSIDE, BUT NO ONE IS AROUND. LET'S GET IN, GET THE GUARD, AND HAVE HIM TAKE US TO THE LAB.
"A NEW LIE."
WE GET WHAT WE NEED, AND GO.
I'LL BE IN THE HOT SEAT.
THEN WHAT? DO WE SPLIT UP, AGAIN?
WE ALL HAVE TO MAKE THAT DECISION, *CHÉRI*.
"WITHHOLD WHATEVER EVIDENCE YOU NEED."
WE BELONG TOGETHER.
THAT'S JUST... HOW IT'S MEANT TO BE.
"SAY IT'S A CULT. GIVE THEM SOMETHING THEY KNOW. AND WHEN NO ONE IS LOOKING, DRIVE A STAKE THROUGH THEIR HEART AND BURN THE BODIES. ALL I WANT..."
DON'T MOVE!
NAAAGH!
"...IS TO BE THERE WHEN IT HAPPENS."
SHOW US WHERE THE BLOOD IS, AND WE WON'T KILL YOU.
MY GOD... I DID IT...
DID YOU HEAR ME, OLD MAN--?

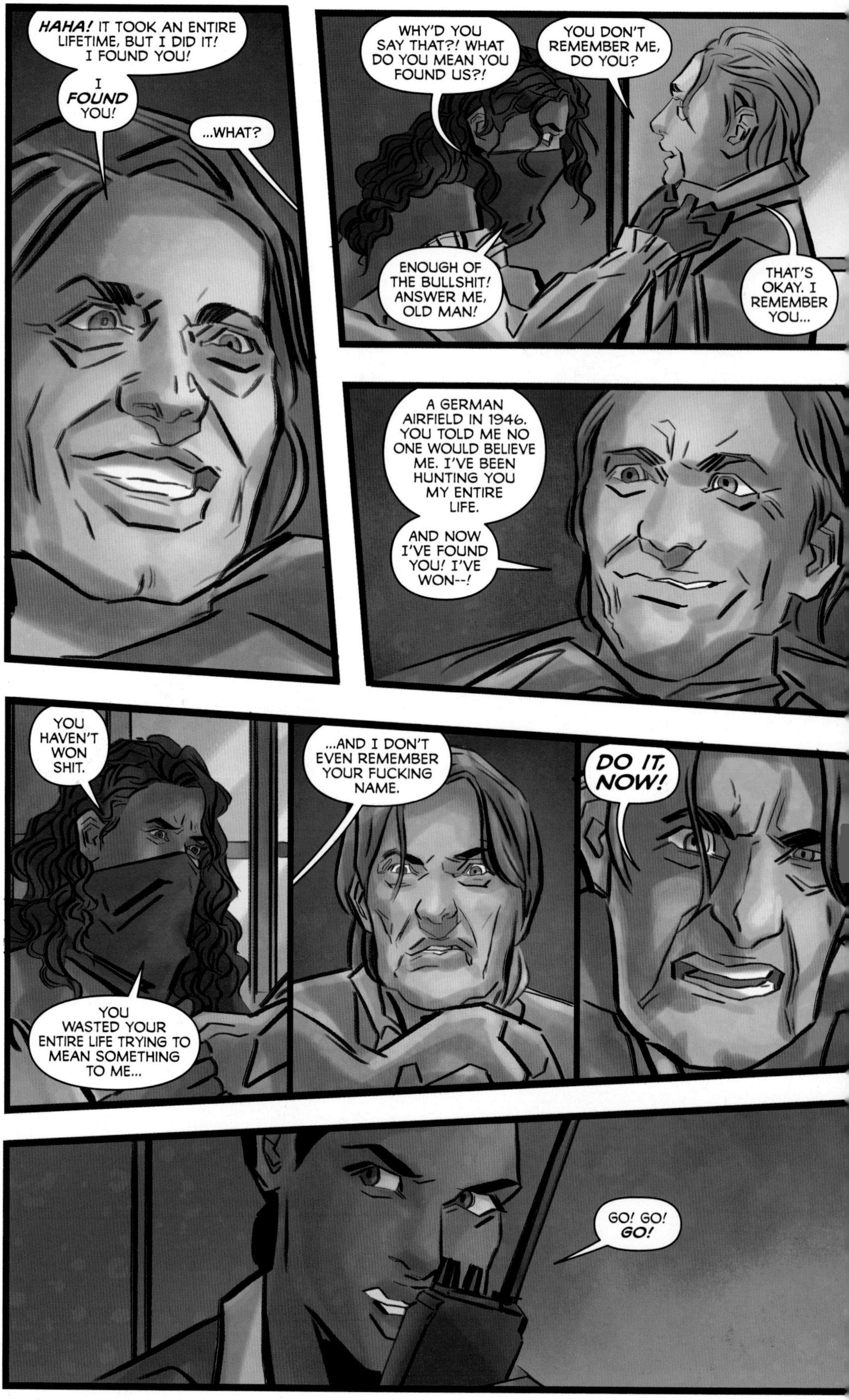

HAHA! IT TOOK AN ENTIRE LIFETIME, BUT I DID IT! I FOUND YOU!
I ***FOUND*** YOU!
...WHAT?
WHY'D YOU SAY THAT?! WHAT DO YOU MEAN YOU FOUND US?!
YOU DON'T REMEMBER ME, DO YOU?
ENOUGH OF THE BULLSHIT! ANSWER ME, OLD MAN!
THAT'S OKAY. I REMEMBER YOU...
A GERMAN AIRFIELD IN 1946. YOU TOLD ME NO ONE WOULD BELIEVE ME. I'VE BEEN HUNTING YOU MY ENTIRE LIFE.
AND NOW I'VE FOUND YOU! I'VE WON--!
YOU HAVEN'T WON SHIT.
YOU WASTED YOUR ENTIRE LIFE TRYING TO MEAN SOMETHING TO ME...
...AND I DON'T EVEN REMEMBER YOUR FUCKING NAME.
DO IT, NOW!
GO! GO! ***GO!***

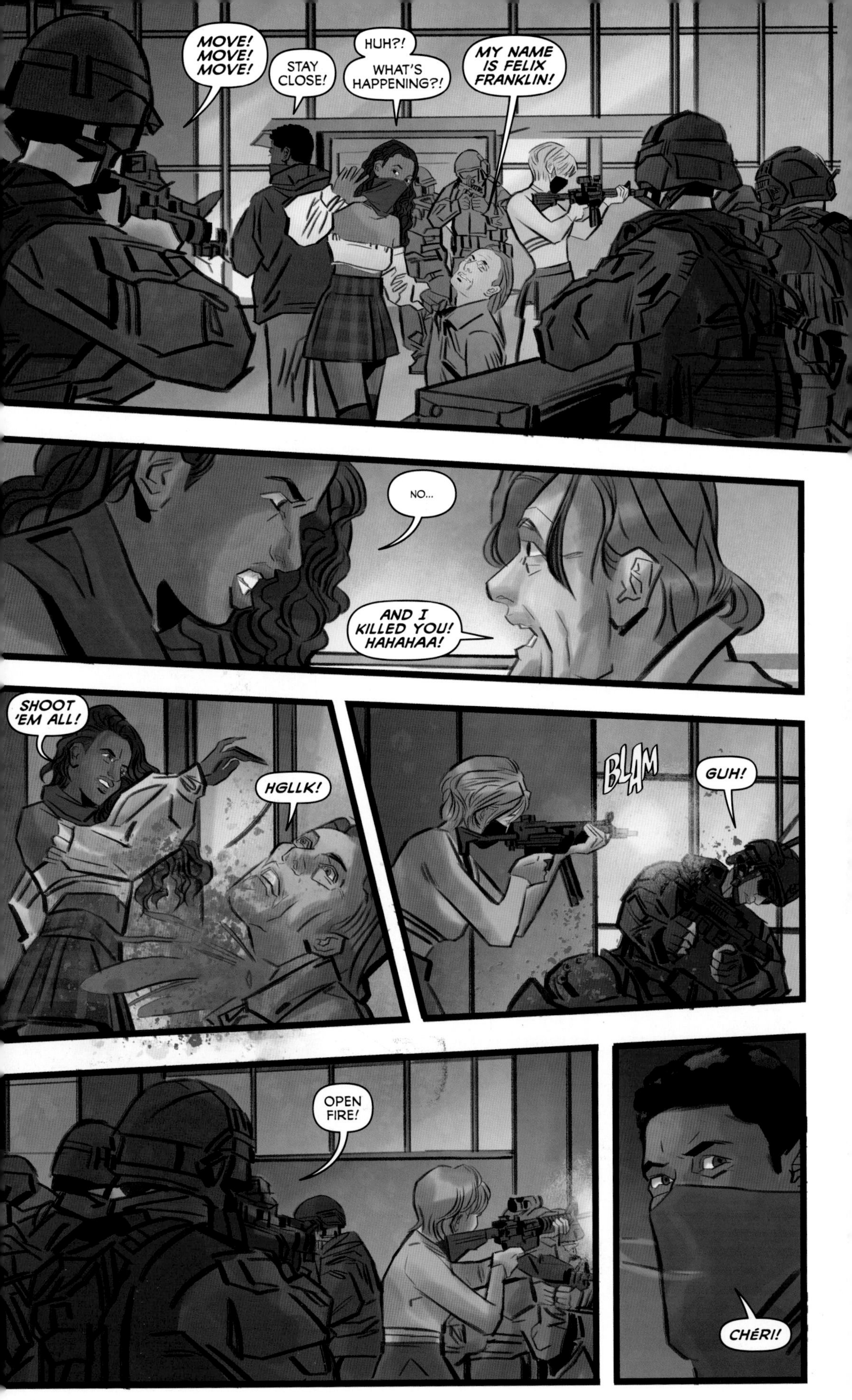
MOVE! MOVE! MOVE!
STAY CLOSE!
HUH?! WHAT'S HAPPENING?!
MY NAME IS FELIX FRANKLIN!
NO...
AND I KILLED YOU! HAHAHAA!
SHOOT 'EM ALL!
HGLLK!
BLAM
GUH!
OPEN FIRE!
CHÉRI!

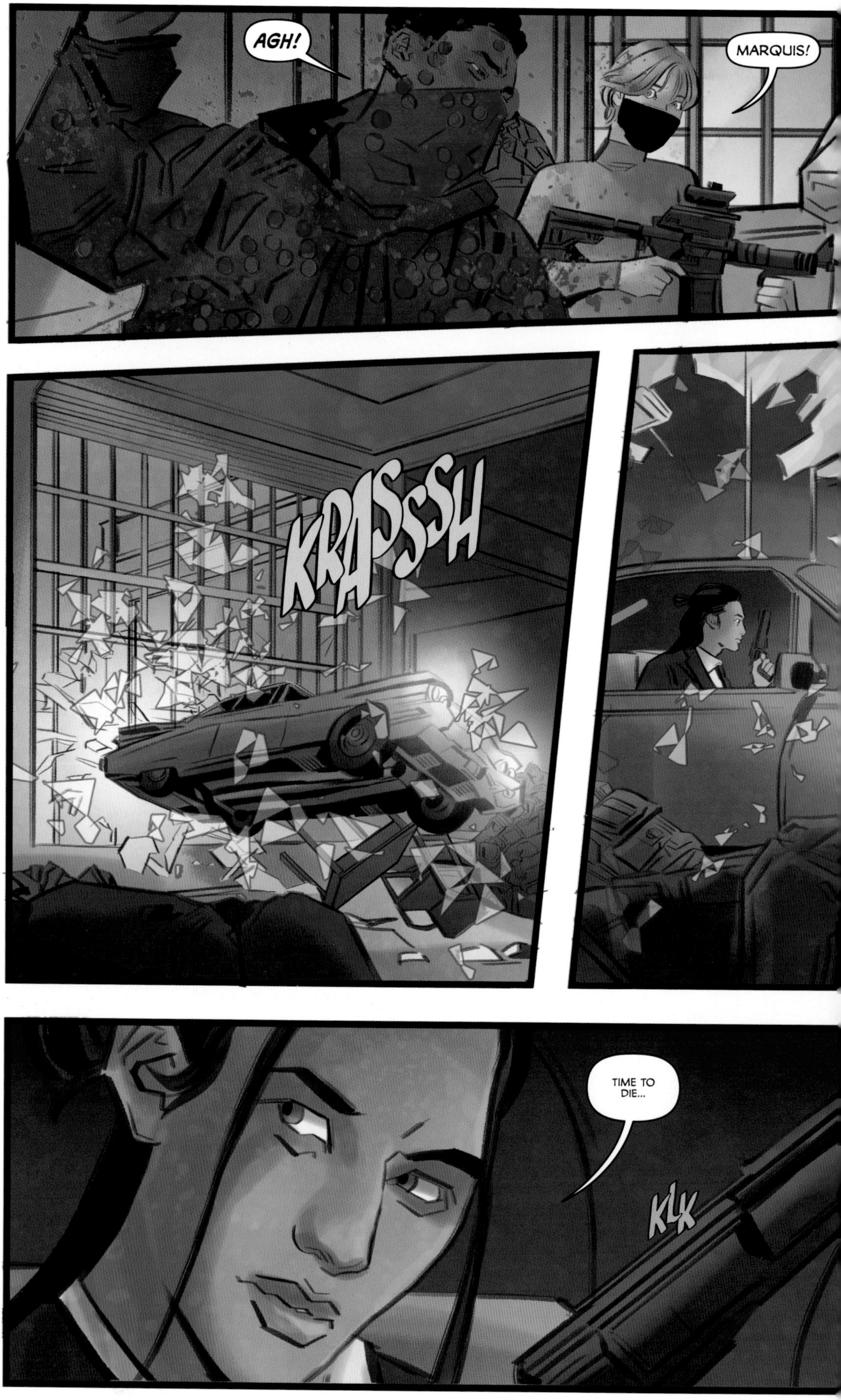
AGH!
MARQUIS!
KRASSSH
TIME TO DIE...
KLK

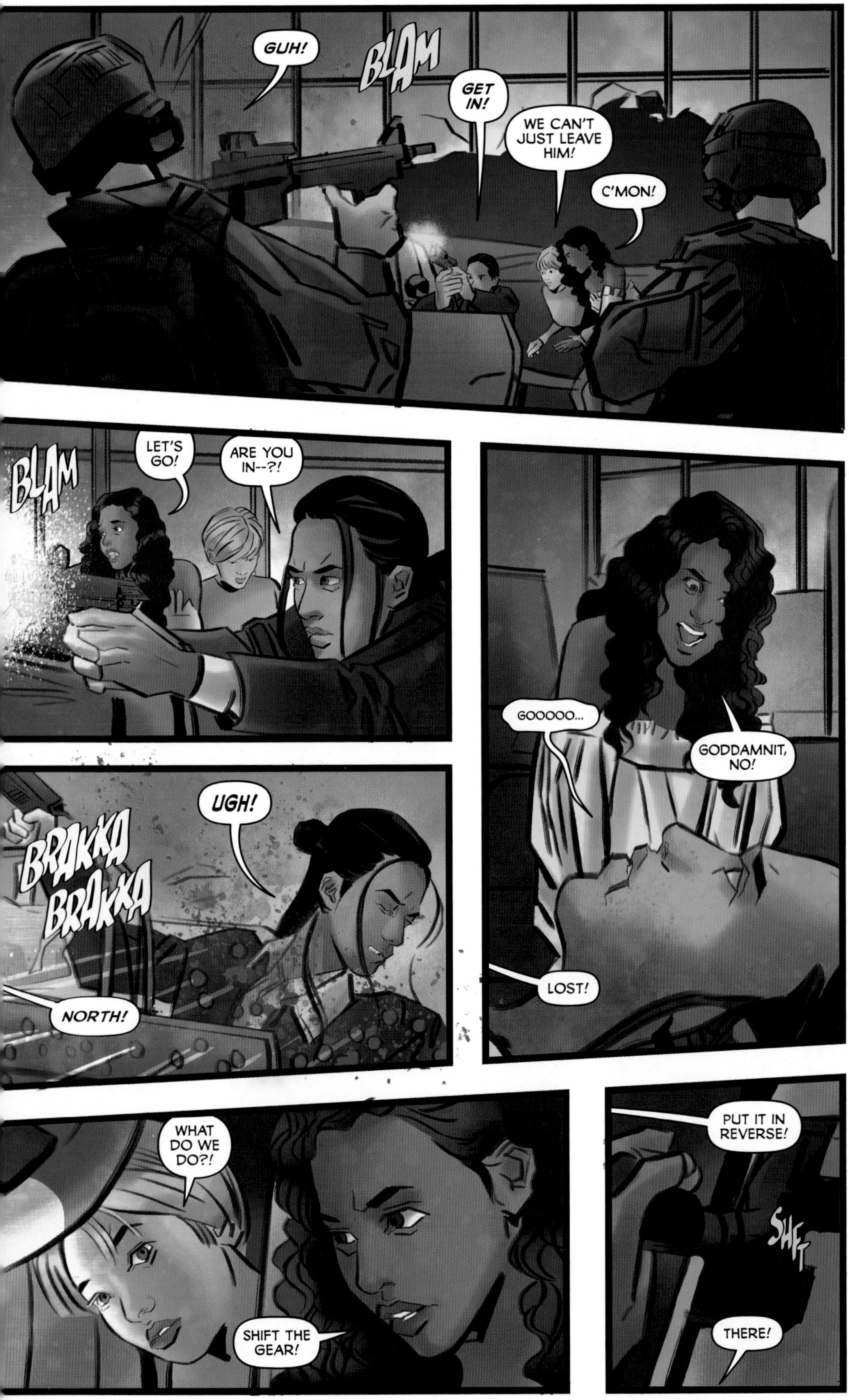
GUH!
BLAM
GET IN!
WE CAN'T JUST LEAVE HIM!
C'MON!
BLAM
LET'S GO!
ARE YOU IN--?!
GOOOOO...
GODDAMNIT, NO!
LOST!
UGH!
BRAKKA BRAKKA
NORTH!
WHAT DO WE DO?!
SHIFT THE GEAR!
PUT IT IN REVERSE!
SHFT
THERE!

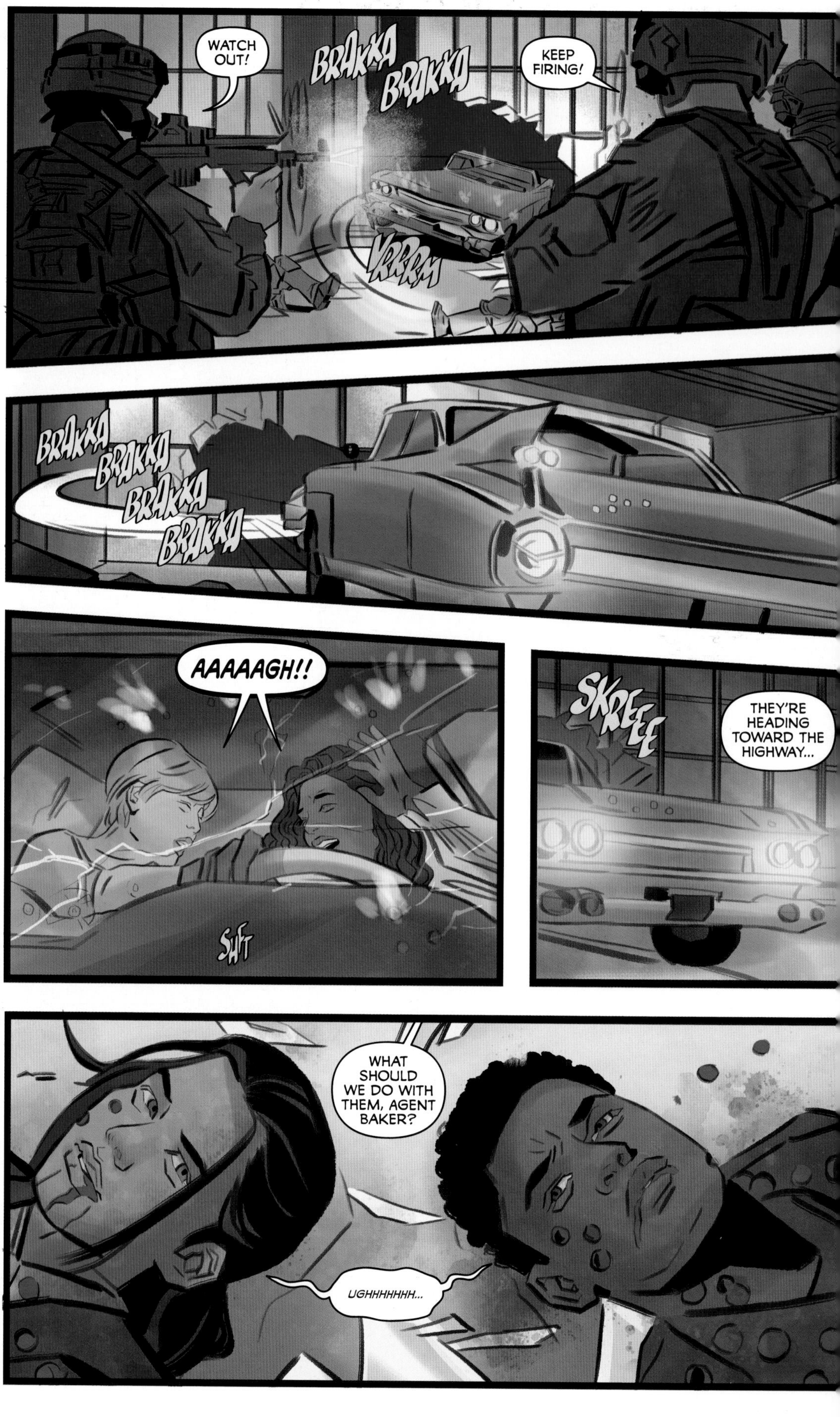
WATCH OUT!
BRAKKA BRAKKA
KEEP FIRING!
VRRRM
BRAKKA
BRAKKA
BRAKKA
BRAKKA
AAAAAGH!!
SHFT
SKREEEE
THEY'RE HEADING TOWARD THE HIGHWAY...
WHAT SHOULD WE DO WITH THEM, AGENT BAKER?
UGHHHHHHH...

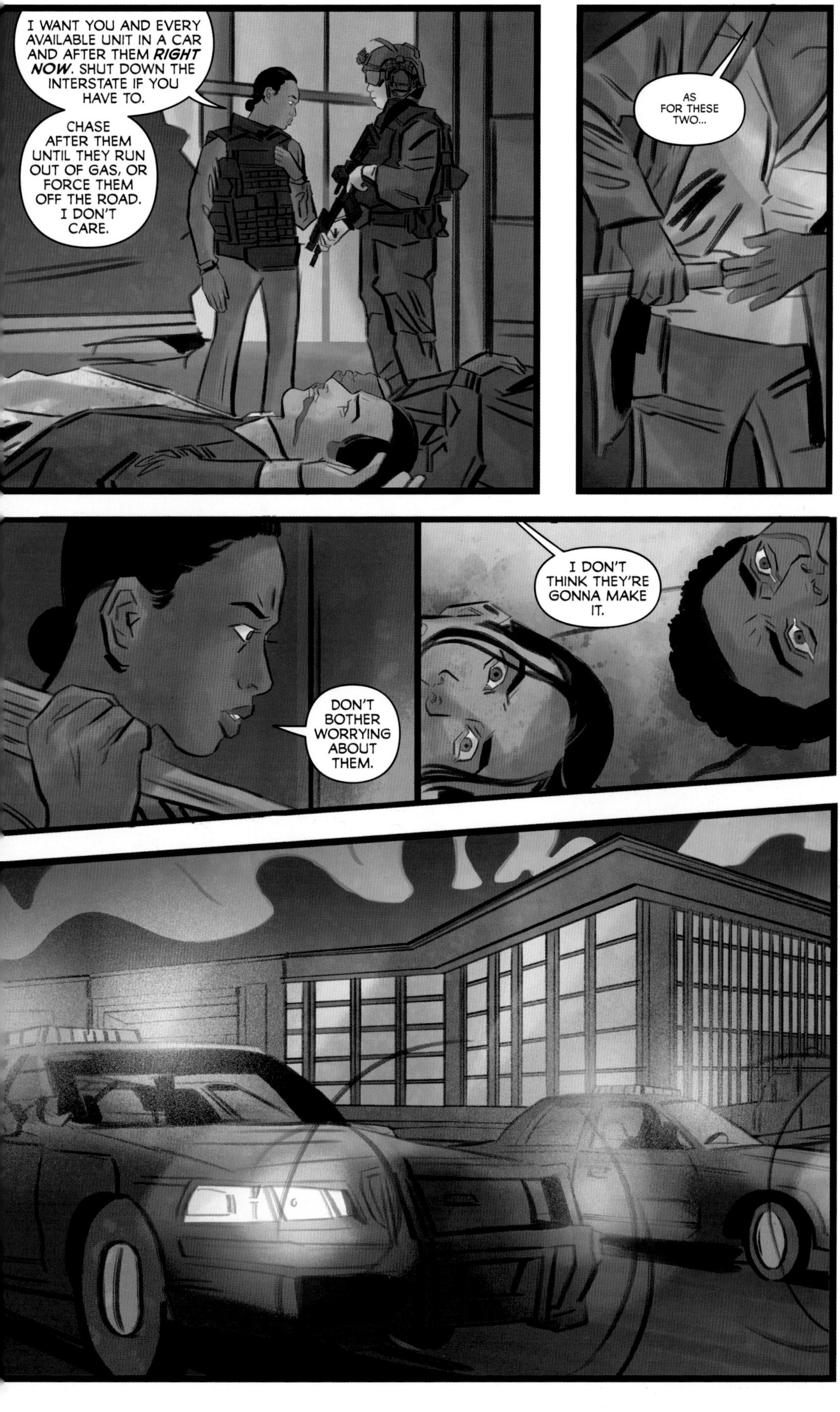
I WANT YOU AND EVERY AVAILABLE UNIT IN A CAR AND AFTER THEM ***RIGHT NOW***. SHUT DOWN THE INTERSTATE IF YOU HAVE TO.
CHASE AFTER THEM UNTIL THEY RUN OUT OF GAS, OR FORCE THEM OFF THE ROAD. I DON'T CARE.
AS FOR THESE TWO...
DON'T BOTHER WORRYING ABOUT THEM.
I DON'T THINK THEY'RE GONNA MAKE IT.

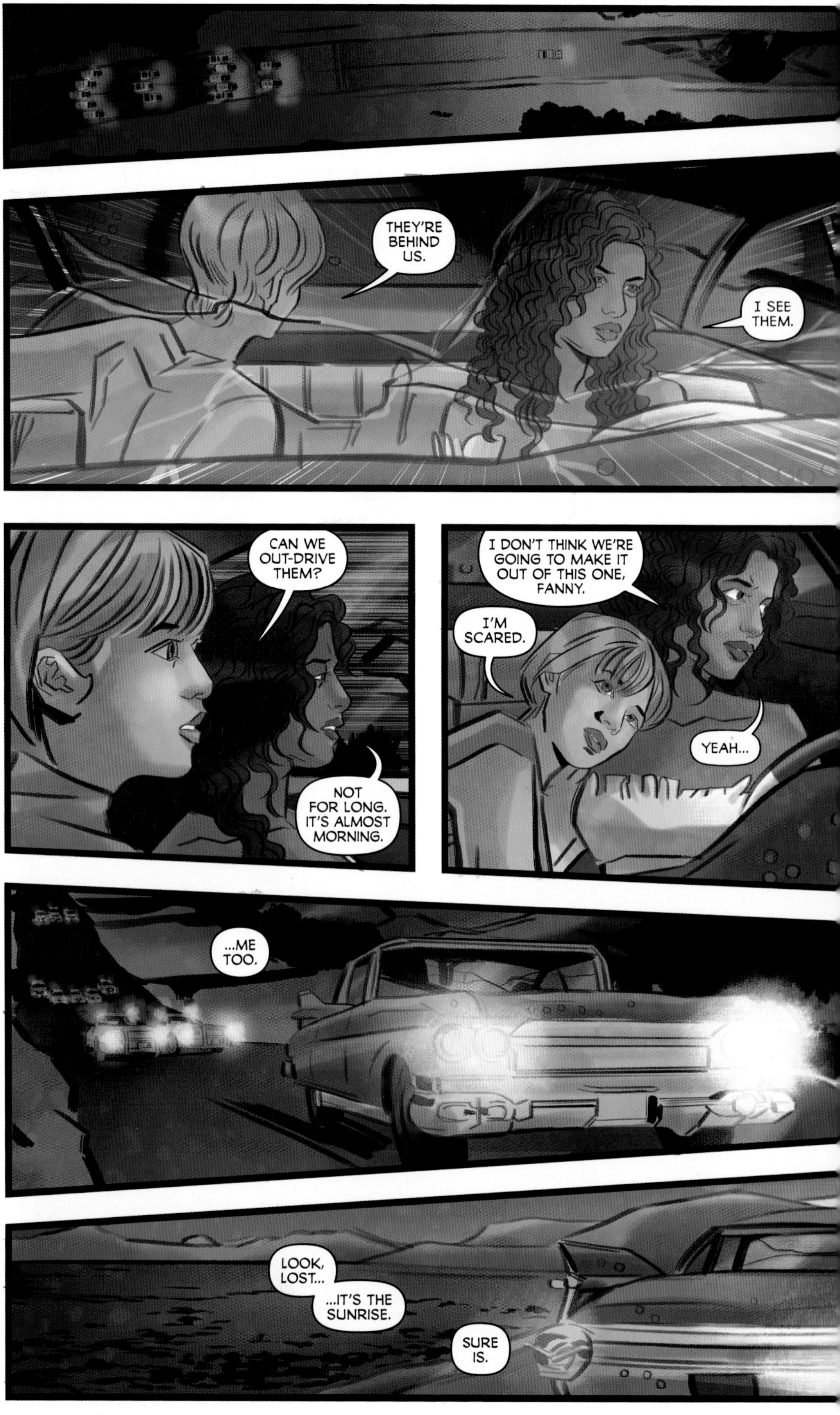
THEY'RE BEHIND US.
I SEE THEM.
CAN WE OUT-DRIVE THEM?
NOT FOR LONG. IT'S ALMOST MORNING.
I DON'T THINK WE'RE GOING TO MAKE IT OUT OF THIS ONE, FANNY.
I'M SCARED.
YEAH...
...ME TOO.
LOOK, LOST...
...IT'S THE SUNRISE.
SURE IS.

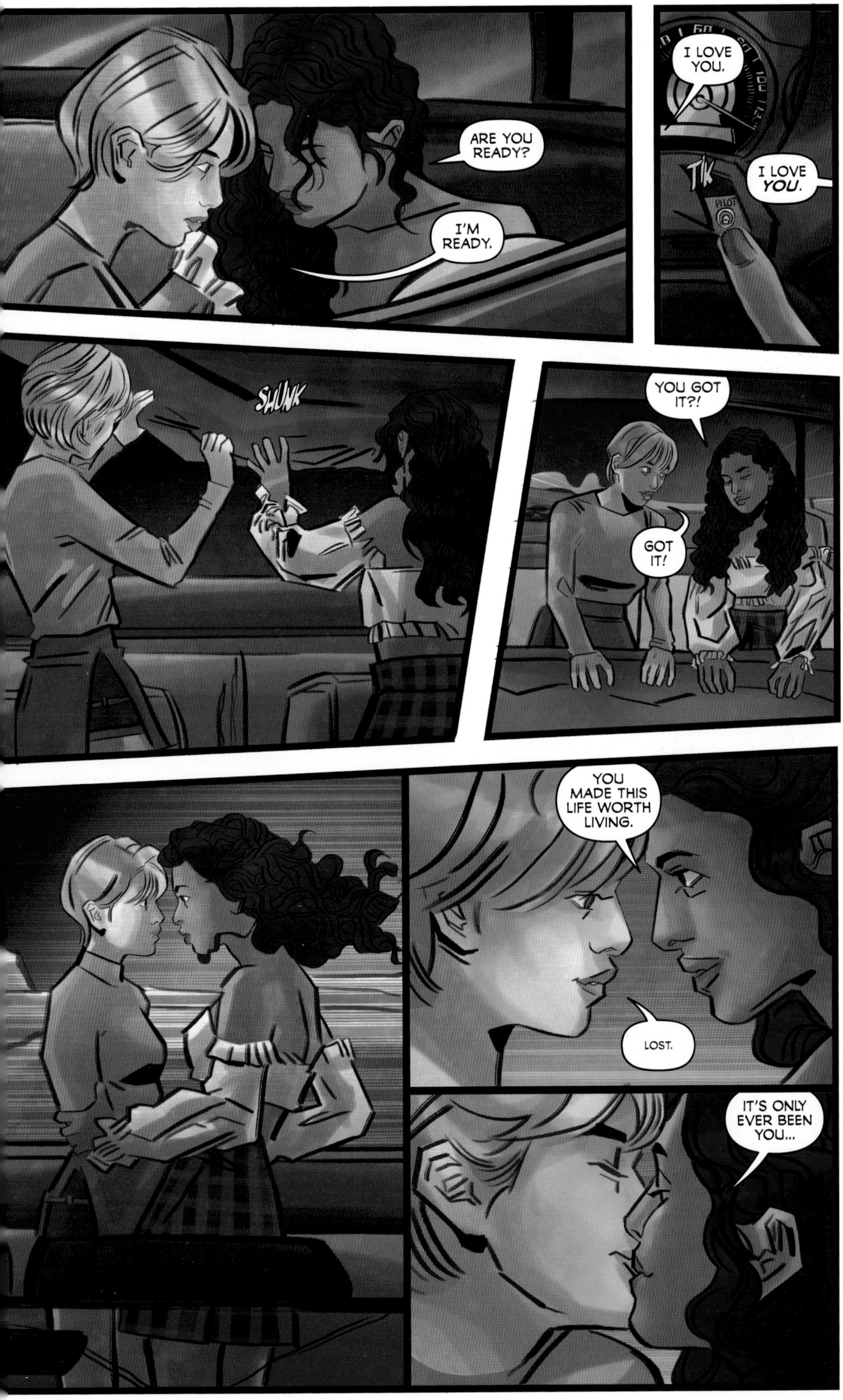
ARE YOU READY?
I'M READY.
I LOVE YOU.
TIK
I LOVE *YOU*.
PILOT
SHUNK
YOU GOT IT?!
GOT IT!
YOU MADE THIS LIFE WORTH LIVING.
LOST.
IT'S ONLY EVER BEEN YOU...

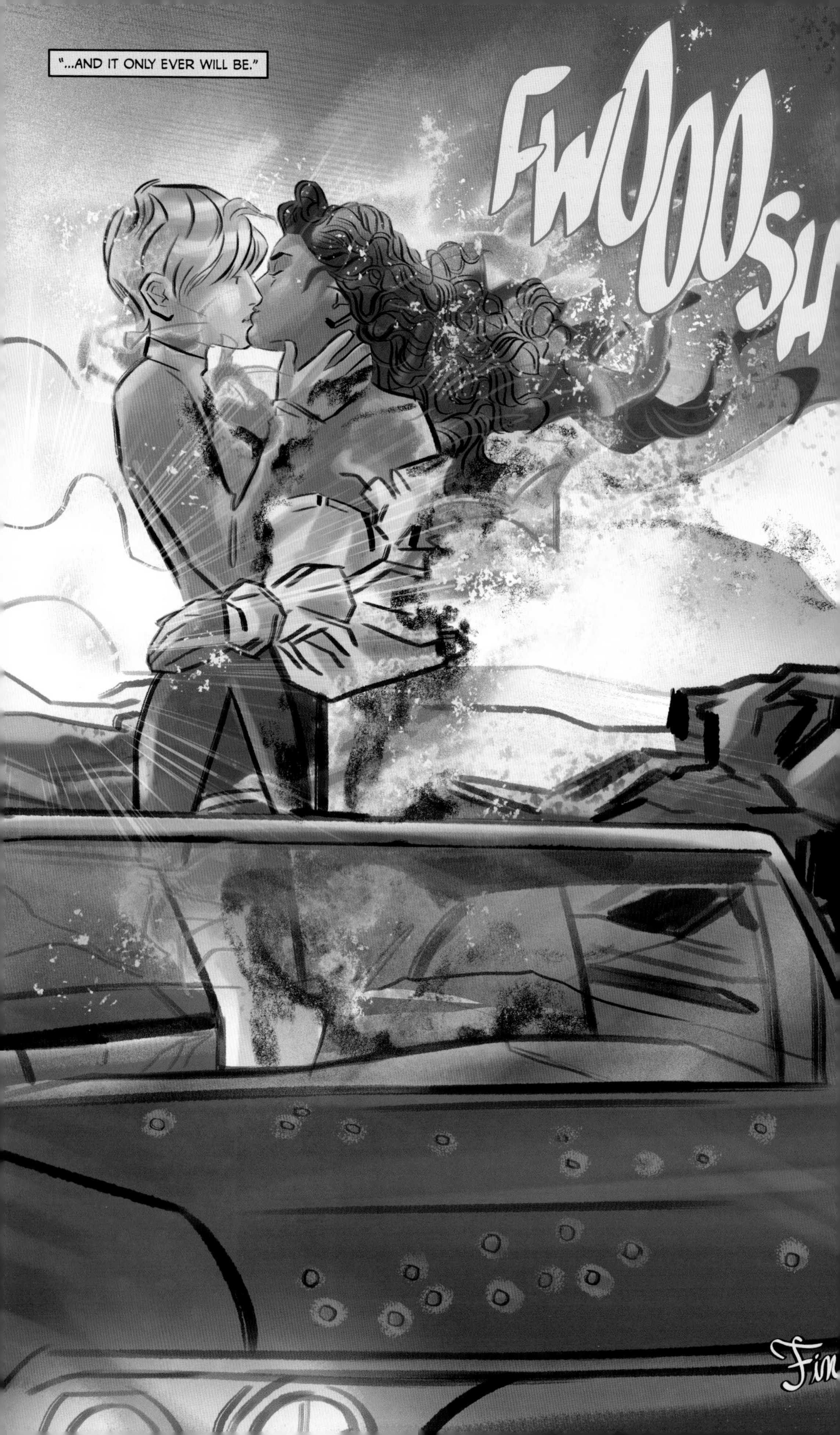
"...AND IT ONLY EVER WILL BE."
FWOOOSH
Fin

COVER GALLERY

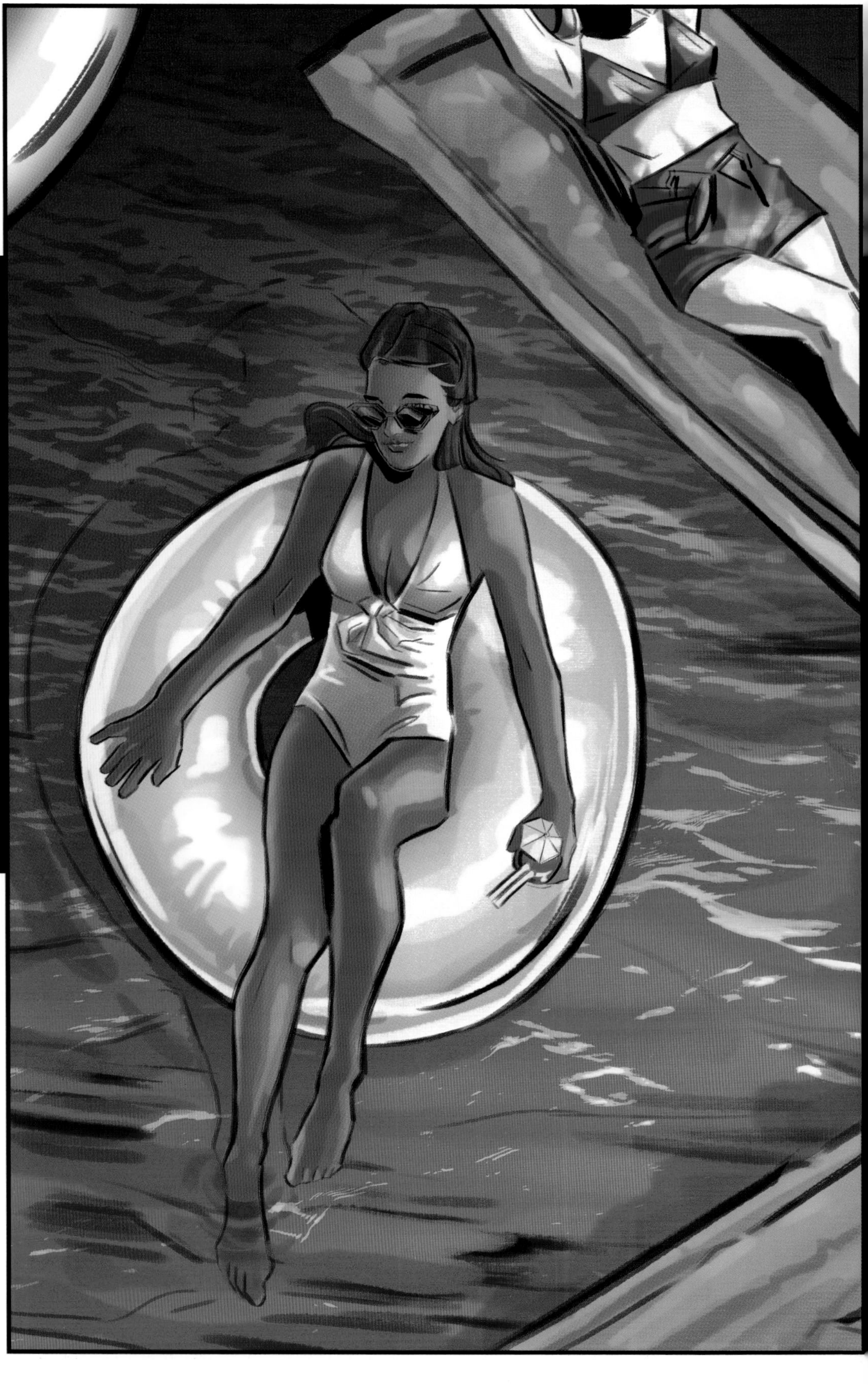

ISSUE #1 COVER ARTWORK BY **EMILY PEARSON** WITH COLORS BY **FRED C. STRESING**

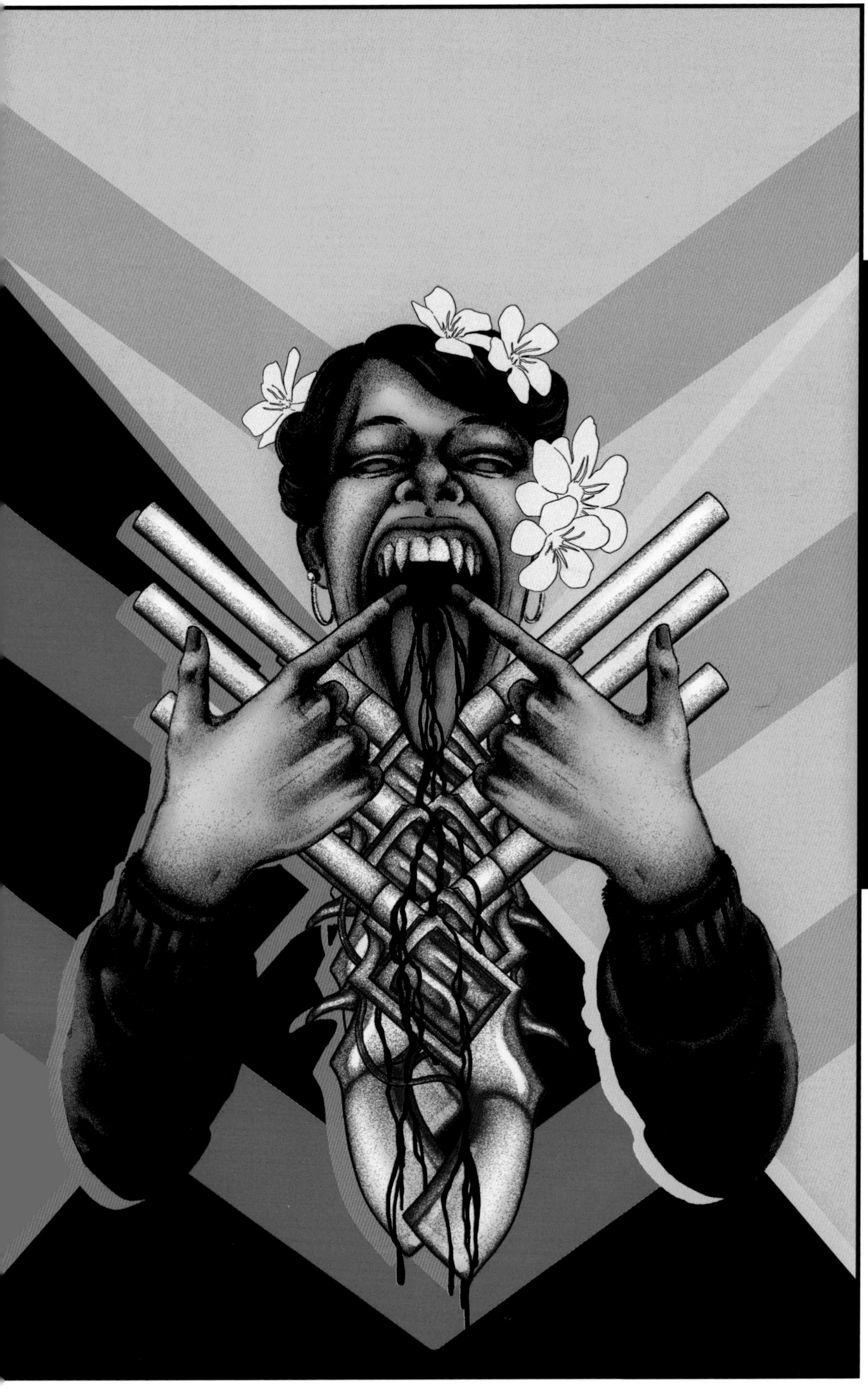

ISSUE #1 VARIANT COVER ARTWORK BY **JENNA CHA**

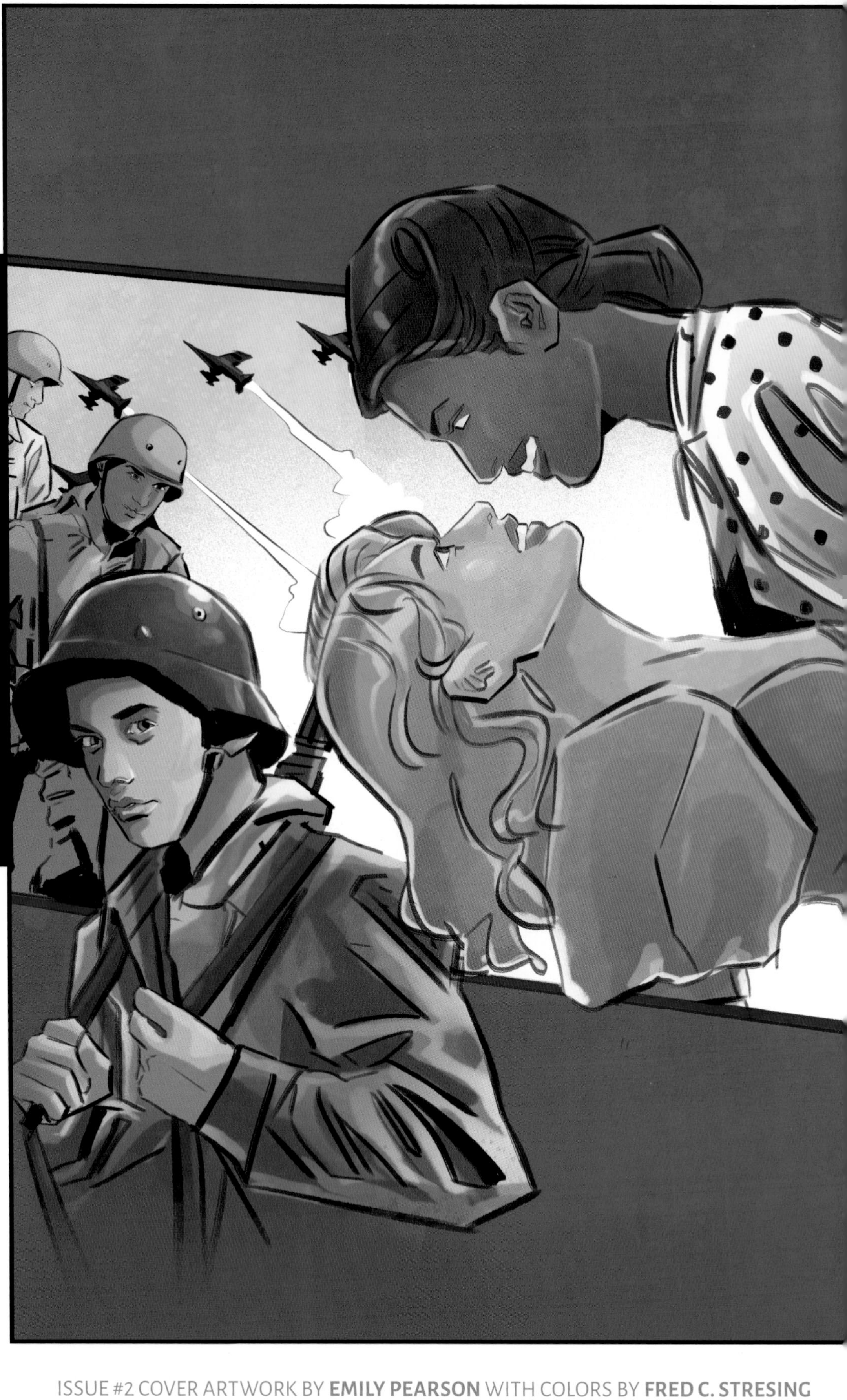

ISSUE #2 COVER ARTWORK BY **EMILY PEARSON** WITH COLORS BY **FRED C. STRESING**

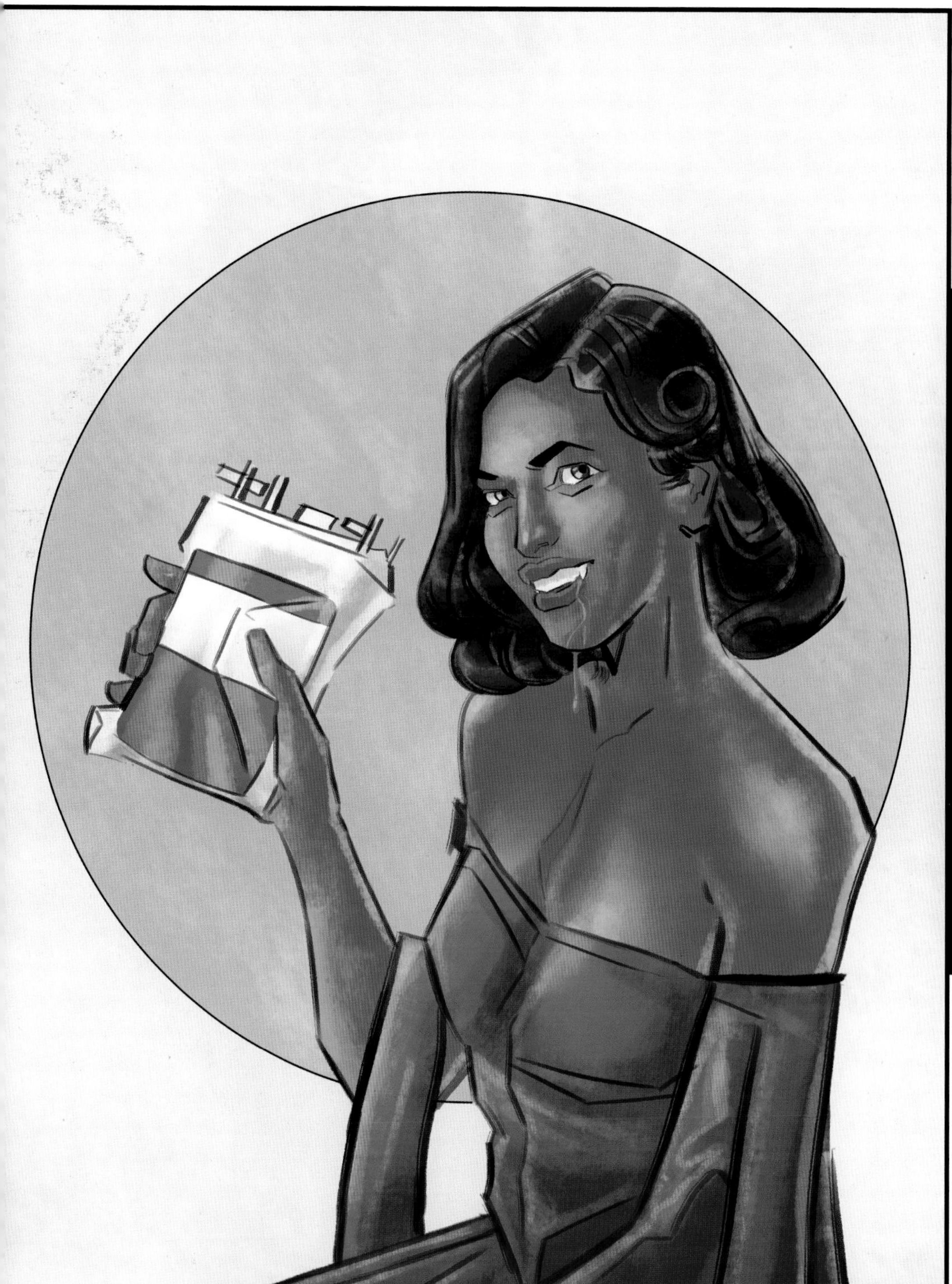

ISSUE #3 COVER ARTWORK BY **EMILY PEARSON** WITH COLORS BY **FRED C. STRESING**

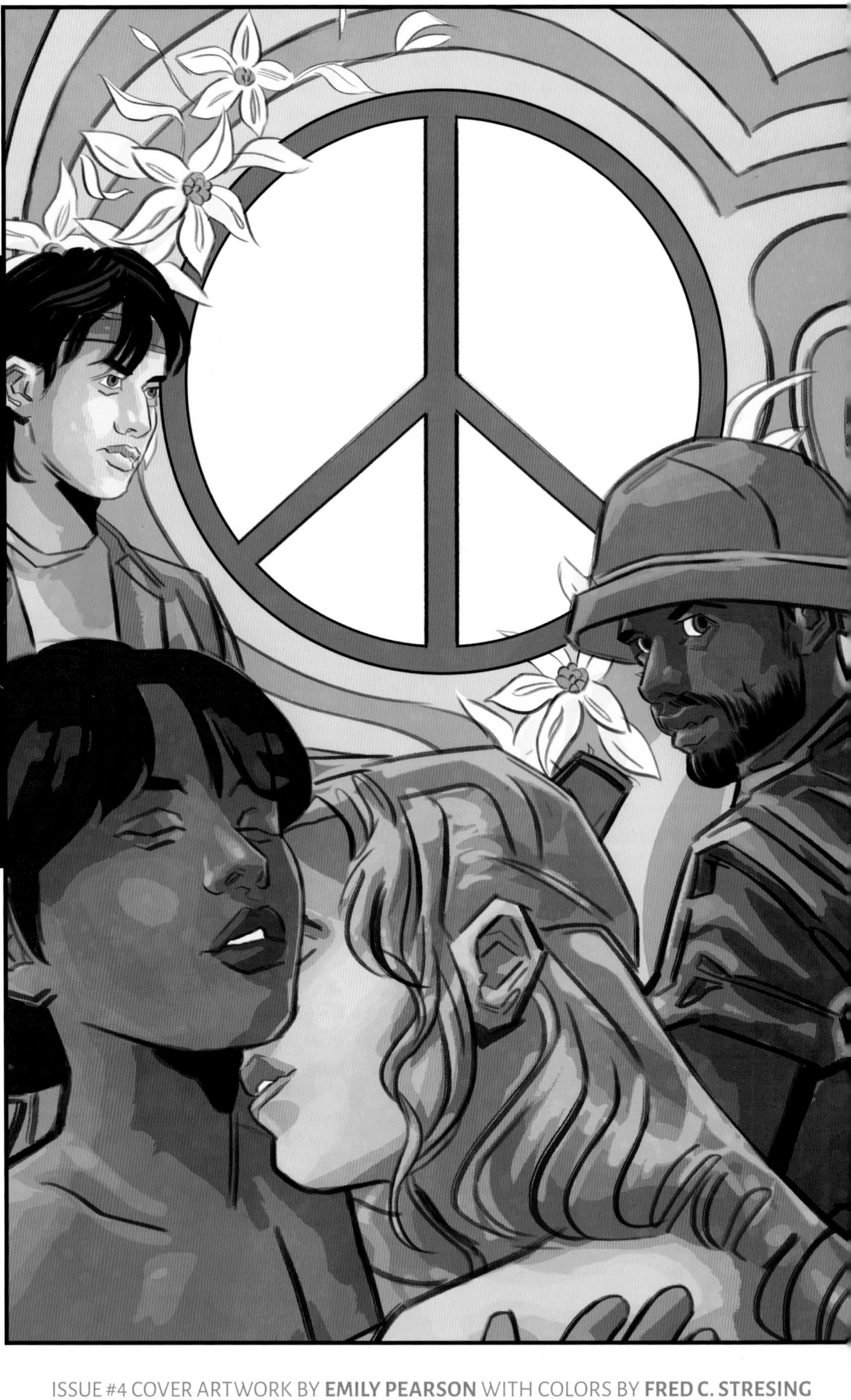

ISSUE #4 COVER ARTWORK BY **EMILY PEARSON** WITH COLORS BY **FRED C. STRESING**

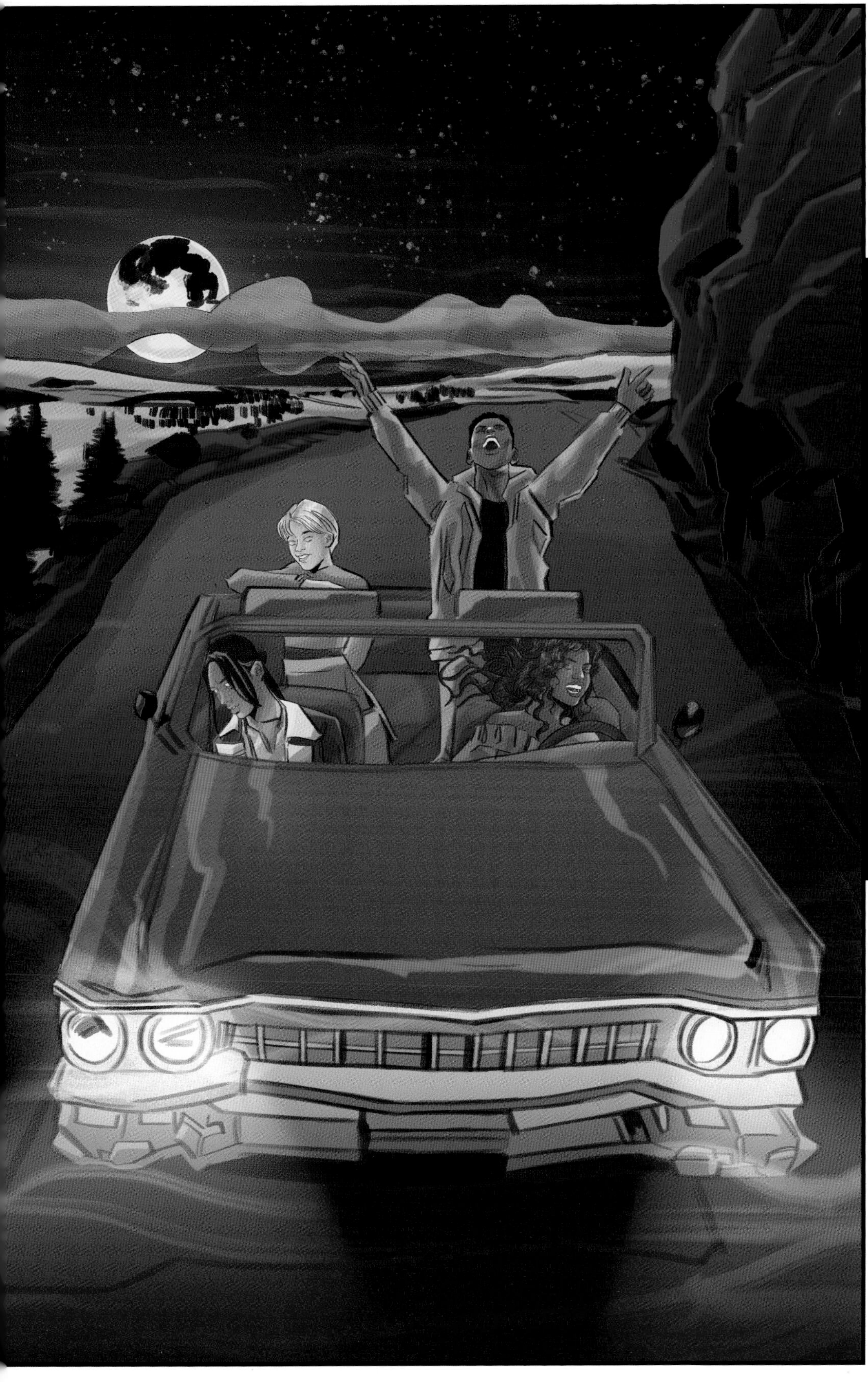

ISSUE #5 COVER ARTWORK BY **EMILY PEARSON** WITH COLORS BY **FRED C. STRESING**

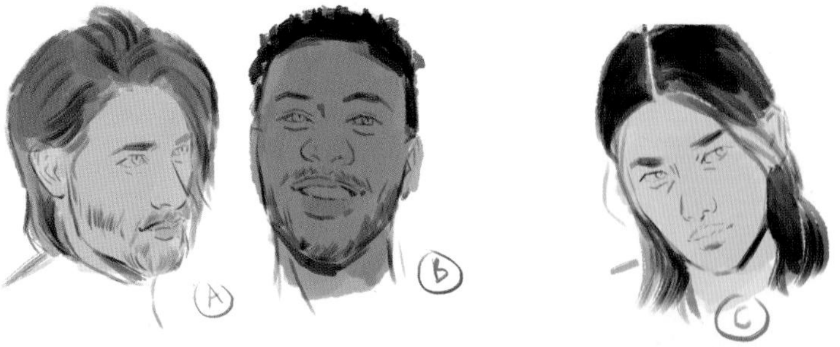
A
B
C

CHARACTER SKETCHES BY EMILY PEARSON

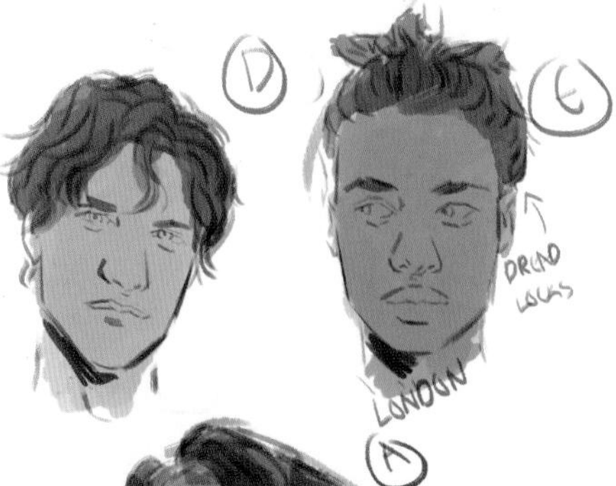
D
E
DREAD LOCKS
LONDON
A

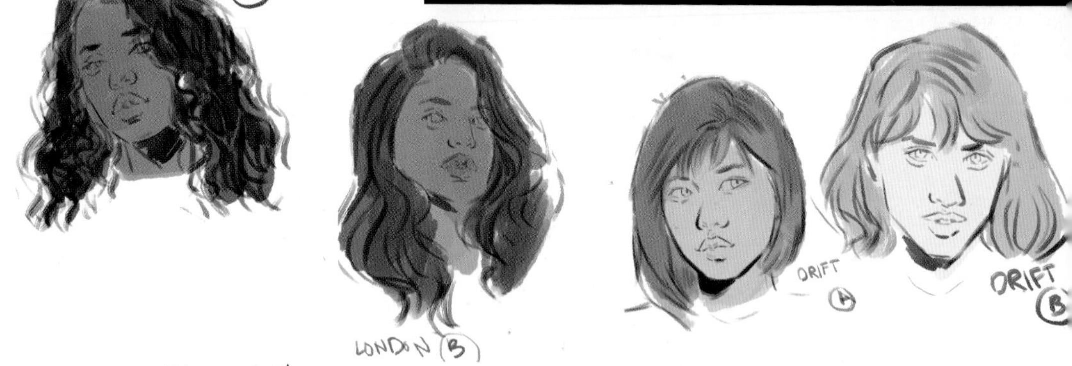
LONDON B
DRIFT A
DRIFT B

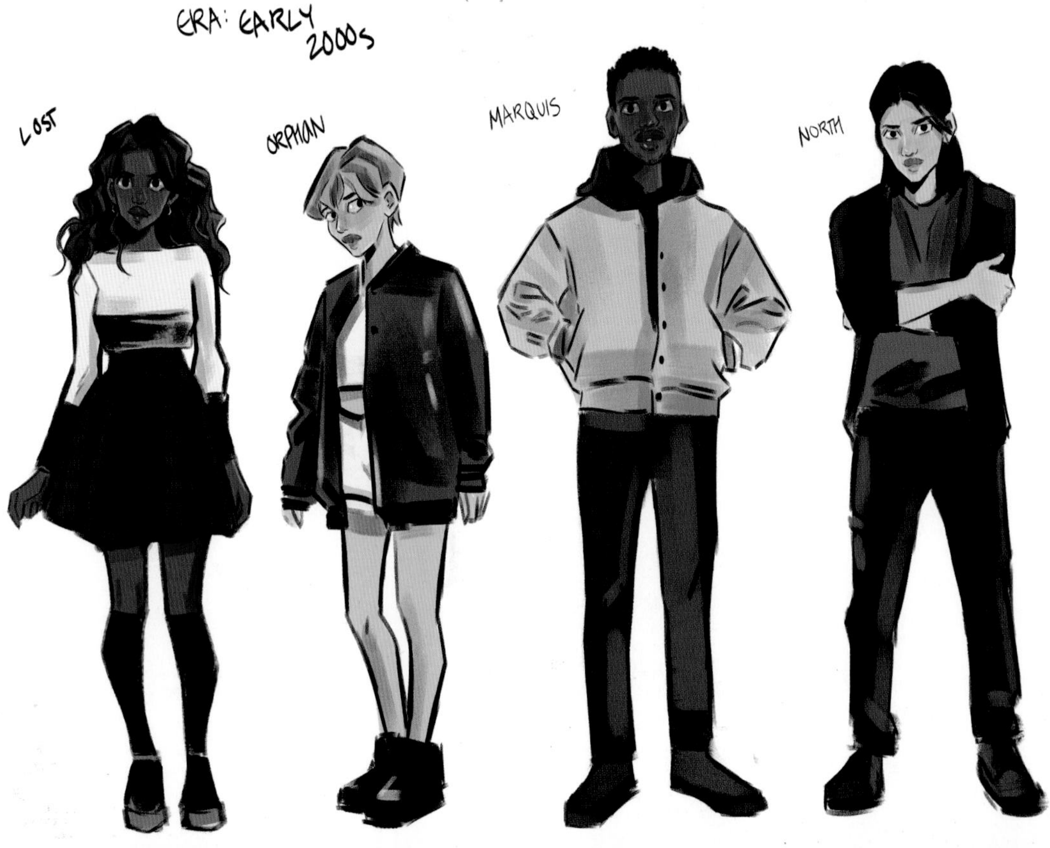
ERA: EARLY 2000s
LOST
ORPHAN
MARQUIS
NORTH

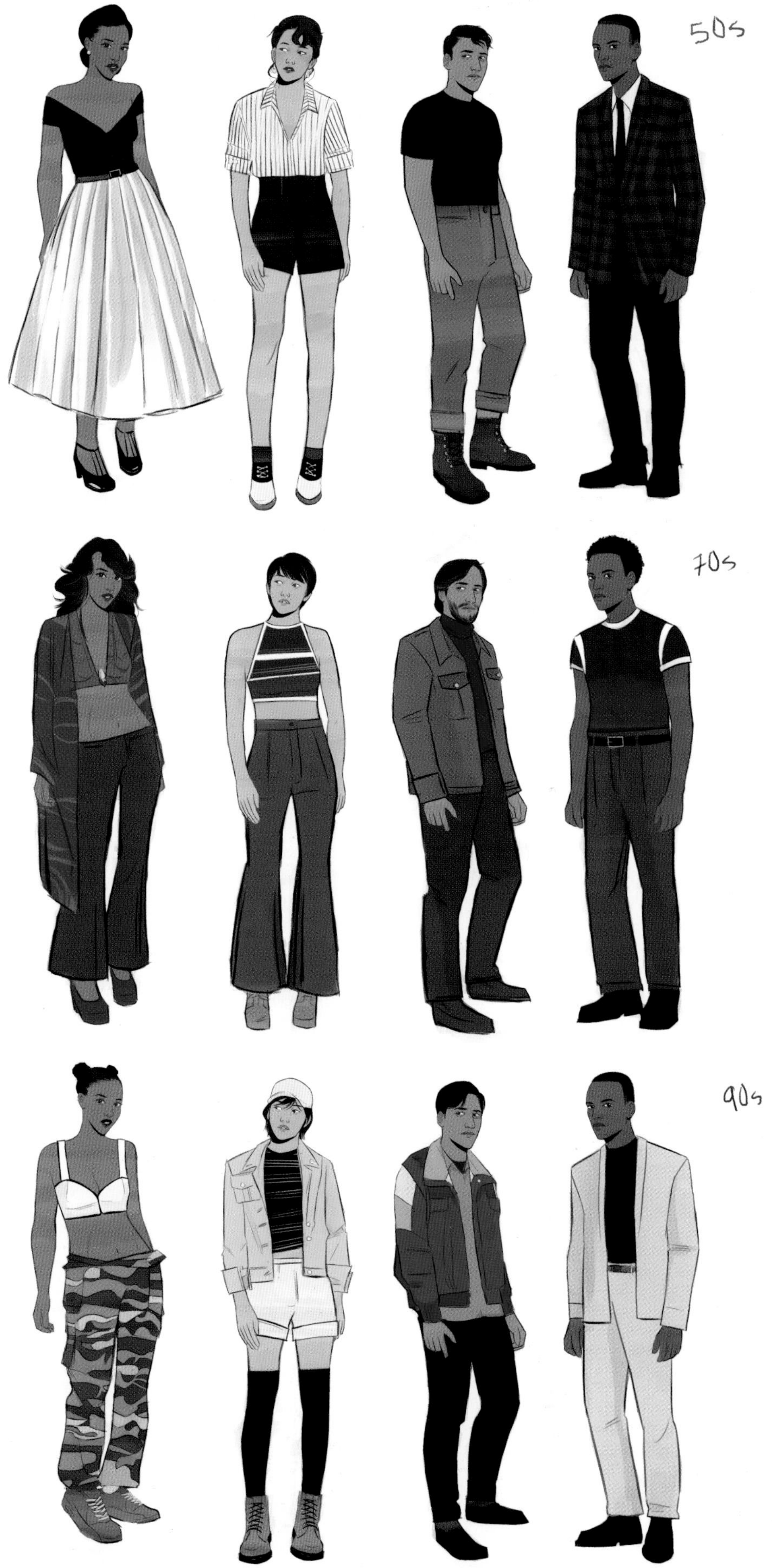
50s
70s
90s

THE BROOD BEHIND *THE VAIN*

ELIOT RAHAL

is a comics writer and creator best known for his work on *Hot Lunch Special*, *Midnight Vista*, and *Cult Classic*.

BLOOD TYPE: Mountain Dew Code Red
FAVORITE VAMPIRE: The Count (from *Sesame Street*).
BEST VAMPIRE MOVIE/TV SHOW: *BUFFY! BUFFY!*
TOP VAMPIRE TUNE: Oh, shit. I know "Free Fallin'" has a line about vampires.
HAVE YOU EVER MET A VAMPIRE? No. Sadly I've only ever met Shadmocks.

EMILY PEARSON

is a comic book artist from California. She has previously worked for Black Mask Studios on *The Wilds*, *Snap Flash Hustle*, as well as the upcoming Vault Comic's book, *Bonding*.

BLOOD TYPE: A+
FAVORITE VAMPIRE: Akasha from *Queen of the Damned*. She's such a heartthrob!
BEST VAMPIRE MOVIE/TV SHOW: I'm a huge fan of *What We Do in the Shadows*. I love subtle awkward comedies, and that movie does it best.
WHICH FAMOUS PERSON DO YOU SUSPECT IS A VAMPIRE? Paul Rudd! The man never ages.
HAVE YOU EVER MET A VAMPIRE? Sometimes, I suspect *The Vain*'s writer, Eliot, is secretly a vampire and this story is an auto-bio. But don't tell him I said that.

FRED C. STRESING

is a colorist, artist, writer, and letterer for a variety of comics. You may recognize his work from *Invader ZIM*. He has been making comics his whole life, from the age of six. He has gotten much better since then. He currently resides in Savannah, Georgia with his wife and two cats. He doesn't know how the cats got there, they are not his.

BLOOD TYPE: A sort of gray, ash-like substance – I mean, uh, C-negative? Is that a type?
FAVORITE VAMPIRE: Not me, as I'm definitely not a vampire.
WHEN'S THE LAST TIME YOU TASTED BLOOD? Uh, haha, never! I'm not a vampire.
DID YOU LIKE IT? Yeah, it was – ahh wait. You almost got me there!
WOULD YOU DO IT AGAIN? Do what again? I've never tasted blood! (Not a vampire).

CRANK!

has lettered a bunch of books put out by Image, Dark Horse, Oni Press, Dynamite, and elsewhere. He also has a podcast with comic artist Mike Norton and members of Four Star Studios in Chicago (crankcast.com) and makes music (sonomorti. bandcamp.com). Catch him on Twitter: @ccrank and Instagram: ccrank

BLOOD TYPE: Oh wow, you've heard of my high-school metal band?!
FAVORITE VAMPIRE: Bunnicula.
DECADE OF CHOICE: Probably the 1920s or the 1930s – all that art deco.
BEST VAMPIRE MOVIE/TV SHOW: *Forever Knight*.
TOP VAMPIRE TUNE: "Nosferatu" by Blue Oyster Cult.